CW00486626

THE CRICKETER'S
PROGRESS
MEADOWLAND TO
MUMBAI

Third Age Press

ISBN 978-1-898576-29-7
First edition

Third Age Press Ltd, 2010
Third Age Press, 6 Parkside Gardens
London SW19 5EY
Managing Editor Dianne Norton

Photographs and illustrations
from the Keith Hayhurst and Richard Hill collections.

The front cover is after a picture from the Richard Hill collection. It is an artist's impression of youths playing cricket in the late 18th century. The back cover is an image of ultra-modern Indian Premier League Twenty20 cricket, full of colour and thrills, and, of course, televised.

Photographs of cricket grounds from Tony Morris's Morphot 'Grounds for Pleasure' series.

Photo on page 297 is by Tom Shaw from Getty Images.

Every effort has been made to trace the copyright sources of the photographs and other illustrations used. The publishers would be pleased to hear of any outstanding copyright permissions in order that due acknowledgement might be made in any future editions.

Cover & layout design by Dianne Norton
Printed and bound in Great Britain by IntypeLibra

THE CRICKETER'S PROGRESS
MEADOWLAND TO MUMBAI

ERIC MIDWINTER

Third Age Press

ERIC MIDWINTER

Eric Midwinter has, for over 70 years, watched and read about cricket, and, after also fitfully playing the game sporadically, he turned to studying and writing about it, especially with reference to its social, cultural and political perspective. In *The Cricketer's Progress Meadowland to Mumbai*, he brings together many of the themes about the origins and development of cricket that have interested him over the last 30 and more years.

A social historian, educationalist and social policy analyst, he has enjoyed a varied career in both the public and voluntary service. Latterly, he was Director of the think-tank, the Centre for Policy on Ageing, Visiting Professor of Education at Exeter University and Co-founder of the University of the Third Age. Throughout his working life and thereafter, he has written copiously. He has published over 50 books, ranging from educational and social policy topics to British comedy and sport, chiefly cricket. In some degree, this latest cricket book is a complementary study to his well-received *Parish to Planet; How Football Came to Rule the World* (2007). Both are intrepid attempts to trace the evolution of a major sport and locate it in its broader historical context. Hailing from the Manchester area, he has, where some are wedded to the church, enjoyed a kind of bigamous relationship with Lancashire County Cricket Club and Manchester United, the emotional foci of this joint sporting interest.

He has written several books for the Third Age Press and is gratefully appreciative of its agreement to publish *The Cricketer's Progress*, its first foray into the field of sporting publication.

CONTENTS

The text is illustrated with appropriate photographs from the Morphot 'Grounds for Pleasure' series, beginning with a modern shot of cricket at Hambledon (above), and one of the Green, Tilford, Surrey. 'Silver Billy' Beldham, one of the early greats, lived in the house on the left – and BBC Television used the Green in the 1970s for its 'England, Their England' programme.

PROLOGUE

With one to win, and the last ball to be bowled, the young man at the striker's end manages to pierce the infield and win the match, at which his veteran partner, who is also his supportive captain, joins him in rejoicing.

It could be a final scene from an old-style schoolboy yarn. It could be a tale of village cricket, penned by an elegant stylist such as Hugh de Selincourt, author of *The Cricket Match*, published in 1924. In fact, it is the 2008 inaugural final of the Indian Premier League (IPL)Twenty20 competition, played before an enthralled and packed house at Mumbai and for a vast concourse of television watchers. The young man is the Pakistani, Sohail Tanvir, of the unfancied Rajasthan Royals, facing the bowling of Lakshmipathy Balaji, of Chennai Super Kings. The young man's mentor is Shane Warne.

That six week tournament was, for good or ill, deemed severally to have radicalised cricket. Detractors, as well as protagonists, recognised the fundamental, the seismic, shift that was occurring. In conception and construction it suddenly changed the constituents and the constitution of cricket. India became cricket's critical mass and the game stood at an historical crossroads. 2008 may well come to be viewed like 1789 in French or 1917 in Russian history, as the seminal year of revolution. As such, it is an apposite time to analyse the social, political and cultural impact of cricket. It is an excellent opportunity to seek to understand cricket's past and to ponder its future.

The Cricketer's Progress has echoes of John Bunyan's *The Pilgrim's Progress*, the first and major part of which was published in 1678, at a time when cricket was, according to many sources, beginning to emerge in something like a rational form. Its very sub-title – 'From this World to That Which is to Come' – might be borrowed by those writing about the face of 21st century cricket. Just as moralistic tags – 'keeping a straight bat'; 'it's not cricket' – have their provenance in the game, so has the Bunyanesque allegory given the world, including its cricketers, a plethora of metaphoric references. From its world-class performers to its lowly knockabout participants, all, even as they have been led by Evangelist, as was Christian, to the Wicket Gate, have experienced the Slough of Despond, the Valley of Humiliation, the Doubting Castle, Vanity Fair, the Land of Vain-Glory, and yet also the Enchanted Ground and walking 'in sunshine and with applause.' Staid traditionalists, looking askance at today's flamboyant cricketing scene, might agree with John Bunyan: 'then I saw there was a way to Hell, even from the Gates of Heaven.'

Above all, there is, with cricket, that similar sense of the arduous journey intrepidly undertaken and having now reached something of a climax. It is that sporting Odyssey which is examined here.

Cricket is a complicated game. The lowest and highest first-class team totals are 12 (poor old Oxford University v MCC in 1877, but do allow for the fact that they were 'one man absent', and North-amptonshire v Gloucestershire in 1907) and 1107 (Victoria v New South Wales at Melbourne in 1926/27). Such a range permits of enormous diversity, a variety much welcomed by cricketing *afi-cionados*. It is scarcely surprising that cricket's history is similarly complex. Whereas the mainstream story of most major sports – and here association football is a prime example – is of a relatively straightforward trajectory from simple origins to a degree of global dominance, cricket has travelled a rather more disjointed track, with by-ways and cut-backs. In the argot of the old-time ballroom, where football has enjoyed the heady, whirling onward dash of the lancers, cricket has picked out the more sedate and recurrent patterns of the gavotte.

The very Twenty20 revolution witnessed in the middle of 2008 in India testified to the oblique, even circuitous, nature of this journey. The IPL event somehow managed to touch on four distinct points of cricket's historical compass.

First, yes, there has been a steady line of progress from bat and ball frolics in the fields of parts of Western Europe in early modern times, via an organised Anglicised version, conveyed effectively to major portions of what was the British Empire, giving modern-day cricket some strong semblance of a world sport.

Second, however, there has often been a strong counterpoint to this expansionist programme, especially in England. A conservationist attitude, particularly evident in the aftermath of World War I, has frequently sought, not without some admirable spirit and perception, to preserve and cherish what had gone before. Thus there is a line, even if a shorter one, traceable backwards, as well as the forward moving path.

Third, whereas most global sports have tended to remain in the chief thrall of European or extra-European (that is, American and Antipodean) exponents, cricket, over the last decades, has experienced a definitive swing of the geographic pendulum. In popularity, media interest, financial undertaking and political bite, the subcontinent, more especially India, has become the central focus for the game. The IPL is but the latest emblem of that massive switch in the impact of world cricket.

Fourth, there has been, in a literal sense, what statesmen are wont to call 'a return to basics', a reversion, no less, to the origins of organised cricket. For we must turn, for a resemblance to the Twenty20 phenomenon, to Hanoverian England. From a myriad examples of 'grand matches', take the fixture at Sevenoaks, on 26 June 1776, when Hampshire beat All England by 75 runs, in a four innings encounter of swirling activity, before a goodish turn-out and accompanied by an uncommon amount of betting, not least by some of the participants. Noting the presence as captain and sponsor of the Duke of Dorset and the cobbled together character of the teams, inclusive of many paid players, and there is even some hint of the 'franchise' mode. Importantly, the whole event was done and dusted in a few hours.

Forwards, backwards, swinging, completing a loop – the geometry of cricket history is indeed intricate. Moreover, there are other dimensions. Most sports that have been organised and professionalised into a component of the entertainment business, especially on anything like a global scale, collect cultural baggage along their way. The financial aspects are obvious enough, as are the varied tribal and nationalistic flavours that become appended to sporting performance. Sometimes there is a social agenda, with some sports appealing predominantly to this or that class or caste, or a political slant, making sport the focus for ethnic segregation or xenophobic adoration.

The economics, the politics and the sociology of cricket give rise to an abundance of such references, providing ample material for historical analysis. Here again, however, one is tempted to think that the cultural nuances of cricket are more variegated than in most other sports. Once more, one is reminded of the complexity of the game in all its styles, formats and manifestations. For example, the ethical value that is often attributed to sporting activity has, on occasion, been heavily and colourfully tinged with religiosity in cricketing circles. Another illustration is the role played by cricket in British imperial endeavour, a curious instance of cricket's political potential.

It might also be contested that the academy of cricket has perhaps more wide-ranging faculties than is the sporting norm. Its archivists and its statisticians, no less its artists and *litterateurs*, as well as its historians and occasional geographers, comprise a formidable bunch. The grove of cricketing academe is long, winding, blooming and not invariably peaceful.

Thus the social context of cricket, in all its gradations and changing hues, is rich and fascinating. Place the ups, downs, halts, swerves and circles of cricket's historical motion against that equally multicoloured contextual tapestry, and one has cause to wonder at the luxuriance of the cricketing experience.

The saga begins in a Harry Potterish maze of myth and mystery, where the reasons why chroniclers have seized on obscure hints at cricket's origins are as fascinating as the conjectures themselves. Indeed, the determination of cricket's chroniclers to indulge in retrospective decisions about the beginnings of the game's major elements forms an essential and interesting part of the record itself. As well as the actual origins of cricket, such aspects as first-class status, the county championship and even the Test match itself have been resolved in retrospect by devoted archivists and dedicated administrators.

If there is a revisionist aspect to this present text, it arises not from any controversy over many of the facts. It is the interpretation of the data that has, on occasion, a different emphasis, especially when that data is located more precisely in its social and political setting, and when the attempt is made to view cricket more neutrally as an element of its time and place, rather than as some special, even unique, thread of activity, untrammelled by the vicissitudes of ordinary contextual influence.

In mainstream effect it was not until the 18th century that, spurred on by the need to bring order to the flamboyant betting of the Hanoverian peerage and gentry, cricket became at all recognisable in modern eyes. Then abruptly and at a point when it had lost much impetus, perhaps almost expiring as a major national sport, it was outflanked by the evangelical advance of the Victorian era and subdued by the roseate essence of distilled religiosity, not least at public school and varsity level.

At the same time, the incursions of industrialism offered an urban arena, serviced by the railways, for the promotion of a national spectator sport, one that, with the aid of the steamship, was conveyed overseas. With W.G.Grace the first-ever international sports star and with the press dancing attendance, Australia and North America were early destinations. Next, cricket became the peculiar creature of Imperialism, the cultural attachment of missionary, soldier and colonial officer. Even today, every Test-playing nation is a former British possession.

The 1914-1918 War broke the spell. Cricket and the cricket establishment found it difficult to break with the past and permit the game to evolve onwards from its Edwardian rapture. At the same time, the sheen remained, as Don Bradman reigned supreme over 'the Second Golden Age' that pushed just beyond the Second World War. The second half of the 20th century brought structural changes at home

– sponsored limited overs cricket, assisted by overseas stars, in the wake of decreasing crowds in the epoch of the motor car and other distractions – and abroad – colonial liberation released a wave of assured international contenders, among them strong West Indian ensembles, as well as troubles, such as the South African problem.

Then the power of the plane and the commercial weight of television, with Kerry Packer a big name to ponder, produced almost non-stop international cricket. In spite of Australia's continued strength, the focus of global cricket gradually transferred to the sub-continent, culminating in, at the beginning of the 21st century, the extravagances – financial, televisual and sportive – of the Indian Premier League Twenty20 franchises.

It has indeed been a plot as convoluted as any sprawling Victorian novel, let alone a journey akin to that of *The Pilgrim's Progress*.

The celebrated comedian, Robb Wilton, used, in the long ago days of the 1930s, to perform a sketch in which, as the fireman behind the desk at the fire station, he dealt lugubriously with the distraught woman, played by his wife, Florence Palmer, who was reporting her house to be on fire. During this exchange of frustratingly pettifogging hesitance and increasingly anguished concern, Robb Wilton would leisurely describe the convoluted route to be taken by the fire engine. The anxious householder protested vehemently that this was an awfully long way round. 'But', explained the fireman complacently, 'it's a prettier run.'

Compared with the social and political history of many sports, cricket's journey has been a longer but also, one has cause to believe, 'a prettier run.'

Chapter One

GENESIS

A depiction of early cricket

Just as, according to Jane Austen, 'a single man in possession of a good fortune must be in want of a wife', then an institution that evokes reverence must be in need of a heritage.

The Hunt for a Heritage

Cricket is just such an institution. Through the years, its devotees, led by dedicated archivists, have persevered in attempts to push the origins of cricket as far back as possible. The longer the age, the greater is the prestige and glory. Were cricket chroniclers chefs, they would concentrate more on vintage wines than fresh chickens. Indeed, an examination of cricket's origins, apart from its own integral importance, is exceedingly useful in throwing light on the cricketing mentality. We may learn here as much about the mind-set of cricket lovers as about the actuality of cricket's beginnings. That is a significant tool in the quest for understanding the subsequent record of cricket's story.

This search for cricket's origins has had two goals. One has been to grasp at the thinnest bones of historical material and garb them in cricketing dress, anything so long as cricket could be seen to have had a lengthy chronology. Cricket, a game subject to reverence and adulation, must have, like all great religions, an ancient lineage. The passage of time grants a form of authenticity.

This purported evidence is both pictorial and documentary. For example, part of an illustration to a Decretal of Pope Gregory IX, dated in the early 1300s, and the illustrated border of the *Romance of Alexander*, a manuscript dated 1340, both contain a couple, one holding a circular object and the other a stick or club of some sort. Each has been claimed as of cricketing provenance. At best, a general recreational explanation might just be plausible, but the cricketing element is present only in the most fervid imaginings of the cricket-obsessed observer.

On the documentary side, there is the often cited instance of 'creag', a pastime mentioned in the *Wardrobe Accounts*, couched in Latin, of Prince Edward, son of Edward I, in 1300. This has been seized upon as a reference to cricket and, as it has no ready connection with any Latin word, the myth was thus fostered. More recent commentary suggests 'creag' is more likely to be related to 'griasch', a kind of nine-pins or to 'greachia', a dicing game, rather more plausible reasoning, given that the worthless ne'er-do-well, Piers Gaveston, was the prince's favoured companion. It is all a trifle strained, although the former prime minister, John Major, in his 2007 compilation of writings about cricket, expressed mock-relief that the detested Gaveston was not involved with cricket's birth, another hint of how cricket must be deemed to have the right moral qualities.

The other aim has been to trace a singular birth for cricket, a discrete and incontrovertible starting-point. This ardent wish to uncover a birthplace, again indicative of the sheer veneration in which the sport is held, is very instructive. It testifies once more to the long-ing among cricket's admirers to settle on a Bethlehem or a Mecca for the game. For long enough, certainly from mid way through the 19th century, Hambledon was called 'the cradle of cricket'. Even if Hambledon contributes a scene, as we shall later remark, to the ongoing drama, it was never the opening act, and yet that heartfelt yearning to establish a named site for cricket lingers on and on.

The sightings of man's first attempts at cricket amid the misty woods and fields of distant time are legion. It is right to pay heart-felt trib-ute to those lovers of cricket who, rigorously and tirelessly, spent countless hours scouring every newspaper, every court and parish and estate record, merely on the off-chance that there might be a mention, however tiny, of the beloved game. Nonetheless, David Rayvern Allen, most sensible of commentators on modern cricket, sounds a warning note: 'where and when did cricket begin?' he asked, in his fine collation, *Cricket; an Illustrated History* (1990) 'No one knows nor ever will. Historians, trying to beat a path through con-voluted cul-de-sacs back to an immaculate conception, have usually lost their way in impenetrable semantic jungles.'

With this alarm bell ringing in the ears, yet in an attempt to sum-marise the pith of these vast researches, it is intended to recapitulate the major interpretations, as presented by the three leading modern exponents of cricket's overall story.

THE INTERPRETATION OF ORIGINS

H.S.Altham's *A History of Cricket; from the Beginnings to the First World War* was first published in 1926, while, after one or two fresh editions, it was re-published, in 1962, as volume one of a pair, with E.W.Swanton penning *From the First World War to the Present Day* as its partner. It could be regarded as the official or orthodox version, for Harry Altham was a President of MCC as well as an historian of much integrity and learning.

He opts for 'the Weald, where we know beyond argument that 'cricket' started.' It was the shepherd boys of the Kentish and Sussex uplands and downlands who first played cricket, and H.S. Altham presents a sturdily Anglo-Saxon case. The Saxon word 'Crick' refers to the rod or crook of the sheep-tending trade, utilised as a primitive bat. The 'wicket' and 'bail', the small hurdle with a moveable cross-bar that formed the narrow gate to the sheep-pen, became the target, the word deriving from the Saxon 'wican' It was something of a sophistication on the even older tree-stump. It is H.S.Altham's contention that 'stumps' was transferred as a synonym for the uprights of the hurdle.

These are all pleasing conceits, persuasively establishing the argument for a very English foundation for the national sport.

A spiky and formidable protagonist, the redoubtable Rowland Bowen spoke up in the next generation, principally in his 1970 book, *Cricket; a History of its Growth and Development throughout the World*. This was, in effect, the nonconformist riposte to Anglican orthodoxy. He argued that 'cricket was an old Celtic game', that it had Irish connections and that 'the first certain reference to cricket anywhere' is from Flanders – 'la boulle près d'une atache ou criquet' – in 1478. Additionally, this region of Northern France, then under the rule of the House of Burgundy, had an eleven-based numbering system, with eleven 'lignes' to the inch and eleven inches to the foot, the explanation, according to Rowland Bowen, of cricket's immortal 'eleven'. As for the word itself, it refers not to the implement but to the goal. It is the Flemish or Dutch 'krickstoel', the low piece of furniture then used in church or on the hearth, perhaps 1.5 to 2ft in length.

It came as a nasty shock to the national constitution to perceive that the English had been engaged in a form of French cricket all these years. There have not been too many fans for this concept.

If one is content to employ the Hegelian or Marxist philosophic device of thesis and antithesis in the less weighty matter of cricket's history, then it was Peter Wynne-Thomas, particularly in his highly sensible account, *The History of Cricket; from the Weald to the World* (1997) who produced something of a synthesis. Calmly, if sensitively, brushing aside some of the clutter of evidential debris, he, first, urged that cricket is indeed a complicated game and likely to have had a slower evolution than games that were founded in but one skill. There is the throwing of the object – initially, a pebble – at the target. Then there comes the idea of defending the target with a stick. Then there comes the notion of hitting the object, the pebble or later ball, as far as possible and running a certain distance while it is recovered. Throwing; hitting; running – it all points, argues Peter Wynne-Thomas, to a later start.

Utilising the log of cricket references built up by his laboriously toiling predecessors, he confirms that the Weald is the likeliest location for cricket's origin. He begins with 1598, with his first accepted reference to the game by John Derrick, who claimed to have enjoyed with 'diverse of his fellowes . . . creckett and other plaies' years before as a boy in Guildford. From 1598 to 1675, he maps about a dozen or more authentic mentions of cricket, and, with a geographer's affection for spatial dimension, he traces a crescent, with a westerly point in Selsey, Sussex, a northerly point in Eltham, Kent and an easterly point in Ruckinge, Kent. The central point of the pattern is Horsted Keynes, in Sussex, and there is an inclination to infer that this may well have been the genuine starting-point for the game.

Although Peter Wynne-Thomas thus seems to side more with Harry Altham than Rowland Bowen as to location, he does not accept the former's charming tale of rustic shepherd boys at play. He regards it as 'a little fanciful'. For example, it is apparent that sheep-rearing is a somewhat isolated occupation, so that, whatever else, there may not have been sufficient lads free and willing at any one site for anything like a team or group engagement. Peter Wynne-Thomas prefers to locate the beginnings of cricket amid the iron and glass industries prominent on the Sussex Weald in the 16th and 17th centuries. There were some 200 such plants at this time, with ample supplies of iron ore and with that densely wooded area available for fuel. These manufacturing sites were usually close to the villages that supplied the labour-force for these and their off-shoot crafts – and it is often those very places that are included on the roster of locales associated with a cricketing reference. It is these iron and allied workers that Peter Wynne-Thomas identifies as being 'much more likely to have played in the first organised matches.'

Because the foregoing tri-part discussion is basically linguistic in motif, it is worthwhile seeking the etymological opinion of the erudite John Eddowes in his scholarly text, *The Language of Cricket* (1997). He kicks away the legs of one or two dubious conjectures – the Old English 'crycc', for instance, otherwise we would apparently have all ended up playing 'crutchet' – before tracing a definitive line of a Franco-Flemish character, initially with the word 'krickets'. He aligns this borrowing with the coming of the Flemish weavers to Kent, where Cranbrook became the trade's centre, from around the last years of the 13th, into the 14th century and on to the 16th century. They came and went by the narrow Channel crossing and along the Pilgrim's Way, 'the most important road in the kingdom', running along the sheltered edge of the North Downs and connecting Dover and Folkestone with Canterbury, Maidstone, Sevenoaks, Guildford and Winchester. John Eddowes points to the proximity of early cricketing mentions to this route. There have also been suggestions that John Derrick of Guildford may have been of Flemish 'Hendrik' stock, while John Eddowes also reckons that the Weald was too boggy in those days for shepherds to play field games.

John Eddowes has the backing of a German scholar, Heiner Gillmeister, who argues that cricket has its roots in the Flemish phrase, 'met de krik ketson', that is, 'to chase with a curved stick', while he also thinks that cricket wickets and hockey goals derive from the sort of chivalric game where a mounted knight defended a narrow passage. Strength was added to the claim in 2009 when an Australian literature specialist, Paul Campbell, unearthed a 1533 poem, attributed to John Skelton but perhaps by an imitator, calling on the Flemish weavers to leave the country. The verse, entitled *The Image of Ipocrisie* rages at the Flemish interlopers in tones modern immigrants into Britain might ruefully recognise:

> *O lorde of Ipocrisie/Now shut ypp your wickettes;*
> *And clape to your clickettes/Al farewell, kings of crekettes*

This makes it, according to this school of thought, the earliest certain reference to 'crekettes', although, once more, no one can be quite certain what they were doing, with the plural 'creckettes' rather confusing the issue.

The settlement of Flemish weavers in Kent places John Eddowes closer, geographically, to Rowland Bowen than Harry Altham, but, economically, his embracing of the weavers' cause, with its attachment to sheep farming, distances him from the iron workers of Peter Wynne-Thomas. Now we are faced with shepherds, iron-founders and weavers as the premier 'kings of crekettes'.

John Eddowes also furnishes us with a discourse on stoolball, like cricket in varied spellings, one of then several extant ball and target games. Stoolball had – and has still, in Hampshire – a target raised about four feet above ground and fixed on a post. H.S.Altham claims it was originally a milking stool. Thus elevated, there is no need for level ground, as one is not required to trundle or bounce the ball. According to John Eddowes, it predates cricket, also has a continental origination and, intriguingly, supports the colourful notion that all these target games are a kind of poor man's chivalric tournament.

This is a tacit reminder that there are scores of references to all manner of diversions in early modern England, some of them enthusiastically associated with cricket by chroniclers. Handyn and Handoute was one of these, dismissed by the careful Peter Wynne-Thomas on the grounds that it was played indoors and involved, for betting purposes, plunging one's hand into a bag. Cat-and-dog and knurr-and-spell are others. As well as the more common place rounders and baseball (spelled as two words, base ball, in *Northanger Abbey* by Jane Austen, published posthumously in 1818). It also appears that Joseph Strutt, in his seminal *The Sports and Pastimes of the People of England* (1801) used the generic term 'club-ball' for games using a racket, club, bat or stick, only for some later scholars to assume that club-ball was a discrete game.

Apart from these confusions, it should be noted that such recreations often appear in longish lists, as in the indignant John Stow's description, late in the 17th century, that 'the more common sort divert themselves at football, wrestling, cudgels, ninepins, shovelboard, cricket, stowball, ringing of bells, quoits, pitching at the ball, bull and bear baiting, throwing cocks, and lying in the alehouses'. Aside from a passing thought as to whether that final activity involved economy with the truth or dalliance with the barmaid, this is typical of several rosters, usually drawn up by irked observers. These generalised recreational accounts move one to wonder how distinguishable one from the other were some of the items. Joseph Strutt worked on the triple basis of club-ball, hand-ball and football games and it may have been sensible of him so to do, given the possible closeness of the relationships.

In effect, practically all the evidence before about 1700 is linguistic in form. There is a negligible testimony to what was actually happening. The press and other references usually concern complaints or lawless incidents, sufficiently telling to warrant inclusion in a newspaper, not descriptions of the game as such. For example, in 1624 at Horsted Green in Sussex, Edward Tye, with other 'husbandmen of West Hoathly' was playing at 'crickett'. He hit the ball in the air and then endeavoured, 'for his greater advantage' to hit it again as it dropped, but Jasper Vinall 'arrived suddenly behind his back' and was fatally struck by a 'bacillus', a small rod, rather than a big bat. This first known cricketing fatality – the report is of the subsequent inquest which deemed it an 'unwitting' accident – was assuredly 'cricket' in name, but utilising a smallish stick, perhaps more like a rounders baton, hindering the field and hitting the ball twice is scarcely cricket, either in a pragmatic or an ethical connotation.

The history of football demonstrates the amazing range of the premodern typology, while, to confuse matters further, not many of those versions included much kicking, at least of the ball. It is probable that 'cricket' or 'crickets', in a diversity of spellings, covered a multitude of, for the censorious Puritan of the age, recreational sins. Indeed, if one mixes in all the incidental bits and pieces identified in the scraps of evidence about early cricket, it becomes apparent that it could, depending on the angle of viewing, resemble lots of games.

'All is flux', said the French philosopher, Henri Bergson. Visualise cricket's swirling profusion of features. A common aspect was the bowling, underarm as in, more literally, the game of bowls, aiming at a target of varying dimensions, as one might find in the skittles or ninepins variant of games. There are reports of a hole into which – hence popping crease – the ball had to be popped before the player had made his ground by thrusting the butt end of his bat in the same hole. A 1680 account to that effect mentions wickets only one foot high and as much as two feet wide. There are single wicket references to the one batsman scampering there and back to complete the equivalent of a run, perhaps with a more circular than 'dash and turn' motion, a clear link with the baseball and rounders variety. Charging, a regular aspect of most football codes, of fielders to hinder them was licit until 1787 and was permitted in a USA and Canada fixture as late as the 1830s. Alternate balls being bowled from each end, and then, for quite a long time, the short four ball over, have the scent of the bowling green. As cricket has been played in any combine from one – single wicket tourney – to eleven against twenty-two, it has also ranged from an individual to a group sport. In some of those earlier instances, when a band of youths were at play, there might have been an individual victor, that is, the one who scored the most 'runs' or whatever the scoring method might have been.

The bard, with his distinguished Warwickshire birth qualification, sang, in *A Midsummer Night's Dream*,

'. . . as imagination bodies forth
The form of things unknown, the poet's pen
Turns them to shapes, and gives to airy nothing
A local habitation and a name.

Perhaps cricket, with some of its anxious devotees over-diligent in trying to confirm its primacy, antiquity and uniqueness, has been such an illustration of this aesthetic tendency.

Clearly, we cannot be sure, until relatively recently, quite what people were doing when their chosen activity was called 'crickets' or something similar, except in the vaguest fashion. Moreover, there is a further complication, one underlying the fact that, cricket, as it eventually emerged, was a late and complex business. The most unusual element of cricket is that it has two targets, like field sports such as football and hockey . . . but the same team defends both individually.

In most dual target team games, of course, the combatants attack and defend a goal apiece. In most single target team games, of which baseball is an example, the batters are pitched individually against their several opponents. In other target games, such as croquet, golf or, moving from the sublime to the ridiculous, marbles, competitors take turn and turn about. The natural propensity, on beach or in garden, is still to play single wicket cricket, and, were tree-stumps or sheep hurdle gates used for targets, it is extremely unlikely that there would have been an equivalent to the first the requisite yard-age away.

Two against eleven: it is really most curious, but it places cricket as much in the hockey and lacrosse as in the baseball and rounders category. Incidentally, when it comes to the naming of recreational parts, as late as 1828, we discover 'rounders' in the east of England, 'pitcher' in the home counties and 'baseball' in the west, all with similar rules – whilst until about 1744 much American baseball was played, rather like cricket, with two bases, not four.

It must also be recalled that the introduction of the third stump was relatively late in cricket's historical process, so that the defence of two uprights and a crosspiece was the regular pattern. Rowland Bowen reports instances of wickets as wide as six feet and only a few inches high, whereas some early football goals were much smaller than today. Factor in the wielding and re-wielding of the bat, in many versions shaped rather like a hockey stick to enable players to hit the often fast moving ball along the ground, plus the charging of fielders, and the connection with the football codes, more especially perhaps with the hockey/hurling formats, becomes persuasive.

When Samuel Johnson defined cricket in his famed dictionary, published in 1755, as a game 'in which the contenders drive the ball with sticks in opposition to each other', H.S.Altham declared this to be a 'less happy' error, but was it? Samuel Johnson, a shrewd if sometimes mischievous observer of life in his beloved London, where, by this time, 'cricket' was well established, may have been witness to a version that encompassed something more like hockey.

The Generality of 'Play'

Thus far we have taken the linguistic route backwards and it is a labyrinthine journey. Time, perhaps, to look at the setting for this confused cluster of labels; time, that is, to go to the social context and march forwards.

First, the concept of 'play' has been properly formulated by Johann Huizinga in his study *Homo Ludens; a Study of the Play Element in Culture* (1938) and by others. He regarded 'play' as 'a thing in itself', the essential 'interlude' or respite between periods of work or other responsibilities, and he recognised its existence in all civilisations. It is the plainness of this clear-cut definition that is significant, for there have been so many rather synthetic attempts – among which cricket has figured quite extensively – to create a plethora of theological or ideological explanations for sport. This sturdy insistence on 'play' as a discrete and straightforward yet fundamental essence of life is refreshingly lucid.

Second, this clear lens enables one to view the recreational landscape of premodern Britain, indeed, Western Europe and observe their inhabitants busily occupying their scarce free time with a 'diversion', defined by the above-mentioned Samuel Johnson with uncanny accuracy as that which 'unbends the mind by turning it off from care'. What Christopher Brooke identified as 'folk-games' in his *English Cricket; the Game and Players through the Ages* (1978) were keenly played, but, apart from the kind of festival football that attracted the attention of chroniclers and legal authorities, much of it was undertaken in complete isolation.

Robert Malcolmson, the expert scholar of popular recreations in early times, underlines this graphically (*Popular Recreations in English Society, 1700 to 1850*, published in 1973). 'It is likely', he explains, 'that these routine leisure activities and family festivities were, in terms of the hours involved, more prominent than the large public celebrations . . . everyday leisure was relatively subdued; it was usually rooted in informal, face to face encounters.'

Such localised romps were patently subject to local rules and conditions, with implements and the area available varying greatly, and with some mix of an oral tradition and the likely intercession of someone, invited or otherwise, giving a lead – a 'star' in the jargon of the sociometrist – and controlling events. One has to imagine a state of 'gameness', a morass of pastimes, all or most of them slightly different from the others, and yet with all or most of them sharing elements, evolving slowly all the time. One might, then, walk from one village to the neighbouring estate and find something recognisable enough to join in readily.

A classic example of this sort of internalisation is the 'fossilised form of cricket', with a curiously shaped club and a small tomb-shaped stone target, associated with Stonyhurst School. A Jesuit college for the sons of English Catholics, during a time when such schooling was frowned upon and banned in England, it was formed at St Omer, some 25 miles from Calais, in 1593. It evacuated to England when threatened by the anti-clerisy of the French Revolution, bringing with it its peculiar take on cricket intact. Peter Wynne-Thomas believes that the boys took the game from their English homes, rather than, as Rowland Bowen, eager to uncover cricketing links in Northern France, opined, picked it up from contemporary French boys. The immediate point, however, is the conservation of a variation on cricket, untouched and unshared, by a secluded community.

Third, amusements were exclusive because everyday existence was isolated. There were about 10,000 manors in England during the reign of Edward I in the 13th century, and the population rose only from 1.5m in 1066 to 5.5m by 1700. By this point there were upward of 15,000 parishes in England and Wales, a honeycomb of chiefly tiny settlements. Apart from the few towns, the majority, possibly 90%, lived in rural habitations and worked at agricultural and allied pursuits. These were small and hard-working groups of people, living in largely self-contained conditions. They took their pleasures locally and together in penny numbers. There was no place, there was no necessity, for generally acceptable regulation of games. By the 18th century there are references to inter-village cricket in the Sussex diaries of Thomas Marchant and Thomas Turner, but there is no hard evidence of such conjoined activity much earlier than that.

Fourth, transport was an issue. It was not that these were, as has sometimes been thought, immobilised communities, introverted and inbred. From the middle ages onwards, there is plenty of evidence of people moving for marriage and occupational reasons. Doubtless news and ideas were conveyed in this fashion, including possible amendments or additions to games, but this was not the same as adopting some regional, let alone national, formula wholesale. These were pedestrianised communities. On foot, it took a long time to achieve a degree of mobility. As late as 1837, the number of annual journeys undertaken by public transport was a miserable four per head. Writing in 1846, the journalist and commentator, Charles Pearson, claimed that Britain's inhabitants were 'chained to the spot'.

Certainly during the decades before 1700 travel was normally on foot. Although there were a million horses in the country, they were chiefly working horses, with only the well-to-do minority enjoying a regular ride on horseback. Especially against the canvas of long working hours, walking any distance for an event and then walking back was rarely an option. Although commentators are correct to aver that past generations were strong walkers, walking is, comparatively speaking, time-consuming. In fact, six miles was the accepted standard for a day visit on horseback, let alone on foot, with fifteen miles very much the extreme. The horse-drawn cart, bearing cricketers, is perhaps a romantic fancy, but this, where and if it happened, would also have eaten up a lot of time.

In 1803 William Pitt the Younger issued an edict calling on able-bodied men to form militias, a kind of home guard, against the hazard of Napoleonic invasion. Two weekly parades were decreed, but the prime minister insisted that no one should have to travel more than six miles from home for his militia service, 'no more than the sturdy English peasantry', he declaimed, 'were in the habit of going when led to a cricket match or other rural diversion'. Even a twelve miles round trip, including military drill, proved unduly gruelling, for it could have taken six hours, after a long day in the fields and when diets were none too nutritious – and this was a hundred and more years after chroniclers have confidently spoken of established rural cricket matches.

It is probably more accurate, assuredly much before 1700, to imagine groups of boys and young men causally assembling for an hour or so in the evening, after an arduous day's toil in field or domestic workshop, for a knockabout relaxation with bat, target and ball, maybe for an hour or so. The notion of them finding the time, perhaps the expense, even the very idea, as well as negotiating some satisfactory compromise on the rules, for a trip to a neighbouring settlement or estate is a figment more of a the modern mind, wedded to the concept of teams playing fixtures.

There is some confirmation of the opinion that cricket did not have a singular birth from the lofty researches of scholars studying civilisations in all their glories. From such works as Felipe Fernandez-Armesto's *Civilisations* (2000), it becomes apparent that, although there is emulation and imitation, there is also spontaneous combustion. Agriculture and writing are but two significant components of civilised life to have arisen independently in different cultures, rather than have been transmitted from a common basis. It is thus easily conceivable that cricket, at its simplest, could have started at many sites. The olde-tyme spelling of 'crickets' has more reason than one to bask in its plurality.

The charitable conclusion must be that the historians and others who have fought the cause of a particular birthplace, what David Rayvern Allen called 'an immaculate conception', for cricket, have all been right. It is highly likely that forms of cricket really did spring up autonomously in dozens of settlements in Western Europe, all as part of that condition of 'gameness', previously described.

Cricket's chroniclers felt obliged, chiefly in the hundred years period from about the middle of the Victorian era, when cricket was coming into its phase of richest and most prominent maturity, to explore avidly for the counterpart of the source of some lengthily straggling and congested river. Some sense of the reasons for this will concern us in more detail later, especially in chapter three, for they are a manifestation of the profound ardour experienced by cricket devotees at that time and, if in lesser degree, since.

The pursuit of a holy grail of cricket, and the construction of varying versions of a cricketing da Vinci code to assist in the search, may reflect some human whim that prefers the immediacy of a Genesis to the muddle of a Darwinian solution. Single causations were a feature of old-fashioned schoolchild history, be it in King Alfred's exceedingly burnt cakes, Robert Bruce's persevering spider, Isaac Newton's downwardly mobile apple or John Watt's upwardly mobile kettle lid. But, in many historical cases, it is a compound of factors and people that has as frequently led to decisive change or movement. Scientific discoveries, such as penicillin, the double helix and even, ironically enough, the theory of evolution itself, are knotted in controversies as to who made which contribution.

The traditional detective story unfolds gradually and unravels carefully, until there is one suspect left standing, clearly guilty of the murder. For the origins of cricket, as for much else in an analysis of historical lore, the better analogue would be that Hercules Poirot mystery – was it in Agatha Christie's *Murder on the Orient Express?* – in which everyone had done it.

There is no Eden, no Bethlehem, no Mecca, and no Hambledon. There is no creation story. The tale is told of the gorilla poring over copies of the Old Testament and Charles Darwin's *The Origin of Species*. 'Am I my brother's keeper or my keeper's brother?' he mused. The origins, in the defiant plural, of cricket offer little scope for such an inquiry. There was no, to deploy the new Bible Belt coinage, 'intelligent design'. Cricket most likely evolved after the standard fashion described by Charles Darwin in his epic 1859 account. It gradually arose from a mess of recreational potage, surviving, by trial and error, by fits and starts, to be one of several sports that came to be widely recognised nationally, where once there had been hundreds, most of them with only localised identities. In the evolution of sport, it is to the New rather than the Old Testament one might turn for scriptural succour. We are told in the gospel according to St Matthew, 'for many are called, but few are chosen'.

Language may have had a subsidiary role. John Eddowes wonders whether 'cricket' was simply a more euphonious term than others, and he submits 'the Marylebone Stoolball Club in solemn conclave' as a sobering alternative. Whatever the case, there was a slow – much slower than is sometimes believed – process of transition during which a mesh of quite complicated actions were unified into a format acknowledged, first, on a regional and later, on a more national scale, to which the title 'cricket' was attributed. Almost as important, there must have been a corresponding procedure, little spoken of because, perhaps, it was a more negative course of action, in which the word 'cricket' in all its varied spellings, stopped being used to label differing formulae that may, in any event, have been dying out.

Turning back to the Book of Genesis, when Adam and Eve were busy in the Garden of Eden naming the animals, they happened on one creature that Adam enthusiastically decided to call a hippopotamus. Eve, inquisitive, as she later learned, to a fault, asked why. 'Because', declared Adam confidently, 'it looks more like a hippopotamus than anything else we've seen so far.'

It is probable that a bundle of sporting actions similarly emerged about the turn of the 17th century and was tagged 'cricket' on something like that Adamite principle.

Stately homes have long had a role in English cricket. Burghley Park, Lincolnshire, (top) is an example of the stately home ground, one of many utilised in the past for 'country house' cricket. At Arundel Castle, Sussex, the ground was established by the 15th Duke of Norfolk in 1895. Lavinia, Duchess of Norfolk's XI are seen here playing the 1990 New Zealand tourists.

CHAPTER TWO
LORDS A-GAMBLING

Cricket at the Artillery Ground, London, in the 1740s

The cautious historian must await the concurrence of the language and habits of cricket before declaring that a game, recognisable by several communities over at least a regional area, is in being. This etymological and practical conjunction requires that a sufficiency of players are conforming with many of the same rules and describing what they do in much of the same argot. This probably occurred later than many cricket chroniclers allow. It was at least the beginning of the 18th century before we may state with rational certitude, that this was the case and that indeed, a form of cricket identifiable as closely linked to the cricket of today, was extant in what, to employ anachronisms, might be termed the Greater London region and the immediate home counties.

From the scanty and scrappy references to pre-1700 cricket, it is difficult to tell – for many of them are concerned with legal, moral or medical rather than purely sportive cases and events – what was occurring. For instance, it is not entirely clear whether cricket was being played as an individual trying to outdo colleagues as opposed to a team game, and that, beyond the throwing and hitting (and per-haps charging), what else was happening, in terms, say, of scoring. The variation, for instance, of touching the umpire's bat or stave at either end, with the 'square leg' moderator perilously close to the wicket, appears to have been common and that has little resonance with cricket as it formally emerged.

THE POLITICAL MYTH

In his seminal history, Harry Altham mused about the Royalist nobil-ity and gentry slinking back to their estates after defeat in the English Civil War in 1646, noticing their servants and the local children at cricket, 'and from sheer *ennui* would try their hand at it and find that it was good'. Although included as a delectable imagining more than a solid statement, it became one of the sources for the myth that the Laughing Cavaliers should be credited for that upper-class adoption of cricket that granted it a more unified legitimacy.

Rowland Bowen, usually a prickly dispeller of orthodoxy, wrote 'of a number of gentlemen formerly prominent about the Court, now back in their country homes with little or nothing to do', where they possibly learned cricket and then took it to London after the Restora-tion in 1660. Even Derek Birley, in his robust assault on cricketing sentimentality, *The Willow Wand* (1979), entertains the notion as genuine. Royalists deemed it, he opines, 'prudent' to remain on their 'great estates' during the Interregnum: 'it was to these havens that the cavaliers retired and it was there, it seems, that the younger set discovered cricket among the labouring classes'. Moreover, there is some agreement among these historians that, by this point, cricket had 'a national appeal' and 'a fast hold' on 'almost all levels of the community'.

Is this a logical inference? Firstly, one must recall the likely absence of any uniform formula for cricket, so that, even if the cricketing cavaliers had spotted, to their sudden surprise, their 'gardeners, huntsmen, foresters and farm-hands' playing the game, it is improbable that they were all watching the same recreation, and that, among all the other folk-games on offer, they would unerringly, and over a relatively brief period of some ten or fourteen years, have chosen this very one to promote in and around London after the Restoration. The case also relies on group myopia among the Royalist upper crust about the delights of cricket on their estates before 1642. The theory is altogether too pat for the vicissitudes of most human behaviour.

Secondly, the Royalist hypothesis depends on what would now be regarded as an unsound social premise. The Stuart historian, Barry Coward, writing in 1980, argued that 'the allegiance of individuals do not appear to have been determined by their social status and wealth. There were prosperous and declining landed gentry, merchants and lawyers on both sides'. John Adamson, in his cogent 2007 account of these events, *The Noble Revolt*, shows that the political dimension of the struggle, for all its allied religious and economic elements, was salient. He underlines the impact of members of the nobility who were opposed to Charles I, men such as the Duke of Bedford and the Earl of Warwick, who were major leaders of the Parliamentary cause. There was also a species of what was called 'neutralism', as some propertied men and merchants just tried to avoid the whole worrying business and carried on as normally as possible.

Thirdly, those estate owners who did defy Parliament were subject to severe censure, especially in the southeast, where, with London in their hands, the Parliamentary forces held supreme control. In part as punishment, but increasingly as a means of funding first the war itself and then the post-war republican administration, many estates were subjected to confiscation and sale, to the liquidation of assets such as timber and lead, and other fiscal measures, such as 'sequestration' and 'composition', scarcely the ambience for a leisurely observing and copying of the servants playing cricket. Elsewhere, in the north and west, where Parliament's writ did not until later run, there was, by common consent, little or no cricket – although one should never forget the warning that, just as 'cricket' may have been a term for varied practices, there may have been games like cricket that were originally called something else . . .

Additionally, Charles II was anxious at the Restoration in 1660 'his enemies to sweeten', evoking the wrath of Royalist opinion by refusing to agree any more than a moderate land settlement. It left the loyalist nobility either without their old estates or with dreadful problems of economic restitution, hardly the atmosphere to contemplate the development of cricket.

It does appear that the idea of a Royalist contribution to cricket's evolution might have been a romanticised and simplistic interpretation of those events, and, in justice to the admirable Harry Altham, his was no more than a speculative rumination. This Royalist legend borders on the well-loved phrases of W.C.Sellar and R.J.Yeatman's *1066 and All That*, published in 1930, wherein this internecine struggle was between the 'The Right but Repulsive' and 'the Wrong but Wromantic'. It owes something, too, to the popular view of dour Roundheads and jovial Cavaliers promoted by such stories as Captain Marryat's *The Children of the New Forest*, very popular from its publication date of 1847.

THE ECONOMIC TRUTH

What should be recollected is that the Cromwellian era was marked by an urgency to encourage economic progress. That distinguished scholar of the 17th century, Christopher Hill, has shown how puritanical zeal for the virtuous life was strongly linked with this wish. Sober farmers, merchants and traders of frugal habit were seen as more likely to sustain the necessary disciplines of economic power. The Puritan outcry against sports and other amusements, for all their moralistic fervour, was always also aimed at that degree of social order and obedience to the work-ethic without which, it was believed, neither social nor commercial value would be advanced. A ban on Sunday travel, when the lower orders might have busied themselves with sportive visits away from their own backyards, was widely welcomed by all the gentry and upper class, regardless of political and religious leanings, because they understood it was about social control.

Chiefly based on the southeast, this progressive economic interest expanded and prospered, the more so after the Glorious Revolution of 1688/89, whereafter the solidity of the kingdom, under a stabilised constitutional monarchy, witnessed a general enhancement of this London-based economy. The relatively ephemeral alarums of the Jacobite Rebellions of 1715 and 1745 were the exceptions to the rule that proved the Orange and Hanoverian ascendancy to be a relatively stolid phase of political and economic retrenchment – if not by any means social calm - after the wild and destructive political excitements of the 17th century. Certainly, by the end of that and into the next century, there were, in material consequence, exorbitant funds in the hands of many of the landed and merchant families of the southern and eastern parts of England.

The Stuart propagandist, William Dugdale, had spun the tale that Oliver Cromwell had been a 'royster', because he had indulged as a youthful student in 'football, cudgelling, cricket and football'. It must be said that, between the forlornly cash-strapped court of Charles I and the bawdily seedy court of his son, Charles II, the magnificence of Oliver Cromwell's own hospitality and spectacle at Hampton Court was much remarked by foreign ambassadors, as was his admirable patronage of the secular arts, dancing, music, painting and literature. He was not to know, even if he gave any thought to his early 'roystering', that it would be, in main part, the funds built up by the estate managers and commercial magnates of his own zealous ilk and their successors, and not necessarily the smaller resources of the downfallen gentlemen among his foes, that would be the more likely to sponsor the establishment of cricket in the coming 18th century.

The post-Civil War period was, for instance, marked by the enlarge-ment of country estates. Through careful marriages, prudent purchases and the mass enclosure of the old-style and somewhat wasteful open and common field modes of agriculture, landlords were busily amassing vast estates. The Duke of Newcastle, for exam-ple, possessed estates in twelve different counties, rewarding him with an income of £40,000 a year. The Duke of Bedford – whose ancestor had so harried Charles I, it will be remembered - was even wealthier, for there was scarcely an acre of Bedfordshire that he did not own. Such aristocrats were often also merchant princes, with overseas trading interests, or intermarried with such families, as the aristocracy, as happens periodically in British economic history, refreshed the landed interest with commercial gains. The genuine establishment of cricket was to depend on both the base of well-to-do estates for emerging cricket teams and on the aristocratic-cum-mercantile connection in London, insisting that the sport should be rationally organised.

THE GAMBLING REALITY

That said, the highly moralistic Oliver Cromwell and his immediate following would not have approved of the use to which this economic surplus was later devoted. Gambling became the distinctive pastime of the upper classes and it spread to the lower regions of the social scale. Gambling had not, of course, been absent from social discourse hitherto, but the degree and weight of the wagering in Hanoverian times was significant. The celebrated scholar of the Hanoverian period, J.H.Plumb, regarded gambling as the public palliative against the exceedingly noisome and harsh condition of a more urbanised existence. 'Gambling', he wrote, 'was an antidote favoured by all classes; the wealthy favoured stocks, cards and lottery tickets; the poor, crown and anchor, pitch and toss, bull baiting and cock fighting'.

Betting was serous and often reckless. Assuredly, never before had such sums been gambled across such a range of opportunities. Gaming at cards or other 'hazards' became common in the rash of clubs that were established in the metropolis during these times. It was not unknown to find sums of several thousand pounds lying on the card table. Does not legend have it that John Montague, 4th Earl of Sandwich (1718-92), patron saint of the English cricket tea, had his cut of ham stuffed between bread in eponymous fashion, in order that he might continue playing cards for heavy stakes, while not greasing a possible winning hand as he replenished his energy? This comestible was named after him from about 1762, right on cue for cricket's true maturation.

Gambling demands order. Without an accepted canon, the likelihood of violent and quarrelsome ramifications was heightened, whether it concerned cards or cricket. It is salutary to note that other sports were as random and chaotic as cricket, and some of these, too, had to be subjected to understandable and acceptable authority, the more competently to control the often heavy betting.

Horse racing is an example, for in spite of or because of its associations with the Stuart royal family, it was a shambles, the less so on the flat, the more so in steeple chasing, initially two horses racing to and from church steeples. One would have thought some of the aspects were straightforward enough, but there was frequently no uniformity about starting and finishing lines and what happened in between times. An early rule commanded riders not to 'open a gate or ride through a gateway of more than a hundred yards along any road, footpath or driftway'. A two hour delay, while punters impatiently awaited late-coming entrants or the outcome of abrasive disputes about conditions, was not uncommon. Shady treatment of horses was taken surprisingly for granted. A gallon of ale to quieten a violent horse or a live eel to enliven a pacific one, or 'feighing' – the insertion of ginger into a horse's rump to produce a show of exhilaration – seemed to have been normal practice.

Slowly, devices were introduced, such as the artificial circuit, the weighing-in of riders, official handicapping and some reliance on the Stud Book. Eventually, the Jockey Club, chiefly composed of influential noblemen and gentlefolk, such as Lord George Bentinck and Admiral Rous, assumed command of racing from about 1750. Its express purpose was to ensure that all was fair and above board, so that valuable prize money might be justly won and that gambling cheats would have their opportunities reduced. It is of interest that the concept of 'form', in relationship to a cricketer's performance, derived from its use for horses and jockeys, and for the same reason of being better informed for gambling.

Similarly, the lawless rough and tumble of boxing had to yield to some moderate decorum that those laying mighty wagers or seeking high cash prizes might not be unduly inconvenienced. It was not easy, for the show tune, *Anything Goes*, might have been composed for early boxing's anthem. The first steps were taken in 1743, when the Broughton Rules were issued by Jack Broughton, whose Tottenham Court Road Amphitheatre was the chief locus for the sport. This brought a semblance of orderliness to a desperately unruly pastime.

Foot racing or 'pedestrianism' was simpler and easier to organise without it becoming unduly acrimonious but football rarely attracted much serious wagering, almost certainly because, at this stage, it was even more anarchic than the other games, often played with massed forces over a wide terrain, usually at festival times, no more than once or twice a year in any vicinity. Of course, as with cricket, there were many differing types of football being played parochially for casual amusement by local and domestic groups. Another point is that football did not come so directly under the directive of the lordly estate owner. What further distinguished his control of horse and foot racing, on occasion boxing, and, as time went by, cricket, was the frequent deployment of estate workers as sporting protagonists.

It was grooms who were the first 'professional' jockeys, likewise, in athletics, it was the footmen, who had to be fleet of foot to run ahead of the carriage to warn of their master's arrival, who similarly obliged. Thus estate workers were the backbone of the cricket sides mustered by the nobility and landowners to fight for their honour and their bank balance. As later happened in association football, the sporting gift sometimes preceded the craft qualification in determining employment. Thomas Waymark, 'the father of cricket professionals' was reputed to have been a groom at Goodwood, the Sussex home of the cricketing Duke of Richmond. Later in the century, the talented Thomas Aylward was bailiff for the sportive Sir Horace Mann on his Kentish estate. As if indicative of the sinecurist nature of the post, we are told that he was a 'poor one'.

Thus it should come as no surprise that cricket, that most complex of diversions, was no speedier than its companion sports in finding some appearance of unity. As for the football codes, these had to await the 19th century for similar orderliness, precisely because they were not adopted earlier by the gentry and nobility. And that was, in turn, because there was little or no major betting on football, for even the most ingenious gamester would have found it difficult to find a route through the crazy maze that was premodern football to define exactly what the gamble was.

Cricket, like horse racing, had the additional advantage that English society, while certainly class-ridden, was not quite so divisive as, say, the more caste-orientated social systems of French or Spanish life. The nobility felt no loss of face in sharing sports such as cricket and racing, where the bodily contact was minimal. Even with boxing, there were occasional forays into the ring by gentlemen. Bowling, what we would now call bowls, was another sport, open to wagering, but also open to some combining of the classes. All this was considered manly. What was usually out of court for the gentry was a football match, often with hundreds scrambling and fighting and struggling. That would have been undignified.

THE INITIAL LAWS

It is, then, no accident that the oldest approximation to a set of laws for cricket is to be found in the 'Articles of Agreement' for two fixtures between teams raised by the Duke of Richmond and Mr Alan Brodrick in 1727. They are described as 'instructions to umpires and team managers', explaining what might otherwise have been disputatious points concerning the betting. Some cricket historians have argued that these implicitly refer back to existing laws, but it may be safer to suggest that they take for granted, not a particular code, but a generalised understanding of what 'cricket' was. It might also be safer to assume that these articles are an illustration of a normal practice, that is, drawing up such documents for individual games where wagers were involved.

Lest it be thought that the 2nd Duke of Richmond had condescended to consort with a commoner, Alan Brodrick, who hailed from Peper Harow near Guildford, succeeded to the title of Viscount Midleton two years later in 1729. Several of the conditions included in their joint agreement indicate what the players could not assume. This adds to the supposition that the overall comprehension of cricket was vague or diverse.

The games were to be twelve a side, the pitch was to be 23 yards in length, 'a ball caught, the striker is out', there was a need to 'touch the umpire's stick' to register a run, and 'the wicket must be put down with ball in hand' for a run out . . . In terms of the later and official laws of cricket, this is a mixture of the contentious and the obvious. Any laws, did they exist, that failed to rule on team size, pitch length, that a batsman could be caught out, how a run might be scored and whether he could be run out from a direct throw, were patently lacking in what later cricketers would view as the fundamentals. There was, for example, much variety of team size, from single wicket, via fives and sixes and upwards. Curiously, it would not be until 1884 that the mythical number eleven, with its purportedly Anglo-Saxon or Flemish derivations, would be enshrined in the laws.

There was also a modern-sounding law forbidding anyone to argue with the umpire with the exception of the noble captains, to whom major disputes had to be referred, as sometimes happens today with off-field umpires. The provenance of the teams was additionally defined, as in the Duke of Richmond's team having to be selected 'from any gamesters who have played in either of his last two matches with Sir William Gage', while Alan Brodrick's players had to have lived recently within three miles of his Peper Harow base. And all this palaver for a twelve guineas bet.

It must be stressed that this is not an argument about whether there was or was not something called 'cricket' being played. The latest compilation – Ian Maun's extremely thorough *From Commons to Lord's*, vol I 1700-1750 (2009) – contains some 200 references to the game. Nonetheless, a major characteristic of all such collections is their variety. The proposition is that the term 'cricket' was much more generic than has been usually believed and that it was only under the compulsion of heavy wagering, that noblemen in and around London were moved, as with horse racing and boxing and at much the same time, to codify the cricketing strands into more or less one format. Another way of looking at the issue, and borrowing from the main 18th century base for gambling, is to see cricket like cards, as in having a game of cards. There was a universally used pack of cards but a hundred ways of playing with them.

To that degree then, cricket, as it now became, was a hand-crafted, even artificial, sport, in that same sense as there was also a synthetic format of horse racing and boxing. Cricket then, is as much a construction, perhaps more so, than that supposed organic plant, nurtured from early English roots, and struggling to survival against the encroachment of alien weeds, so deeply loved by its more romanticised adherents.

In 1752 the laws are mentioned in *The New Universal Magazine*, 'as settled by the Cricket-Club in 1744, and play'd at the Artillery

Ground, London'. The 'London' laws of 1744 are thus the first of which we have cognisance. As Derek Birley, in his *A Social History of English Cricket* (1999) indicates, they bear a resemblance to the tone and style of the Broughton Rules for prize-fighting of much the same time and which, interestingly, required that 'the principals' should choose two umpires 'who shall absolutely decide all disputes'. Their cricketing counterparts were to be the judges, like football referees today, of 'all outs and ins, of all fair and unfair play or frivolous delays, of all hurts real or pretended.' They are highly specific regulations, with as little as possible left to chance, and the whole timbre is of gentlemen wearied by the constant bickering that had obviously attended many of their 'plays'.

Some historians, perhaps eager to demonstrate the longevity of cricket's saga, urge that this set of laws is a 'recension' to, that is, a retrieval from, a previous code of long usage. They point in support to the durable Saxon derivation of the language of stump, wicket, notch and so on. This is not entirely convincing. It is equally likely that these laws were either a sophisticated version of one of several codes or an essay in compromise of all or most of them. On the negative side, for example, they do not allude to the 'popping' hole between the wickets, in which the ball had to be deposited for a run out in one apparent variation of the game, and this possibly tiny aberration is rarely again mentioned. On the positive side, the measures of pitch, wicket dimensions and so forth were now strictly codified. Just as, a little over a hundred years later, leading football organisers had to formulate a code to enable teams to play regularly and competitively the one against the other, so were cricket's exponents faced with the same problem.

Even then, one might re-read the 1752 magazine item – (cricket) 'play'd at the Artillery Ground, London' – as leaving the description open to the interpretation that these laws were particularly drawn up for games at that venue and, were one especially wary, for that year.

What is most evident is that almost despairing edge to the wording of these new laws, as, especially when money was at stake, the contentious condition of the game had somehow to be moderated. There cannot have been much prior agreement to a common oral tradition if that degree of squabbling had to be resolved. It was, therefore, a major step forward in 1774 when a group of 'noblemen and gentlemen' from London and the neighbouring counties, and chaired by General Sir William Draper, met at the Star and Garter tavern on Pall-Mall (then boasting a hyphen) to revise and unify the laws. Again, the site is London and the tone is authoritative. It is the voice of leadership issuing its dictates, resembling in sense and style the Jockey Club's edicts. It is the declaration of a committee that was ready to adopt the role – perhaps was already regarded as – 'the Cricket Club'.

In practice, a major change in the laws was the introduction of the LBW rule. In the past, the 'hockey stick' bat had left the batsman standing apart from the wicket, while, with speed the chief weapon of the bowler, few had been tempted to risk damaged ankles and limbs. The changing shape of the bat brought the batsman closer to the target, and, possibly under the pressure of competition for heavy wagers, spurred him on to place his legs in jeopardy. However, no LBW decision has been discovered prior to 1795. It was also in the last quarter of the 18th century that the third stump was included, to the satisfaction of bowlers who had watched their finest deliveries whistle between the two uprights. This was a gradual process from about 1776. It was 1785 before the three stumps device is mentioned in the laws, so it may not have always been deployed hitherto.

THE FIRST DESCRIPTIONS

Eventually, there are actual description of recorded games of cricket, with a code of rules explicit within it. Language and action are joined. The County of Kent and All England played out a mighty match, the former team narrowly winning, at the Artillery Ground in London, in the same year – 1744 – that the first set of laws was published for cricket at that venue – they may even have been con- cocted to control this very match. It is the first game for which the scores have been fully preserved, while James Dance, writing under the pseudonym of James Love, was paid to describe the encounter in the hyperbolic terms of Latin heroic verse. The ostentatious description of an ordinary event or mundane condition was very much a Hanoverian literary conceit; witness Alexander Pope's *The*

Dunciad (the first version of which was published in 1728), which satirised 'Dullness' in lines of formal elegance. Nonetheless, James Love's tongue is only pressed slightly into his cheek, as he extols the cricketing paladins in battle.

What is difficult to judge is whether his detailed 300 line narrative, *Cricket; An Heroic Poem,* is intended to inform authentically or impress aesthetically. Nonetheless, it floridly depicts a recognisable cricket match, one in which the modern essentials are present, even unto the very modish element of gambling:

> *But while the drooping play'r invokes the Gods,*
> *The busy better calculates his Odds.*
> *Swift round the Plain, in buzzing murmurs run.*
> *'I'll hold you ten to four, Kent – Done, sir – Done.*

A precursor ode, also in Latin, dates from 1706. William Goldwin, an Old Etonian and later a schoolmaster and vicar in Bristol, published a set of poems, *Musae Juveniles,* among them a 95 line verse called *In Certamen Pilae* or, very crudely, 'in contest over a ball'. Friendly pens, have, as with James Love's poem, translated this charming piece, which begins:

> *Springtime comes, with mild and limpid air*
> *Smiling, with kindness coaxes earth to bear*
> *And active feet to sport where fields spread wide;*
> *A team of youths with crocken bats supplied.*

What attracts the historian's attention, however, is that, before the teams are engaged, there is a dispute about which local rules shall apply. They turn to a 'Nestor' figure, after the brave and wise Grecian chief who participated in the Trojan Wars, to pass judgement and he imposes the 'Justes Leges' that both sides find acceptable. Although H.S.Altham tries hard to see this as 'the established code', his head perhaps conflicts with his heart as he allows for the possibility of it meaning 'a reasonable compromise'. That is probably a more realistic opinion, whereas, by the time of James Love's extravagant poesy, there is little doubt that, at least in the London region, one code has been fairly generally accepted.

Just recently another mock-heroic poem, in manuscript form and dated 1723, has been found in the East Sussex Record Office. Its authorship is unclear. It has been published in brave translation and with comments, by Martin Wilson and Martyn and Jeremy Butler, in *The Cricket Statistician,* no.148, Winter 2009.

It is titled *Clava Falcata Torsio* or 'Playing Ball with a Curved Bat'. It is a pick-up match, in which 'true friends divide into two lines', and it might be noted that it is a one innings affair. Control is in the hands of 'four men of whom two safeguard the laws of one wicket and two the other'. Martin Wilson wonders whether this mistakenly embraces the two scorers, although it does not seem likely that there would have been a scorer for each end, and the occasion may have pre-empted the quartet of officials of the modern Test match. There is betting, for a hundred pounds, and Martin Wilson rightly draws amused attention to the modern-sounding 'goading, tantrums, triumphs and celebrations' of the players. Again, there are idiosyncrasies. The bowler instructs the fielders to 'stand behind me and throw the ball back that flies past me, giving some impression of a rounders field setting and its mode of returning the ball to the bowler. To score a run, the batsmen 'touch bats', with some ambiguity in the Latin as to whether it is their own bats or bats held by two of the umpires. Significantly, there is no standard practice. Before the game begins, 'clothes are laid out and rules agreed.'

Whether specific or diverse in formula, the tempo of cricket in the southeast certainly quickened during the 18th century. Newspapers and other organs, such as journals and diaries, are, compared with earlier decades, awash with items, faithfully collected by dedicated archivists such as H.T.Waghorn, F.S.Ashley-Cooper or G.B.Buckley. The printing of scores assisted the serious punter, as he could study the 'form'. Gambling remained a major motif. There must have been, of course, a continuation of what now would be called the recreational game, with clusters of young men enjoying cricket-orientated diversions in villages and towns, but the serious, more controlled and higher level of the sport remained at the behest of its funders.

The manner in which cricket threaded into the interstices of Hanoverian society makes for a complex tapestry, probably best described in David Underdown's judicious *Start of Play; Cricket and Culture in 18th Century England* (2000). In summary, however, it was the sponsors who made the running, and, as they came and went, so did the cricketing emphasis shift slightly within its southeastern ambit.

Thus the influence of the 2nd Duke of Richmond (1701-1750), resident in Goodwood House in West Sussex, gave that area something of an initial edge, either through the recruiting of his own estate workers, plus some allies, or through his backing of the cricketers of Slindon, a village adjacent to Goodwood.

Later in the century the 4th Earl of Tankerville (1743-1822) of Mount Felix, Walton-on-Thames, in Surrey, and the 3rd Duke of Dorset (1745-1799), who owned the Sevenoaks ground, together with Sir Horatio Mann (1744-1814), who also controlled two or three cricket grounds in Kent, switched the focus rather towards those two counties. There was even some royal patronage, in the somewhat unprepossessing figure of Frederick Louis, Prince of Wales, the eldest son of George II, an inveterate gambler. Reports suggest his death in 1751 resulted from a blow from a cricket ball, although Horace Walpole said it was a tennis ball. Horace Walpole, aesthete and youngest son of Sir Robert Walpole, was no games lover, but one is tempted to wonder whether we find ourselves still amidst the clutter of premodern games where one ball might have served differing purposes. There are also those who have pondered the difference that alleged direct hit might have had on English (and American) politics had the prince survived and ascended the throne rather than his son as George III.

By this time there were players who were gaining in at least regional acknowledgement. These included Richard Newland of Slindon and England fame, 'Lumpy' Stevens and William Bedster, who had Tankerville connections, and the Duke of Dorset's employee, John Minshull, scorer, on behalf of the Duke's team in 1769, of the first recorded century.

THE HAMBLEDON INTERLUDE

A further example of the compound of patronage and locality was Hambledon, made famous by John Nyren's *The Young Cricketer's Tutor*, edited by Charles Cowden Clarke and first published in 1833. The author's father, Richard Nyren, a nephew and protégé of Richard Newland, had captained the Hambledon team, and these tales of the old Hambledon cricketers, among them 'Silver Billy' Beldham, Tom Walker and David Harris. Unlike almost every other such agency, the records survived of the Hambledon club, showing, for instance, that, in 1791, 52 subscribers – all listed as 'gentlemen' – paid a three guineas fee.

John Nyren's enchanting story, together with Rev James Pycroft's affirming text, *The Cricket Field*, published a little later in 1851, led to a belief, still sometimes difficult to deny today, that Hambledon was 'the cradle of cricket'. Much has been written and argued about Hambledon, with possibly the most authentic account being *Hambledon; the Men and the Myths* (2001) by John Goulstone, one of the most diligent scrutineers of sporting archives of his generation. In effect, and especially in the 1770s and 1780s, Hambledon was the focus for a large slice of the top-class cricket of the day.

The chief organisers and backers of the Hambledon fancy were Rev Charles Powlett and Philip Dehany, a Bristol businessman. There is some evidence that they would lay off money 'pretty quickly' against Hambledon, if the contest were going in favour of the opposition, but that was regarded as sensible among the betting fraternity. Some of the claims about the amounts wagered are rather implausible. It has to be recalled that promoters were inclined to exaggerate the sums 'depending' on the outcome of a fixture to boost the excitement. John Goulstone shows convincingly that the figures were more often in the hundreds, and less than in the thousands of guineas, fairly low by the amounts sometimes wagered in other pursuits. Nevertheless, the high and lowly alike were drawn by the urge to bet. It should also be remembered that, as well as the overall purse at stake, a stream of other monies was gambled, as in the modern mode, during the progress of the match.

According to John Arlott, 'a match was the subject of a wager while a game was not'. There were a lot of matches. Hambledon may not have been the Bethlehem of cricket, and, while it might be extravagant to call it the Las Vegas of cricket, there was more of the casino than the cradle about that famed cricketing location.

It is sometimes suggested that Hambledon was off the beaten track of Georgian society – but it was no more so than, say, Newmarket in respect of horse racing. That is maybe the genuine kind of comparison to offer. It was situated across the Hampshire boundary from the West Sussex cricketing sites of Goodwood and Slindon and, for gentlemen inclined to enjoy a day or two in the country, as they might for racing, not too strenuous a journey from their nearby estates or from London.

There are confusions over the relation of Hambledon and Hampshire, a mirror image of the same ambiguity elsewhere at this time, where the mix of clubs, counties and teams named after noble patrons was equally ambivalent. This was partly to do with the fact that, as with the hyped high wager, the posters that cried Kent rather than Sevenoaks were more likely to attract the crowds. To take two less colourful examples, the Oldfield club of Maidenhead and the Hornchurch club would sometimes raise Berkshire and Essex sides respectively. It is also true that many citizens identified much more closely with their county at that time than would be the case today and probably found some positive enjoyment in this nomenclature. Furthermore, it is salutary to recall that some of the patrons actually owned a sufficient proportion of the shire in question to justify them labelling their team accordingly.

So there were plenty of Georgian fixtures involving Kent, Hampshire, Surrey and so on, to say nothing of England and All England teams. Not least because of the itinerant nature of the best players, many of them paid for their services during this time, and of other vagaries of selection, it would be misleading to concede that there was anything remotely like 'county' cricket, let alone 'England' cricket, in any institutional form. Peter Wynne-Thomas quotes the tale of the Duke of Cumberland, brother of the future George III and infamous as the 'Butcher' of Bonny Prince Charlie's Jacobite host at the Battle of Culloden in 1746. In 1751 he ordered the best twenty two players to practise before him; he picked his 'England' eleven; and the rejects then routed Cumberland's select. The cynic might suggest that selection policy has not progressed much since that juncture, but the haphazard fashion of the day warns against reading too much into the labels fastened on teams. There has been a tendency in the literature to use the term 'county' without this linguistic health warning, a practice that has sometimes led to readers surmising wrongly that there is a strong affiliation between 'county' cricket then and now.

London, throughout, retained the genuine allure. There is a sense in which the delights of other foci, such as Hambledon, are ephemeral. Hambledon has more of a claim on the heart and soul of cricket than on its flesh and blood. That is not said lightly; the sentiment involved with any cultural activity is often as significant as its practice, but the metropolis had the enduring pulling power. In terms of the history of cricket, Hambledon and London illustrate a telling dichotomy. One pulled at the heart strings, the other at the purse strings. Top-grade cricket would thereafter be an urbanised diversion with rural yearnings.

From 1730 leading matches were played at the Artillery Ground in the Finsbury area of London. The lessee, George Smith, also managed the Peel Horse tavern in neighbouring Chiswell Street. This was a stock arrangement that lasted many years, whereby a landlord utilised cricket, as well as other sports, to attract customers. It was here that, according to Peter Wynne-Thomas, the 'London Club' was established and where the Kent and All England game of 1744, celebrated in John Love's heroic verse, was played.

Later the chief, if not the exclusive, focus moved a little northwards to fields adjacent to, inevitably, another inn, White Conduit House, in Islington. The (London) Cricket Club rented the ground several days a week and doubtless made full use of the neighbouring facility, while its members also dined at the Star and Garter hostelry in Pall-Mall, where, it may be recalled, the revision of the laws was discussed in 1774. From about the end of the 1770s, a young and competent cricketer, Thomas Lord, acted as a kind of groundsman-cum-coach for the club. As with other clubs of the day, a considerable amount of members' usage of the ground would have been for internal practice matches and the like, rather than just for fixtures.

In 1786 its treasurer, the Earl of Winchilsea, told Thomas Lord that Colonel Charles Lennox, later the 4th Duke of Richmond, himself and others, were interested in developing a private ground for the club. The felt need for an enclosed arena for the gentry, and apart from any natural wish for independence, may have arisen because of disputes either with other users of the Islington ground or, as occasionally happened amid the tumults of the Georgian era, among attendees at matches. There had certainly been earlier reports of fighting between the players and the spectators at the Artillery ground. Thomas Lord was asked to consider creating such an amenity and he readily agreed.

In fact, he created not one but three grounds. He was the ideal cricket organiser, for he was as successful in the wine trade as in grounds-manship. One who kept wine and laid turf with equal capability was a cricketing treasure. In 1787 he took the lease on an inn and field in New Road, by what is now Dorset Square, in Marylebone. When that curse of urban sporting venues – building development – encroached, he constructed a second ground some 800 yards to the northwest in 1809. The New Road ground was yielded up to the builders in 1810, but the second ground was itself menaced by the construction of the Regent Canal. In 1814 Thomas Lord pushed another 400 yards to the northwest and opened the present Lord's ground to the north of St John's Wood Road.

To the despair of orthodoxy, Peter Wynne-Thomas, relying mainly on a 1784 broadsheet kept in the Leicester Record Office, persuasively argues that there is a continuum from 1744 of a 'Cricket Club', akin to the Jockey Club; indeed, he even has the temerity to suggest that the former might have fathered the latter. The broadsheet includes the 'Star and Garter' laws and the club's rules and membership. An intriguing sideline is the confirmation from these that much of the activity was internalised, that is, members assembled for pick-up games. Basically, Peter Wynne-Thomas urges that the geographic descriptors – London; Star and Garter; White Conduit; Marylebone – mislead, except if they are regarded merely as addresses for the 'Cricket Club'. He points out that a 'White Conduit' team playing at Lord's in 1787 were all members of the 'Cricket Club' - and so were the team called the Marylebone Cricket Club in 1788.

Very quickly, what we might respectfully and impartially label the Cricket Club at Marylebone became nationally, as well as regionally, accepted as the source of legitimate authority, and what cannot be disputed is that the leaders of the old guard, men like Colonel Lennox and the Earl of Winchilsea, were the premier defenders of the new faith. And when they re-published the laws, with little more than an extra minor polish, in 1788, it was under that very heading of 'the Cricket Club at St Marylebone'. MCC worthies reject the theory that the club was not instituted in 1787, one of the few instances in cricket's history when those closely involved are unwilling to attribute an earlier date to its progress. Certainly it was 1787 when Lord's ground was opened for business and there was definitely a golden jubilee ceremony at Lord's in 1837, presumably with a few ancients engaged who might have recollected the beginnings.

The random pavilion fires – Lord's in 1825, for example - that have mysteriously destroyed so many cricket annals may have hindered the debate. Whatever the case, it is certain that, from the mid 1740s, almost from the point where cricket became a serous and organised concern, the authoritative hand of a few leading noblemen and rich gentlemen, with London their natural habitat, was and would remain in supreme command. The prestige of Lord's grew and there was a drift thereto of most of the important matches.

Slowly, what might be safely termed the 'London' cricket code spread to other parts of the nation. Cricket is a complicated game and there was nothing of the wildfire expansion of association football that followed the unification of football's laws in the mid-Victorian era. These kicked at the open door of a widespread incidence of types of football and did so at a time when economic factors, such as transport, urbanism and industrialisation, were helpfully ripe. But the earlier epoch was one when it was said both men and horses were drowned in potholes in the Great North Road, the country's main thoroughfare. There were, very probably, plenty of cricket-orientated diversions played outside of the home counties, but, as yet, the pressure to compete with outsiders according to an ordained set of rules, no less the opportunities of doing so, were less likely to be found outside the southeast where lay the most prosperous and progressive portion of the kingdom.

Rowland Bowen's intensive researches suggest that it was well into the 19th century before there was at least one reference to cricket in each one of the English counties. East Anglia, where Thomas Lord learned his cricket, was perhaps the first area removed from the direct influence of London to develop a formal interest in the game, followed by the Midlands and into Yorkshire and Derbyshire, although the aristocratic oversight was less common in these areas.

There were signs of cricket overseas, but these invariably involved English soldiers and sailors or expatriates. In 1789, the cricketing patron, the Duke of Dorset, was the British ambassador in Paris, where English and French lordlings occasionally played at cricket. He famously attempted to have arranged the first-ever cricket tour, but the team got no further than Dover, for what would now be called security fears intervened, courtesy of the French Revolution. It was to be a fascinating precedent.

The south eastern imbalance remained enormous. Of the known games in the 18th century, four-fifths were played in the five counties of Essex, Sussex, Kent, Surrey and Middlesex, including London, that is, only about 350 of roughly 2000 games had been staged outside that region, with neighbouring Hampshire, of course, responsible for quite a lot of those. Rowland Bowen speaks of 'unofficial laws' that 'enshrined local variations of long standing' circulating into the 19th century, 'and it seems more than likely that different versions of the game were played in different parts of England during most of the 18th century, and that it was only in the 19th century that there was something near uniformity.' In the same passage, he adds that versions of the game being found on the continent about the turn of the 18th century 'were not due to any English importation but to the existence of the old game of cricket which seems to have been played in one form or another over most of Europe.'

This provides a further reminder of the hypothesis of a kind of soup of 'gameness' or of a much more variegated and unsystematic nature of 'play' than is usually visualised. On the whole, organised cricket, something recognisable as a genuine forerunner of the approved form, was chiefly restricted, apart from a few fragmentary pockets, to London and its surrounds until well into the 19th century. Betting was a crucial, but not an indispensable, aspect of the sport, which was closely controlled by a noble and plutocratic cabal. Although there were often occasions when principal matches, featuring notable players, were spread over two or three or more days, scores, while increasing as the century drew on, remained fairly low. Many two innings games were completed in a day, especially if the weather held good. Looking a long way ahead, one may point to some of these features reoccurring in the modern commercial presentation of cricket.

It is with that perspective in mind that possibly the most important date in 18th century cricket may be pronounced. In 1744 the first known admission charges were made. It cost twopence to obtain entry to the Artillery Ground for a great match. In 1743 'checks' for re-admission had been issued but it is not sure whether they were priced and when the prices were raised to sixpence for another fixture in 1744 there was a furore and down they tumbled to twopence. Beforehand the commercial practice had been to rely on the sale of food and drink, plus other franchises and doubtless handouts from the patrons.

The actual charging for admission placed the whole enterprise on a different footing. Now it was an unqualified commercial entertainment and the sporting aspect could no longer take pre-eminence. The cricket authorities were not quick to accept the distinction. When the England and Pakistani Test at the Oval in 2006 was halted on a cricketing technicality, however significant it might have appeared to the authorities, a grave injustice was done to both the 20,000 spectators there present and the 14,000 who had bought tickets for the following and last day. Another example, by no means the only one, was the abandonment of an England and Australia Twenty20 match at a crowded Old Trafford in 2009 by reason of parts of the ground being wet. The views of the umpires and players, their *amour-propre* imperilled by the thought of playing what was basically a short-term romp in difficult but not impossible conditions, were allowed to take precedent over the wishes of the audience. Since 1744 theirs had been the prior if sometimes ignored claim.

These and other matches should have been continued in whatever fashion and it was scandalous that the customers, despite the solace of any rebates, should have been so badly treated. Forget the palaver about the ethics of umpiring, ethnic pride and prejudice and legal hocus-pocus. The cricketing authorities should have ensured that the Oval Test of 2006 was played, for to do otherwise was a grim dereliction of commercial obligation. Thought should have been given to the two pals who travel a long distance to meet once a year at the Oval for a day's international cricket or the dad taking his youngster for the first time to a big cricket match. It might have occurred to someone in authority that, but for the gate money and the media revenue paid by the public, Pakistan and England would not have been playing professional cricket at the Oval in the first place. Imagine the uproar if the actors playing Portia and Shylock had a row at the interval about a mistimed cue and the theatre management refused to stage the last act of *The Merchant of Venice*.

The show must go on. Cricket, like theatre, was suddenly a public entertainment as well as a private recreation. Indeed cricket, from practically its onset as an organised venture, has been cast in those two separate forms.

Village cricket has long played a part in both the real and the imagined cricket of England. The top picture is of the Recreation Ground, Churt, in Surrey, on land gifted as a First World War Memorial, while a northern example, below, is Pott Shrigley in Cheshire.

CHAPTER THREE
WHITER THAN WHITE

Harrow cricket ground in the 19th century

Then there was a lurch in cricket's progress. The game, at least in its formal mode, languished. The dualism of the recreational and the official game continued, as it does to the present time, although 'generic' and 'formal' might be better descriptors for that early stage. One must remain wary of some of the allusions to cricket upcountry and away from the southeast. Some commentators are inclined to ascribe these to the spread of cricket, implicitly of the formalised variety, from the London region but they may be the first written or printed reference to longer standing samples of localised 'rough' cricket.

THE NEAR EXPIRY OF CRICKET

The sudden decline of orthodox cricket has been rather vaguely attributed to agricultural and trading difficulties, some of them connected with the long French wars that dragged on, with a slight break, from 1793 to 1815, with an aftermath of social discontent. Nevertheless, other sports, such as horse racing and pugilism, prospered during this time and, come war, come famine, the rich who sponsored cricket were hardly ever incommoded in their pursuit of leisure. Further, the Hanoverian period, in spite of some solidity of structure and economic gain, was no stranger to social tumult. Apart from military action, as at the time of the two Jacobite Rebellions, there were plenty of disturbances, such as the terrifying Gordon Riots of 1780. The Riot Act itself was passed in 1715 and government in the 18th century was, according to one wit, 'oligarchy moderated by riot'.

If one accepts the distinction drawn in this analysis whereby the formal game was relatively recent and restricted in fashion, one might rather speculate that organised cricket had been something of a craze, a freak gambling mini-mania, which subsided as quickly has it had risen. It had not, in its official formula, struck down countrywide roots. A comparison might be ventured with tenpin bowling, which emerged from a mesh of typologies of skittles, just as cricket had emerged from a similar *mélange* of diversions, including, of course, skittles. Backed by technical wizardry it took much of the western world by storm in the 1960s. It was one of the first games to find a regular and popular niche on television; bowling alleys sprang up and national competitions were mounted. A few years later the tenpin tempest had died away, leaving a desultory series of venues for pleasant but rather understated recreation.

Whatever the reason, there was a dwindling of interest. In microcosm, the termination of the Hambledon Club, which had always been a clubbable outfit, with cricket its major but not its exclusive concern, indicated the trend. The club minute book for 25 September 1795 reads simply 'no gentlemen present', leaving the historian to ponder the theological enigma as to who – one other than a gentleman, perhaps – recorded that blanket absence.

Using *A Guide to Important Cricket Matches Played in the British Isles 1707-1863* (1981) and *Complete First-class Match List vol 1 1801-1914* (1996), both published after several years of onerous research and earnest debate by the Association of Cricket Statisticians and Historians, it may be demonstrated that having, from 1720, built up to sometimes twenty games a summer, formal cricket collapses. Between 1802 and 1840, important matches never reach double figures in a season – then in 1841 there are eleven such fixtures. In 1801, 1803, 1814 and 1818 there are only two matches each year. In each of 1802, 1811, 1812 and 1813 there is just one 'important' fixture.

Moreover, the venues for such matches were very restricted in location. The First-class Match List, for which users of are advised by the compilers to term individual pre-1860 games as 'important' or 'great', includes 115 fixtures for the years 1801 to 1822 inclusively. Of these no fewer than 82 were played at Lord's, leaving but 23 played on other grounds. Almost all of these were situated in the southeast, with Cambridge latterly coming into the picture and hosting some five fixtures from 1817. It was to be 1825 before, on an eight-three basis, there were more matches elsewhere than at Lord's in this phase. It was 1826 before the first great northern encounter is recorded, when Sheffield and Leicester played Nottingham at Sheffield.

Firstly, there was, in those twenty-two years, precious little 'important' cricket at all; secondly, Lord's hosted over two-thirds of such games played; thirdly, almost all the rest were played in the southeast. Just two matches – one involving a Nottingham and Leicester eleven and one a Norfolk side – involved teams from very far outside the Home Counties. Whatever the incidence of other grades of cricket up and down the country, this is the story of a practical monopoly of 'important' cricket by the London region, and especially by MCC.

The belted earls and other gentlemen who had urged Thomas Lord to establish his famous ground had been keen to find some relative privacy for their pastime, and it should be remembered that, as with most clubs and grounds at the time, one of Thomas Lord's main functions was the provision of facilities for practice, for internal play among the membership and for minor games against local clubs. For all the near monopoly, 82 'great' fixtures over 22 years, barely four a season, was uneconomic, but, apart from the minor cricket and practice activity, Thomas Lord hired out his ground for pedestrianism, ballooning, pigeon-shooting and other events. In 1822 Benjamin Aislabie became the first secretary of the MCC and in 1825 the MCC took possession of the ground. Thomas Lord, tempted by the lure of building on his land, was persuaded instead to sell the lease for £5000 to the wealthy cricket enthusiast, William Ward, himself a fine batsman. His 278 for MCC versus Norfolk in 1820 was the first double century in a major game.

This retreat of the well-to-do behind the fences of Lord's, together with a sixpenny entrance fee for games which was intended to detract the boisterous element, marked a reaction against that combustible mix of alcohol, gambling and large crowds that was so explosive in the 18th century. Gambling often begets corruption, which, in turn, often involves the participants. The craftsmen professionals of the day were well paid by the standards of their contemporaries in the manual and agrarian trades. In the second half of the 18th century a guinea (£1.05) was usually the pay for a major match, with, as time drew on, liberal match fees of as much as five guineas for a win and three guineas for a loss recorded. This compared well with the average weekly agricultural working wage of ten shilling (50p). That said, it was small financial beer when the wagers on the games are considered, even allowing for some natural exaggeration of the sums by the promoters. The notoriously unpleasant Lord Frederick Beauclerk, descendant of Nell Gwynne and the leading upper crust player of his age, reckoned to make 600 guineas a summer, betting on himself and others, while, it should be remembered, gambling was covered in the actual laws of cricket at this time.

The professionals foregathered at the Green Man and Still tavern in Oxford Street, London. It was where they were hired – and it was where they were bribed. As late as 1817 the Nottingham and England game at Lord's was said to have been sold on both sides, allowing for the intriguingly Carrollian sight of bowlers trying not to take wickets and batsmen attempting to be dismissed. It would also seem that bookmakers remained a constant around the Lord's pavilion well into the Regency period.

The apparent if short-lived – its public usage was halted in the 1750s – success of the Artillery Ground as a commercial cricketing venture was followed by other schemes. Well into the 19th century, entrepreneurs developed enclosed grounds in big towns like Brighton, Sheffield, Leeds and Leicester, where, on the relatively rare occasion of major games, large crowds could quickly and easily assemble. They were variously sustained by rentals from local clubs, from membership subscriptions, with the more ambitious ventures including wider recreational facilities, and from the inevitable retail of alcohol. Apart from the splendid exception of Trent Bridge, few of them endured for long. Like many of the bingo halls of mid-20th century, they came, blazed fitfully for some years and then succumbed to cultural and economic pressures. They mainly lacked the identity and focus that regular sports fans came to demand, whilst other commercial initiatives, such as the regular scourge of building development, proved more profitable.

The undertow of the history of sport, perhaps of all leisure, has been a rumbling chorus of disapproval from the righteously inclined about its effects on morals, on social conduct, on political stability and on the economy. Sometimes these critics have been in the ascendant; sometimes they have had good cause for their concerns. Frequently, the consequences have been patchy, with a parson or squire being here a lenient games-lover and a punitive games-hater there.

In 1793 the *Gentleman's Magazine* voiced its worries about the assemblage of urban crowds of up to 20,000 following sports, including cricket. Such activity, it was averred, 'propagates a spirit of idleness at a juncture when, with most industry, our debts, taxes, and decay of trade, will scarcely allow us to get our daily bread'. That kind of critical voice was not new but it perhaps indicated a mood-swing. Important cricket was, in a sense, hidden away at Lord's. It fell away. For a generation, cricket drifted into a feeble condition. It took a step back, an unusual course for what would later be a major global sport and business. Of course the linkage via Lord's and its adherents to the old days of cricket would prove invaluable. Nonetheless, it is sometimes forgotten that the prescribed cricket that evolved during the Victorian era was essentially a novel construct.

THE VIRTUOUS RECOVERY OF CRICKET

Its chief progenitor was the reformed public school movement. One of the prize features of the northern Renaissance had been the 'free grammar schools' established to such a degree that few boys in England were not within what, for then, was reasonable walking distance from home to school. For the remainder, the schoolmaster might have taken a handful of scholars into his own accommodation, sometimes on a week-by-week basis, a device that would prove to be a fatal flaw in the system. During the 18th century the grammar schools fell into extreme decay, so that barely a hundred were left, offering a service to only about 3000 pupils in total.

It was at this point that a parasitic takeover began of a few of these schools, many of them founded by charitable acts for poor local children, to board and educate the boys of the rich on a broad geographical base. The lodging of a handful proved a stimulus to providing accommodation for the majority or for all of the pupils, which ended much of both the local and the charitable provision. As a convenient example, a local grocer, Lawrence Sheriff, founded Rugby School in 1567, and, when it was switched to that other purpose, there was opposition from neighbouring farmers and others. Thus, from among the desuetude of the many, emerged the new life of the few, the 'public' appellation and, to this day, their spurious clinging to advantageous charity status, an incongruous and, indeed, offensive reminder of their benevolent past. Later, 'private' or 'proprietary' schools were purpose built to join them, so that schools like Marlborough and Cheltenham complemented the ancient piles like Eton and Harrow. The evolution of such a national series of insulated citadels was attended by a rise in the starting-age from seven or eight to thirteen, with a range of 'preparatory' schools opened for the younger boys.

Unluckily these 'great' schools were by no mean free from the vices of their host society. They were, in the words of Thomas Bowdler, editor of the censored Shakespeare canon of 1818, 'nurseries of vice', where the masters beat the boys, where the older or stronger boys beat and bullied their younger and weaker brethren, save when they were terrorising the local neighbourhood, where fearlessly youthful arrogance ruled and teachers exerted little control, and where rebellions, at least one of which, at Westminster school, required for its thwarting the attendance of soldiers with fixed bayonets, were frequent. By comparison, the worst performing secondary school in the most violent and deprived district of the UK at present must look like a haven of serene academic sedateness.

A critical element in the urge to reform these schools was a new generation of pupil, the sons of the masters of industry and trade, their fathers keen to emulate the landed gentry but less eager to throw their money away foolishly. Prime Ministers such as Robert Peel and William Gladstone were the children of commercial profit who were educated at, respectively, Eton and Harrow, before moving on to Oxford. It has been powerfully argued that elitist schooling of this brand, rather than blue blood, quickly became the emblem of the ruling classes, as, not for the first time, landed and commercial wealth intermingled. Some of the intermingling was by marriage; for instance, John Gladstone, William's wealthy father, married into the noble Glynne family.

Another crucial component was the arrival of a bunch of energetically reforming headmasters. Although Thomas Arnold, the much lauded head of Rugby, is properly hailed as the exemplar, his Christian outlook was not wholly sympathetic to sport. It was rather his admirers and disciples who really pressed for games, cricket foremost among them, to be 'compulsory, organised and eulogised'. They admired Arnold's motto of 'Godliness and good learning', but they were also the champions of a social conformity, among which school uniforms, school magazines, school songs, school chapel, as well as games, were utilised to create the manly product. Edward Thring, at Uppingham, introduced the first public school gymnasium, and relished 'the fool in form ' who could manage a decent 'hit to leg', Charles James Vaughan, at Harrow, H.H.Almond, at Loretto, enthusiast of the open window and the cold bath, E.W.Benson, at Wellington – these were to the fore in this vast reformation of the public schools.

'Fortitude, self-rule and public spirit' were the watchwords. They seized what were little more than confined herds of wild boys and attempted to construct junior versions of Oxbridge colleges, almost medieval in a monastic insistence on the experience being secluded and uncompromising. It was the educational gloss on the evangelical mood that was so evident in Victorian life and work. Thomas Carlyle, the great apostle of the Victorian era, wrote in 1840 that 'we do not believe there is in the world a community so religious and so sober-minded as the middle-classes of England' – and their schools were moulded accordingly.

The cult of Athleticism was adroitly encouraged. Cricket fuelled the sense of allegiance to form, house and school; cricket was a diversion away from what Edward Thring, in booming sermonising, called 'the worm-life of foul, earthly desires'; cricket, unlike some previous boy-led field sports, such as hunting and shooting, could be reasonably supervised within the school precincts. It grew close to anti-intellectualism, the anxious wish to avoid producing what, in 1872, were branded 'effeminate, enfeebled bookworms'.

There was not much fear of that and, needless to say, the ideal was not always realised – Lord Salisbury, later to be a long-serving Conservative prime minister, was removed from Eton in 1845 because of his sufferings at the brutal hands of bullies – but it was a step forward, and the shrewd use of games as an honourable channel for physicality was a clever stratagem. What the reformed schools did was to domesticate the pupil-managed games of the older order, clean them up, bring them inside the purlieus and under the superintendence of the authorities, and fit them snugly into the conformist pattern. Games, once the signal of vicious rebelliousness, became the token of devoted orthodoxy. Just as the Christian calendar demonstrates some agile borrowing of pagan festivals and dates for orthodox ends, so did cricket similarly feature in the reconstruction of the public schools.

'By the 1880s', wrote Correlli Barnett, 'the playing field had become what the parade ground is for the army – a powerful instrument for inculcating common responses, values, outlook . . . The purpose of this ritual elaboration of ballgames was a debased version of Arnold's ideal of Christian education.' In books like *The Audit of War; the Illusion and Reality of Great Britain as a Great Nation* (1986), Correlli Barnett, a scholar of both military and economic history, has, indeed, blamed this evangelical mind-set for its deleterious effects on British foreign and industrial policy.

Gradually, there were official - as opposed to the pupil-run, unofficial and often rowdy – fixtures with other schools, the old boys and so on. The first, and clandestine, inter-school match recorded was Charterhouse and Westminster, in 1794, but, by the 1820s, the annual Eton and Harrow game was a regular and increasingly fashionable feature of the Lord's programme, while Winchester, where a fierce emphasis on fielding was the norm, had also evolved into a notable and competitive cricketing school. The seasonable weather made exchanges between schools easier than for winter football, when transportation was frequently hazardous. Eventually, the MCC/school game would be the high spot of the season, and one of those early matches gained in prominence from having a fictitious revisiting, what would now be called a docudrama.

This was the MCC trip to Rugby in 1841, which was 'unfinished', a more accurate term, it must be said, than 'drawn'. According to Arthur Haygarth's indispensable *Scores and Biographies*, 'Marylebone' made 136 and 99, and the school 120 and 102 for 8, left, excitingly, requiring 14 to win. The amiably corpulent Benjamin Aislabie, himself played. Rugby's captain was, famously, Thomas Hughes. He opened the batting and, with 29, top-scored in the first innings, although he was out for a duck in the second. He contrived to stump one and take three wickets in the MCC second innings.

When Thomas Hughes came to write the semi-autobiographical *Tom Brown's Schooldays* in 1857, Tom Brown skippered the school eleven in a similarly close-run game that had the school needing eight runs with two wickets standing. The match is, apart from an epilogue mourning the death of Thomas Arnold, the end-piece of the book, which became, of course, the template for thousands of schoolboy stories. Interestingly, the older boys were still in charge, albeit under the august authority of the headmaster. It was the end of term and Doctor Arnold was off for his usual respite at Fox How in the Lake District. – but not before giving various permissions as to what might or might not happen.

Benjamin Aisalbie makes a straightforward appearance in the book; Johnson, the school's most successful bowler, was based on the Honourable Arthur, later 3rd Viscount Wrottesley, who took ten wickets in the original game; Tom Brown was also partly based on Augustine Orlebar, later to be vicar of Willington parish church, Bedfordshire, for over fifty years; his fictional opponent in the famous fight in the story, Slogger Williams, was another clergyman to be, Bulkeley Owen Jones; 'the young master' was George Cotton, destined to be the reformist head of Marlborough . . . and so fact and fiction intertwine.

In a telling passage, Tom Brown discusses cricket with 'the young master', who tells Tom and his 'Christian' alter ego, Arthur ('Scud' East being the 'Muscular' counterpart) 'what a noble game it is too'. 'Isn't it?' answers Tom, 'but it's more than a game. It's an institution'. Arthur chimes in with a statement that suggests, given organised cricket's relatively modern origins, that the history teaching at Rugby is below par, calling cricket 'the birthright of British boys, old and young, as *habeas corpus* and trial by jury are of English men'. 'The discipline and reliance on one another it teaches is so valuable', affirms the master, apostrophising cricket as 'an unselfish game. It merges the individual in the eleven; he doesn't play that he may win, but that his side may.'

That little case study of Tom Brown is mightily significant, for it was by a combine of fact and fiction that the love of and for cricket was engendered, and this was the opening shot in a major cultural campaign. All of a sudden, and in a nutshell, the lesson of cricket was encapsulated. It was all present and morally correct. Cricket taught a swathe of fine virtues; excitement, good fellowship, character building, discipline, dependability, team-work, leadership – it was a kind of ethical cure for all moral ills.

In passing, one might mention the New Zealand based research, published in the *British Journal of Sports Medicine* in 1996 that found that 15-year-olds with high sporting levels were twice as likely as their less sporty counterparts to be delinquent at the age of 18, with the finding stronger for girls than boys. 'Our study', concludes the research team, 'does not support the view that involvement in sporting activity is a panacea for delinquent behaviour; if anything, it may exacerbate the problem.' What the researchers call 'the deterrence hypothesis' fails because, they argue, successful involvement in sport encourages aggressiveness and even cheating

As for the energetic Thomas Hughes, he combined the qualities of East and Arthur to become a 'Muscular Christian', a credo he defined as 'the protection of the weak, the advancement of all righteous causes and the subduing of the earth that God has given to the children of men.' Games were a moral and physical preparation for the cause and Thomas Hughes continued playing cricket as a student and afterwards. Thomas Hughes' beliefs overlapped into Christian Socialism, advocated by Charles Kingsley, author of *The Water Babies* and other novels, and by Frederick Denison Maurice, the true originator of the movement. Thomas Hughes earnestly and busily answered their call for a more co-operative spirit in the earthly application of religious tenets.

THE COMPONENTS OF REFORMED CRICKET

This comparatively rapid switch in the valuation of cricket was a kick-start for a new and virtuous vogue for cricket. There graduated from the schools a junior cricketing corps that carried the game into several social arenas that were themselves very influential, and so the new game, new that is, in spirit, spread quickly. There were four chief such modes; the universities; the church, the army and the amateur touring sides, all of them manned or led by ex-public schoolboys.

Firstly, there were Oxbridge undergraduates who had met one another in inter-school games even before the reform era and they were anxious to maintain the interest. College cricket began to sprout. A major turning point was the concept of the varsity match. Oxford's Charles Wordsworth, nephew of the poet, and the Old Etonian, Herbert Jenner, of Cambridge, contrived, in the face of some suspicion on the part of the authorities, to organise the first such game in 1827. There was another just before the first university boat race in 1829 but then there was a gap until 1836 after which this Lord's fixture became an annual highlight of the dawning new era. In 1830 the universities began their annual tryst with MCC, and varsity fixtures were to be accorded first-class status, a convention that still applies sometimes today, in spite of serious doubts about its validity.

This was the decorative topping on an elaborate edifice. The impact of university cricket was widespread, simply because cricketing graduates returned to the public schools and increasingly, as the century wore on, to proprietary schools and to the more prestigious day schools, as teachers, where, in turn, they propagated a commitment to cricket. In sum, the total of such schools had increased from about forty in mid-century to a hundred by 1900.

Secondly, just as significantly, there were hundreds of Oxbridge graduates who became clergymen and many of these carried cricket into districts untouched by the direct influence of the public schools. As missionaries, some carried cricket even further afield. Vicars like Augustine Orbelar and Bulkeley Owen Jones, with their simple, ebullient faith in 'Muscular Christianity', were responsible for much of the spread of cricket in town and village in the Victorian era. From Charles Wordsworth, Bishop of St Andrews, to David Sheppard, Bishop of Liverpool, it was to be a well-endowed connection. What a far cry they were from such a rascally cleric as Frederick Beauclerk, errant vicar of Redbourne in Hertfordshire.

Gerald Howat, among his many astute researches, showed that, of the 795 varsity blues of the Victorian period, 209 were ordained, seven of whom rose to bishoprics. 59 varsity men of the cloth, not all blues, played county cricket during the same era; the large parish of St Mary's, Southsea was able to field an eleven of curates, while thousands of others donned the pads in many of the 15,000 parishes of England and Wales. The caricature of the curate on the village green is no idle fancy.

Thirdly, there was the army, no stranger to sporadic cricket, but now commanded to regulate and extend its interest. In 1841 Viscount Hill, the Commander-in Chief, issued an order insisting that all barracks in the United Kingdom should lay and maintain cricket grounds, and that 'no carriages or horses be suffered to enter them'. Those with even minimal martial experience may recall the gap between the solemn edict from on high and the actual practice at the sharp end where evasion was ever an art-form. Nonetheless, there was a sufficiency of response, doubtless because of the welcome the order would have received from the younger breed of officers conversant with the new public school ethic. Indeed, 1841 also marks the first year of the Sandhurst and Woolwich series of matches, the teams inclusive of many officer cadets.

Officers benefiting more than NCOs and other ranks is another common fact of army life. Thus it was in respect of barrack ground cricket, with the rash of regimental teams, boosted by this high endorsement, almost all of commissioned rank, ready to play, not just each other, but against the other amateur elevens of the day. In a final reminder of the rooted traditions of the military life, it was 'the troops' who were charged in the order to pay for any repairs, it having been assumed that they would have been responsible, 'as in the case of barrack damages'. That said, there might have been internal use of the barrack cricket grounds on an inter-troop or company basis, involving the lower ranks. Like the estate teams of the 18th century, where cricket was sufficiently genteel to allow master and servant to play together, the military hierarchy also permitted of some blending of officers and men on the barrack cricket ground. Certainly, this encouragement of army cricket was to pay dividends in terms of the spread of cricket overseas.

An illustration of the possible mingling of officers and men may be found in the game at Prince's ground, London, in 1879, between the Royal Artillery and the Household Brigade. Among the officers and gentlemen, marked by military rank or the tell-tale 'Esq' often found on older score sheets, may be discovered Musician J.J.Boys, representing the artillery, and the initial-less Private McIntyre, who in the best 'professional' tradition, did a lot of bowling for the Household Brigade and took ten wickets in the two innings match. Later, 'mister', or some other social ranking, would signify the gentleman, while in more modern scorecards the use of initials fore and aft of the surname, for gentleman or player respectively was the required device. Making his batting debut in 1949 at Lord's, the youthful Middlesex off-spinner, Titmus, heard the public address system solemnly inform the watchers that his initials, F.J., should be after rather than, as falsely printed, before his surname on the erroneous scorecard.

Fourthly, and from that same roll call of public schoolboys and Oxbridge students and graduates, there arose a series of nomadic teams. Deliberately homeless, these wandering clubs drew their personnel from all over the nation, giving former school and varsity chums a chance to re-group and meet one another. I Zingari (the Gypsies) was formed by Cambridge undergraduates in 1845, and they were the model for the likes of the Quidnuncs (1851), the Harlequins (1852) and the long-lived Free Foresters (1850). Although one or two stand out in the annals, it must be stressed that there were scores of them, with life-cycles short as well as long, all offering an opportunity, especially in vacation time, to promising amateur cricketers.

Their fixtures were, obviously enough, arranged from others within these four categories, namely public schools and old boys' clubs, university or university college teams, regimental teams and, on occasion, clergy sides. The wandering elevens played a vital role in another adjunct of the new tamer and more domesticated cricket of the day. Great estates had boasted cricket grounds in the 18th century but now there was a major expansion as wealthy families found themselves urged by the dictates of fashion and their cricketing scions to lay a cricket ground, something after the style of the accessory swimming pool of today. No great household could count its social calendar complete without a week's cricket, tricked out with accompanying lunches and dinners and pretty ladies. Patently, the visits of the well-known nomadic clubs were an integral aspect of this doubtless enjoyable experience.

Vast land-holdings had been built up, as was noted earlier, during the 18th and into the 19th century, some of them through 'town-made wealth'. By mid 19th century 4000 landlords owned half the soil of the nation, including 200,000 tenant farms among their possessions. The stately homes of England were the political and cultural centres of the elite. Was not Chesney Wold, the gloomily damp home of Sir Leicester Dedlock, in Charles Dickens' *Bleak House*, the location for a meeting to decide who should form the next government?

It is a distinct mark of cricket's social progress that the grandees in their 'rural palaces' should sponsor the game so fully, adding battin', bowlin' and fieldin' to their huntin', shootin' and fishin', and maybe giving the fox , the partridge and the salmon some respite thereby. In an intense piece of research, Eric Snow, that first-rate recorder of Leicestershire cricket, identified no less than sixty country house grounds in Leicestershire and Rutland alone, plus eleven minor sites. Country house cricket was not a minor element; some commentators have argued it delayed, by its prior claims on promising amateurs, the proper development of any county competition. Over the years, hundreds of games must have been played.

A rough and ready personal spotting of the professions and careers, where stated, of about a thousand amateurs in the hundred or so years before the end of the gentlemen/player distinction in 1962 appears to demonstrate what would the continuing strength of those major sources of cricketing renewal. No less than 40% were connected with the armed services, whilst another 12% led clerical careers, almost all in the Church of England, and 10% were school-masters, all professions well-placed to encourage cricket at home and abroad. About 10% were landed gentry or farmers, something under 10% were businessmen of varied kinds, with law at some 5%, the civil service, including the colonial service at about 4%, and, perhaps surprisingly given the conspicuous example of the Grace family, medicine at a low 3%. This leaves a miscellaneous group of roughly 6% in range of other posts and jobs, such as the arts, journalism and so forth. The public school and Oxbridge ethos is, of course, prominent across the entirety of this sample and, need-less to say, there were many other well-heeled amateurs who laid no claim to a career.

A central focus for many of these ventures remained Lord's. MCC hosted key school and university matches, as well as fielding teams to play the top regiments and wandering teams. MCC was the fount of the laws and many of those involved with these four branches of amateur cricket were, of course, MCC members. MCC had scarcely consolidated its position when the waning of cricket occurred, but it survived in good order and was quickly restored by these novel outlets of the amateur game.

Most of these renewed sectors of cricketing activity demanded expert support, not so much for playing purposes but for coaching and attendant duties, like groundsmanship. Many of the great schools, the Oxbridge colleges, the crack cricketing regiments and the country houses hired professional cricketers for longer or shorter periods.

The Lord's professional staff grew and as county grounds, such as the Oval, were constructed, they, too, employed professionals. Thriving clubs took on one and, in some cases, two professionals. It was a real shot in the arm for a craft that had dwindled into obscurity during the decline of the old brand of cricket. Peter Wynne-Thomas reckons that, about 1830, there were no more than twenty cricket professionals in England. By the 1850s there were several hundreds.

The cream of this revivified echelon composed the itinerant teams, known, without varnish, as the Exhibition elevens. These were the seasoned tradesmen of the craft. The originator was the shrewd Nottingham operator, William Clarke, who, having established the enclosed cricket ground by his Trent Bridge Inn, diversified his activities on a nationwide basis. From 1846 his All-England XI journeyed to all parts of the kingdom, playing against odds of up to twenty-two, and conducting an exhausting programme of fixtures, peaking in 1851 with 34 games. William Clarke usually received a £70 fee, plus hospitality for the team, and most or all the revenue at the gate. He paid the then going rate of £4 to £6 a match, a regular if not princely income for the more experienced players, and John Arlott has winningly described how he would pay off his team-mates, and then, with a muttered, 'and £37 for me', sweep the remainder of the cash into his tall hat.

George Parr, accomplished batsman and competent businessman, later took on William Clarke's mantle, while other 'Exhibition' teams were formed, the leading two being John Wisden's breakaway southern outfit, the United XI of England, in 1864, and, a year later, the United South of England XI, for which W.G.Grace was to prove a spectacular draw-card. They all undertook strenuous lists of games, day in day out, aided by improved travel conditions and welcomed wholeheartedly by local pressmen and traders. For close on forty years – quite a proportion of recognized cricket's history - they dominated the spectator side of the sport, often to the detriment of other major fixtures, for these were the most expert cricketers in the country.

It was players of this calibre who had inaugurated top-class representative games, such as the North and South series, the first two of which were played at Leicester and Lord's in 1836, with the emergent cadres of Nottingham-based professionals dominating the Northern eleven. The North also had regular fixtures with MCC and later Surrey.

Because county cricket came to predominate on the domestic scene from the latter part of the 19th century until well in the 20th century, it is easy to forget that, for a solid generation, these touring teams were professional cricket's lifeblood. For the first time mainline cricketers visited the most outlying parts of the nation, demonstrating skills, building interest and lifting standards. A by-product was a demand for cricketing equipment and literature, with sports firms run by cricket professionals like John Wisden and Frederick Lillywhite the satisfied beneficiaries. At the same time, the soil was not entirely virginal. In large part because of the exertions of the other contributory and chiefly amateur groups, there were, clearly, eager clubs and keen organisers prepared to find the up-front fee and twenty-two stalwarts prepared to have a go.

The British public, for its part, was habituated to travelling entertainment. On the cusp between the fledgling industrial revolution and the complete urbanisation of the nation, social, as well as economic, life was something of a bubbling and unsettled crucible. Soon there would be more consolidation, and with that would come more permanent localised amenities, but for now entertainment was frequently mobile. Charles Dickens painted fairs and circuses in gorgeous pigmentation. Vincent Crummles and his fit-up theatre in *Nicholas Nickleby*, Mrs Jarley, *inter alia*, and her travelling waxworks in *The Old Curiosity Shop* and Mr Sleary and his circus troupe in *Hard Times* are fictitious compadres of the redoubtable William Clarke. The arrival of an 'Exhibition' eleven in town had much the same effect as that of the travelling fair, where local heroes would take on the professional bruiser in the ring – and with very much the same results.

While far removed in social status, the two planes of activity, amateur and professional, contrived in amalgam to ensure that cricket was not unknown in any nook or cranny of the land. There is no doubt that the activities of the country house and Exhibition elevens emphasised the existing division of the social grades already apparent in the 'estate' and allied teams of the 18th century. The first Gentlemen and Players matches, two of them, were in 1806, not followed by another until 1819, this being cricket's phase of decline. In any event, and for many years, the professionals out-did their purported betters by large margins despite playing odds matches against eighteen amateurs, loaning their rivals a couple of paid assistants or even having to defend larger wickets. The games survived at Lord's, principally because MCC members, rather like the townsfolk anxious to take on William Clarke's wily spin, wanted to test themselves against the experts.

The social divisiveness this engendered and the problems it stored up for later cricketing development, are plain enough. Nonetheless, given that the whole of society was strictly constructed on class lines, it could be argued that cricket, by allowing even this degree of familiarity between the social classes, was a shade ahead of the rest of most 19th century cultural evaluation. Just as on the landed estate and in the regiment, cricket did permit of some meeting of the hierarchical opposites. Other sports, other occupations and recreations, could not boast even as much as this somewhat patronising conjunction.

As the century wore on, be it amateur or professional, it was cricket played to an increasingly higher standard both as a spectator sport and as a local diversion. Importantly, it was played according to an acknowledged set of laws, hitherto the property chiefly of the south-east of England. Just as important, it was cricket that, in the main, was played in accordance with an unwritten ethical diktat. That this was not always obeyed, any more than there are not occasional lapses among the godly apropos the Decalogue, was predictable enough. It was no less a significant ideal and aspiration.

It would not be true to state that cricket had died and had been born again. Naturally, there was some overlap of the ancient mode and the new dispensation, with the angelic ambrosia of Victorian gradually diluting the devil's brew of Hanoverian cricket. For all its decay around the time of the Regency period, it did not come too close to vanishing, but possibly a period of atrophy, with less noise and hullabaloo, had been necessary for cricket to be reorganised on these more virtuous lines For its new ethos was a stunning change.

If Resurrection were too theatrical a term for the reformed game then possibly Renaissance would be apt.

In 1796 Eton played a covert match with Westminster School, and, on their return from a miserably heavy defeat on Hounslow Heath, the Eton eleven were roundly flogged by the headmaster, a distinct case of adding injury to insult. This was for their defiance and probably for their subsequent misbehaviour, as drunken horseplay 'après-ski' was a feature of early schoolboy cricket. Similar incidents were common after other schools matches of the time.

In 1861 700 carriages and 7000 spectators paraded at Lord's for the Eton and Harrow match, already a must on the fashionable calendar and an event that would be lengthily reviewed in the best newspapers. Moving on a little, an Old Harrovian, John Galsworthy, chose the Eton and Harrow match at Lord's for one of the most poignant moments in *The Man of Property*, the first volume of *The Forsyte Saga*, published in 1906. The grievously introverted Soames Forsyte lunches at and perambulates around Lord's. Among 'six thousand top hats, four thousand parasols', he spots the lovely, to him, frigid Irene, the cynosure of admiring attention. He is the loner in the crowd among the pomp of a glittering London occasion and the dash of a public school encounter. It is not an idle choice of venue.

In microcosm, one observes cricket's precipitate conversion from vice to virtue. If *Tom Brown's Schooldays* offers a picture of upper class youth in the 19th century, its 18th century parallel was Henry Fielding's *Tom Jones*, published in 1749, the picaresque tale of a spirited, imprudent, hedonistic lad, prone to mischief and misadventure. In idealistic concept, and, in due order, realistic fulfilment, the cultural translation of cricket and cricketers from wicked to good is personified by the two heroes.

Tom Jones had become Tom Brown.

The public and allied schools made a vital, perhaps indispensable, contribution to the makings of English cricket. Featured here are, top, Marlborough College, Wiltshire, founded in 1843; and Reading School, re-founded by Henry VII in 1486 (the photograph was taken in the school's quincentenary year of 1986).

Chapter Four

PERSISTENT SHIRE

*Lord's Cricket Ground from a design on
a silk handkerchief in 1837*

The traditional history of cricket is largely a rhapsody in retrospect. The romantic keenness to reveal origins and developments earlier than sensible analysis allows has already been noted; later the phenomenon of determining international cricket by backward-looking judgement shall be discussed. The *post hoc* resolution of which matches should be declared first-class has already been mentioned. Indeed, as Peter Wynne-Thomas has sagely reminded us, 'first-class' was originally applied to batting averages and, slightly later, bowling analyses compiled by Fred Lillywhite, publisher of cricketing annuals from about the half-way mark of the 19th century. It was by this arbitrary route that the teams and games from which he personally took these performances became in turn, first-class. *Wisden Cricketers' Almanack*, published from 1864, also began to include a 'First-class Records' section, which brought added respectability to the concept.

CRICKET'S PASTORAL IMAGE — THE SHIRE

The same is true of county cricket. As we have observed, there were many examples of teams being tagged as county sides, where a well-endowed local landowner chose loftily so to do, where a wily promoter sought an extra marketing buzz by so doing, or where an ambitious club gathered a few additional neighbouring players to its ranks to justify making such a claim. The preposition 'of' was frequently utilised, as in 'eleven of Kent', as opposed to any falsely definitive descriptor, such as 'the Kent eleven'. The sporting press and later the cricket annuals joined in, often declaring a particular 'county' the champions, to the point where some modern commentators have felt able to erect a roster of county champions way back to the 1820s.

Sussex had something akin to a formal club, with Surrey the next in line, while Kent and Nottinghamshire were well-organised teams, but it was the 1860s before others, such as Lancashire, Middlesex and Yorkshire really joined them as equals, whilst several other counties drifted in and out of the embryonic first-class list. The sporting press, which incidentally, was by no means as widespread in circulation as today's newspapers, attempted to range the counties in some order. The strength and weakness of the opposition was one yardstick, with, in earlier years, an element of the previous holder having to be beaten to obtain the title, in the same traditions of boxing championships. That was the same convention as the 'cock' house notion of influential public school custom, whereby the 'cock' had to be toppled from its midden by a rival. Originally, the FA Cup, first competed for in the 1871-1872 season, was planned on similar lines, and still includes the word 'challenge' in its title. Although by the mid-1870s, there were enough counties and enough games to allow for a more consensual approach, there was naturally much room for differences of journalistic opinion.

It all makes a for a pleasant conceit and is harmless enough to conjecture about but it is, on the other hand, confusing for those who might be tempted to think that there is more than a nominal comparison between such activities and the evolution of properly constituted county cricket clubs participating in a formally recognised competition with all on an equal footing. This was a later design, quite different in institutional format and competitive formula.

Indeed, the truer continuum is the cricketing club rather than the cricketing county, for it was in effect, the former that led to the latter. Admittedly, the prior interest in 'county' matters, helped by newspaper urgings, had saved the notion from dormancy. The power of the county should not be underestimated – but it was the device of the 'county club' that was novel and influential.

The English shire has an impressive lineage. Some counties had been kingdoms and others earldoms, and they remained highly significant administrative units. In Stuart England and even later, people sometimes referred to their 'county' as their 'country'. In George Eliot's *Middlemarch*, set around 1831, Josh Rigg threatens his delinquent stepfather with dreadful punishment, 'if you dare to come on these premises again, or to come into this country after me again.' That cleverly analytical historian of Hanoverian England, Lewis Namier, shrewdly called them 'county commonwealths'. The one-time doyen of local history, A.M.Everitt, writing of the Victorian shire, judged it to have been 'the matrix of local society in which political opinion was formed'.

The quandary of communication already alluded to as a dampener on the development of cricket as of other affairs, must be recognised. Unless there had been some show of localised authority the pursuit of any type of national governance would have been impossible. People thought and acted within more confined limits before the age of rapid transit. Thomas Hardy, who readily comprehended the restricted life of most of his fellow-countrymen even late into the 19th century had this to say when Tess Durbyfield, in *Tess of the D'Urbevilles*, published in 1891, wanted to get far away from her home village. 'It was not quite so far off as might have been wished but it was probably far enough, her radius of movement and repute having been so small. To persons of limited spheres, miles are as of geographical degrees, parishes as counties, counties as provinces and kingdoms.'

It was in the 'limited spheres' of the counties that the judicial system, from the magistracy to the assizes, had a long-standing and firm base. The regimental configuration of the British army had strong county roots. As new administrative patterns were formed during the 19th century, the county was utilised, if not exclusively, with the 1839 and 1856 County Constabulary Acts, which established the 'new police' forces, being a distinct example.

There were then, plenty of reasons why cricketers should turn to the shire for organisational succour. Other sports would emulate cricket, although most – rugby union, hockey, football among them – established associations of clubs with actual but relatively infrequent county matches, the teams being selected from the clubs in the county alliance. The emphasis was more on the organisation of county-wide club competitions and activities. It seems to have been cricket alone where the concept took hold of autonomous county clubs in regular competition forming the major tier of the domestic game.

So familiar is the concept of the club to the modern mind that its seminal role in the development of cricket is sometimes overlooked. One thinks for instance, of 'county cricket', even to the point, as has been observed, of linking random pre-club 'county' activity over-closely with the forthcoming club model. It is the county 'club' that is really significant. The 'club' idea, for its fruitful part, was essentially an 18th century concept, its common denominator lying in the acceptance of a subscribing membership, usually with voting rights to elect a committee and so forth, seeking the benefit of mutual enjoyment of some diversion or another.

There had been precedents in earlier times, such as the dining association, the Apollo, founded by Ben Jonson in 1616 and located in the Devil Tavern at Temple Bar, or, on the sporting front, the Tudor archery companies, such as Prince Arthur's Knights. The coffeehouse culture of the later 17th century witnessed some growth in the movement, with clubs enjoying the hospitality of particular venues and taking on distinctive characters. It was now that the term 'club' came into common usage and in a way the modern mind would understand it. Said the eminent diarist John Aubrey, 'we now use the word clubbe for a sodality in a taverne', a sodality being an association. In 1755 Samuel Johnson defined a club as 'an association of good fellows, meeting under certain conditions.'

It was not, of course, applicable only to cricket or other sports, with such 'certain conditions' as politics, music, literature and the arts being only a choice few of the interests that led men, less so women, if at all, to form and join clubs at this time. During the 18th and 19th century, the number of clubs increased profusely and rapidly. The range was extraordinary. From majestic edifices like those on Pall Mall, such as the Reform, established in 1834, to the tiniest of village cricket clubs, it was a social appliance of spectacularly wide convenience. Clubs are here defined briefly, but that brevity should not be seen as a measure of, henceforward, their impact on and contribution to the strong British tradition of voluntaryism.

Clubs like Hambledon and Slindon and Hornchurch, with their minute books and other administrative paraphernalia, had given something of a lead, but, especially throughout the decades of cricket's rejuvenation, cricket clubs grew in number and incidence. The combination of the factors described in the last chapter – the post-public school and post-Oxbridge manifestation of a cricketing interest through church, teaching, the armed forces and the touring amateur elevens, plus the formidable presence of the Exhibition teams – was a massive boost for club cricket. The country as a whole, was soon profusely dotted with them, some deriving from the outreach activity of churches and if less so, of firms and businesses, but many arising simply from the desire of groups of young men in a given locale to share in the delights of cricket.

Much of this activity was initially secluded, that is the club, rather like a golf or squash club today, was an amenity for its members to practise and play together. Gradually, and as the number of clubs mounted, it became increasingly natural and simple for each to plan a programme of friendly inter-club games. History repeated itself in so far as the public schools had played internally before branching out to add inter-school fixtures to the more in-bred pattern of net practice and house or other intra-school games.

It was the application of the 'club' principle to the next level of cricketing provision that, without precedent, gave English top-class cricket its fulsome and exceptional flavour. The process normatively began with representatives of leading clubs within the county pale discussing the possibility of a county profile. There was a general feeling that, by founding some joint enterprise, the standards of local cricket could be improved. In almost every case, and although there may have been peripheral motivations as well, that rather wholesome rationale was uppermost. Once more indeed, the initial activity in several instances, tended to be internalised coaching and practice rather than the arrangement of a lengthy fixture list, let alone the avid hope of attracting lots of spectators and making a commercial profit.

Unlike most other sports, where the county constitution would encompass chiefly clubs as members, as in the manner of the county football or hockey associations, the county cricket clubs tended quite quickly to opt for individual membership, firstly, and naturally, of playing subscribers, but, increasingly, again after the manner of the local club, of friends and supporters. As the number of games played grew and especially when, informally and then officially, a county championship was at stake, the latter figure increased even more.

By the end of the 18th century, nine of the current first-class counties had had teams play under their banners and others followed suit in the 19th century. However, when one turns to the inauguration of county clubs *per se*, the picture is rather different. It also has to be recognised that some county clubs, like some local instances, were established but faded and collapsed, possibly to be re-started at a later date. Some had slightly different objectives. For a time Kent boasted two differing organisations, with Canterbury offering a solid cricket club bastion of playing members and a Maidstone-based group utilising the subscription list approach to finance the activity. In any event, much of the evidence is blurred and any summary should be accepted as a guide to what happened rather than as a precise account.

It would seem that the Oxfordshire county club has been extant since 1787 making it the oldest of county clubs at large, although its modern format dates only from the 1920s. If one takes as a prime sample the sixteen counties that until 1921 with the advent of Glamorgan and then 1992 with the coming of Durham, lorded it, a few of them rockily, over the first-class domestic scene, their sequence of establishment is roughly as follows, according to the annals of the *Wisden Almanacks*. In a handful of cases there was a substantial revision of the club, a major reshaping, that is, not a complete fracture of the institutional line. The years of these recastings are in brackets in this chronological series of the formation of the sixteen counties.

Northamptonshire	1820	(1879)
Sussex	1839	(1857)
Nottinghamshire	1841	(1866)
Surrey	1845	
Kent	1859	(1870)
Yorkshire	1863	(1891)
Hampshire	1863	(1879)
Middlesex	1864	
Lancashire	1864	
Worcestershire	1865	
Derbyshire	1870	
Gloucestershire	1871	
Somerset	1875	
Essex	1876	
Leicestershire	1879	
Warwickshire	1882	

It is a 19th century, by and large, a mid-Victorian phenomenon. Including the bracketed revision dates in the sequence, then Surrey, founded in 1845, is the longest surviving and non-reconstituted county club, with all the others dating, on that same criterion, from a period of some 31 years from 1857 to 1891.

They enjoyed what geographers sometimes call the impetus of a start. Although one or two others – Cambridgeshire, for example – flirted with the mighty, what came to be called the 'Minor Counties' tended to have a slightly later year of origin, either late Victorian – Buckinghamshire in 1895; Devon in 1899 – or Edwardian - Cheshire in 1908 – or even later.

There is little of the colourful variegation about the foundation of the county cricket clubs that one enjoys in the exotic series of starting points for what became England's Football League clubs. There were works teams, church teams, pub teams, school-based teams, and mixtures of several sorts, not to mention football teams started by cricket clubs. Not so the county cricket clubs, almost all of which began life in something close to tedious uniformity.

The evolution of the county circuit was a further and major stage in the amateur revival described in the foregoing chapter. Clusters of clubs in a given county were keen to raise the bar of excellence higher. Representatives of these clubs met, normally in a convenient hostelry, and took the decision to establish a county club, usually with a call for subscribing members. Sometimes there were failed attempts and later another effort would be made. All it required was sufficient middle class gentlemen to pay the fees and play the cricket. When, as soon happened, fixtures were arranged, some such titling of 'the Gentlemen of Loamshire' was devised. The county clubs also wished to hire professionals, for coaching, for groundsmanship, for bowling practice and, eventually, to bolster the shire ranks in match play.

Examples include meetings at the Horns Tavern, London, in 1845 to inaugurate the Surrey club; at the Queen's Hotel, Manchester in 1864 to launch the Lancashire club; at the London Tavern in 1864 that led to the formation of a provisional committee for the Middlesex club; at the Bull Inn, Rochester in 1870, with the autocratic Lord Harris in the chair, to help the establishment of the Kent club; at the George Hotel, Winchester in 1879, when district representation to manage the Hampshire club was determined; at the Angel Hotel, Cardiff in 1888 to establish the Glamorgan club . . . and so on.

The impulsive coming together of local clubs to form county clubs must not be exaggerated. In its much smaller fashion the process was often more like the Unification of Italy and Germany at much the same time. There was, encouraging and encouraged by popular nationalistic dreams, the *Realpolitik* of a strong and ruthless component; Piedmont-Sardinia in Italy and Prussia in Germany. Some would claim that those cricketing unions were more the expansion of the dominating element that an organic and visionary uprising of the whole.

Thus many county clubs had one or two strong leading contenders, the Montpellier club in respect of Surrey, for example, or the Swansea and Cardiff clubs in regard of Glamorgan, the South Derbyshire club, based at Chaddesden, the Canterbury club in Kent, the West Gloucestershire club, Sheffield in Yorkshire and so on. Sometimes there were rivalries where two or more clubs felt themselves to be the chief protagonists but slowly but surely, as with Piedmont-Sardinia's Cavour in Italy or Prussia's Bismarck in Germany, there were often strong-minded individuals who grasped the reins of development, or, like the Graces in Gloucestershire or the seven Walkers of Middlesex, strong-minded families. Lancashire is a pronounced case of the county and club argument, for at Old Trafford there was little that separated the Manchester club and the emerging county club, including the players picked. In 1880 this common law marriage was legalised with official nuptials as 'The Lancashire County and Manchester Cricket Club', an intriguing and portentous geographical title.

The closest to a difference in overall county organisation was with Nottinghamshire, Yorkshire, and, to a lesser extent, Sussex, all strongholds of professional cricket with subscribing membership lists to fund the activity. There was occasionally conflict between proletarian player groups and bourgeois subscribers and committees, but eventually, through, for instance, the firm leadership after 1883 of Lord Hawke at Yorkshire, the prototypical relationship of capital and labour was resumed. A specific instance of this was the notorious 'schism' in 1881 at Trent Bridge, when the county secretary, Captain Holden, encouraged by the authorities of the other counties, quelled a rebellion of the Nottinghamshire 'pros' against the decision to stop the players arranging games outside the county's jurisdiction.

That was the last throw, at county level, of professional independence. The 'Exhibition' elevens, some of which had been run alongside the relatively sparse county programme, faded away, and the richer county clubs became the safest haven economically speaking, for the aspiring paid cricketer. Not all counties wanted or, more to the point, could afford waged cricketers, although, slowly, those with ambitions soon realised that cricketing life would be demanding without at least a professional sprinkling. Inside the sacred arena of what might tacitly be called first-class cricket, the eleven without a professional or two became rarer and rarer, although, of course, the amateur rule mainly held sway for the larger realm of all the lesser county clubs.

There would always be some tension between playing and supporting membership, with the latter rather keener to watch something a little more enterprising than 'the Gentlemen of Loamshire'. Some counties – Lancashire and Surrey are perhaps examples – began to think more in terms of a team for rather than of the county, sides, that is, which would provide a superior form of entertainment for the membership. Thus did the circle revolve. The demand for classier county staffs meant more money and although counties relied heavily on subscriptions and, indeed, aristocratic handouts – the Duke of Devonshire baled out Derbyshire on a yearly basis at one time – there was pressure to develop a county ground and build up the numbers paying at the gate.

Very soon the format was to be seen everywhere of gentlemen members in the pavilion and paying spectators around the ground and on the terracing, many of them from the working classes, watching a similarly class-divided team of Gentlemen and Players playing first-class cricket. The formula, for all the quiddities and oddities of local eccentricity, was remarkably similar. Obviously, the England team would, in time, play first-class matches, as did visiting tourists, Oxford and Cambridge Universities, alongside a handful of other elevated fixtures, such as Gentlemen and Players or Champion County versus the Rest of England, some late summer friendly Festival games, one or two MCC matches and occasional outings involving the classier amateur elevens like Free Foresters and Combined Services.

Nonetheless, in terms of regular domestic first-class play, the equivalent if you will, of football's First Division, later Premiership, the only route was to form a distinguished county team. It was the

County Championship. It was not open to a town club or a bank or the army or a brewery to organise a talented team and somehow make its way into that upper echelon. That was – that is – the degree of dominance of the county tradition in English cricket.

This sometimes gave a spurious air of regionalism to the top tier of cricket, especially when compared with the later emergence of the much greater incidence of town-based football, rugby league and, to some degree, rugby union clubs of excellent order. Association football later developed an often exciting tadpole philosophy, with hundreds of teams vying to be one of the frogs of the Football League, itself 92 strong by early in the 20th century. Cricket was not quick to follow that route, leaving many settlements remote from reasonably proximate first-class cricket. Late in the 19th century, league cricket took on some prominence, especially where high-class professionals were encouraged, usually one per team. Even so, the excitement was localised. There was no national network and no hope of advancing further than the top of that local alliance of clubs.

Cricket's Pastoral Image – 'the Medieval Dream'

This clinging to the county structure might perhaps have been influenced by what has been called 'the medieval dream'. This was, basically, a negative response evoked by the ugly grimness of industrialism, a yearning for a pastoral idyll that had, frankly, never been. It was a backward-looking dream that has already been observed in the zeal of Victorian cricket archivists to reveal pre-modern roots for cricket.

It was a widespread and insistent mood. The cogent left-wing historian E.J.Hobsbawm has castigated 'the characteristic mythical Britain of the travel poster' and shown how 'the heavy incrustation of British public life with pseudo-medieval and other rituals, like the cult of royalty, dates back to the late Victorian period as does the pretence that the Englishman is a thatched-cottager or a country squire at heart.'

The 'chivalry' of the 19th succeeded the 'decency' of the 18th century. There was a fashion for the historical novels of Sir Walter Scott, such as *Ivanhoe*, of Charles Reade, such as *The Cloister and the*

Hearth, or of Charles Kingsley, such as *Hereward the Wake*, in all of which the heroes act like ideal Victorian gentlemen. In the arts and in architecture, gifted men, like Augustus Pugin, restored a 'vibrant medievalism' – the Houses of Parliament; St Pancras Station – to their designs. There was a vogue for the often Gothic fairy tales of the Brothers Grimm or of Hans Christian Andersen, while there was a revival of 'folklore', itself a Victorian coinage, which reached its zenith in the Edwardian era, when Cecil Sharp was a key influence.

The medieval knight was the model of the Victorian gentleman, a template for which was Tennyson's *Idylls of a King*, published in 1859. Public school headmasters and their staff were compared to the knights of the Arthurian round table, while knights in armour proliferated in school trophies, stained glass windows and war memorials. Courtly love was in evidence at the highest levels. Queen Victoria had Prince Albert depicted in full armour both before and after his death, while her premier, Benjamin Disraeli – 'he is full of poetry, romance and chivalry', penned the much-moved monarch – adopted the medieval role of 'cavalieri serventi', of pure devotion for and duty to a married woman, in, as he asserted as he knelt and took her hand, 'loving loyalty and faith.' Disraeli's approach well may have embraced an element of play-acting. A more sincere example may have been that of Colonel Oliver Montagu, younger son of the Earl of Sandwich, with his 'chivalrous devotion to a beautiful woman' in the regal personage of Princess Alexandra, wife of the Prince of Wales, later Edward VII, around whom scandal swirled. It was said that Montagu 'shielded her in every way, not least from his own great love, and managed to defeat gossip.'

Politically, medievalism stimulated both the Young England movement, closely associated with the mercurial Benjamin Disraeli and the radical pre-'Norman Yoke' concept, with its appealing notion of an Arcadian past unmarred by commercialism. In 1893/94 750,000 copies of Robert Blatchford's left-wing tale, *Merrie England*, were sold. Later there was the Primrose League, bringing widespread support to the Conservative Party, with its pseudo-medieval nomenclature. 'Habitations', such as the 'King Athelstan' at Malmesbury, were branches and 'tributes' were subscriptions. In historical research, the great constitutional academics, William Stubbs and F.W.Maitland, busily tracked down Anglo-Saxon and Anglo-Norman origins for English legal and institutional devices.

Approaching closer to the pastoral image of the cricket sward, there was the English love affair with the garden, with its trim lawn, according to Walt Whitman, 'the handkerchief of the Lord.' The poet should have given some credit to Edwin Budding, inventor of the cylinder mower in 1830 – a delightful example of the diverse parts played by the industrial revolution in the evolution of the purported pastoral salience of the lovely cricket ground. Until the lawnmower was developed and accepted, the scythe held sway. At Loseley Park, near Guildford, one of the homes of the cricketing Christopherson family, nineteen gardeners rose at 4.0 a.m, until the Edwardian era, to scythe the cricket field preparatory to a day of country house cricket. Stanley Christopherson, fast bowler and President of MCC throughout the Second World War, was one of ten sons, who, led by their father, could muster a full eleven.

Cricket in general, and in particular the shire allegiance and also the tradition of 'village green' cricket naturally benefited from this illusory falsehood about a charming rural existence before the advent of industrial blight. One does not have to pretend that the urban existence was, especially initially, pleasant, but the migration from the countryside to take up urban trades was, while sometimes enforced, often a preferred option. Rural life was very harsh and cruel. For example, child labour, so frequently, and rightly, seen as an early industrial evil, had long been a dreadful sore on the rural economy.

What proved to be a significant ingredient of the 'medieval dream' has already been mentioned. This was the allure of landed status among the newly moneyed commercial men. W.H.Smith, son and grandson of stationers and printers, made his fortune with his news agencies and kiosks, bought himself an estate for £30,000 and became an able cabinet minister in a Conservative cabinet. Richard Cobden, leader of the Anti-Corn Law League and chief protagonist of 'Manchesterism' and the free trade movement, was horrified. Had not the Free Trade Hall, headquarters of the successful League, been deliberately erected on the site of the Peterloo Massacre in

Manchester, that emblematic event in the struggle for parliamentary and allied reform? His radical Liberal allies, like the politician John Bright, and himself had believed optimistically that international free trade would be the basis for global peace and that, on the foundation of commercial wealth the great industrial cities would nobly create new Florences and Venices, places of artistic and humane value. Manchester would be 'the Athens of the North'.

He was dismayed and disappointed at the degree of political apostasy. When the new Manchester Corporation decided to emulate the medieval style of its antiquated City of London predecessor with mayoral and aldermanic flummery and ritual, he was truly shocked. He dismissed his fellow 'shopocrats'' weakness as 'glorying in being the toadies of a clodpole aristocracy', satisfied with 'the very crumbs from their table'.

In practice, the toadies were never to be quite so subservient, for they brought hardheaded commercial tenets to bear as they brought new money to back the bargains they struck with the ancient regime. The reform of the public schools is but one of many examples of this 'Forsyte' effect. Their impact on local government is another and more significant illustration.

For all that, Richard Cobden was right in cultural and social terms. The adoption of county cricket by this nascent upper middle class is an instance of that. From scores of cases, two might be chosen to illustrate the point. Reginald Hargreaves was the son of Accrington calico printers. The family's industrial fortune was such that he was educated at Eton and Christ Church, Oxford and was enabled to purchase a 160 acre estate, Cuffnells, in the New Forest, Hampshire. There he became the doyen of the local Conservative Association, his house the centre for gentlemanly sports and activities. He was President of the Hampshire County Cricket Club and played twelve first-class matches for the county. He stands proxy for many like him, rich children of the Industrial Revolution.

His cricketing career was moderate, but he claims more fame from his (rather unhappy) marriage to Alice Liddell, the original Alice in Wonderland. This was after, first, as is now believed, her parents, the Dean of Christ Church and his tuft-hunting wife, had irascibly squashed Lewis Carroll's own timid attempt at betrothal with the young Alice, and second, a non-amused Queen Victoria had refused to permit her fourth son, also a Christ Church student, Prince Leopold, to wed Alice. This former-day 'Student Prince' married the Princess Helen Frederica of Waldeck-Pyrmont instead, while Alice settled, somewhat unconvincingly, for 'Regi'. The Dean's wife omitted Lewis Carroll's wedding present from the official list, Alice wore a valuable brooch, a gift from Prince Leopold, on her wedding dress, and nobody seemed to live happily ever after.

Apart from any idle interest the tale may have, it does demonstrate how far the Hargreaves family had risen from the relative rags of some cottage calico printing to the riches of rubbing shoulders with royalty. As for Lewis Carroll, it was remarked by his captain of the sole ball he bowled playing cricket at Rugby that, 'it would have been a wide, had it reached the other end'.

The second personification of the joint commercial-landed interest and cricket is at the other end of the sporting gamut. The family cotton mills in Blackburn financed Albert Neilson Hornby, seminal captain and influential president of Lancashire County Cricket Club. He was educated at Harrow, where, tiny of stature, he earned the nicknames 'Monkey' and 'the Little Wonder' and developed a taste for the *al fresco* life. After a fleeting acquaintance with Oxford, he, too, married and soon found himself a county estate, Parkfield, Nantwich, amid the lush dairy meadows of Cheshire. There he had his own country house cricket ground and his stable of lively horses, for he hunted with the energetic abandon that he brought to the cricket arena. He boxed and dealt pugilistically with rowdies on both Manchester and Australian cricket grounds; he played soccer for Blackburn Rovers; he captained England at cricket and, by dint of nine rugby union caps, became a double international; he had a captaincy in the East Cheshire Militia . . . Richard Cobden he was not.

The parvenus of the Lancashire textile districts sought a place in the patrician courts of old England. In 1842 the Manchester club paid its first visit to Lord's – and was humiliated by MCC. The visitors were all out for 59, after which, according to a press report, the Mancunian bowling proved 'very deficient, it being of the old-fashioned under-hand school, which afforded the MCC gentlemen much amusement in hitting it away' to the tune of 200 or more. Although round-arm bowling had been belatedly legalised in 1835 and practised assiduously hitherto, we again observe the ascendancy of the southeast in these matters and the absence of a national norm. Lacking the technique either to defend against or attack with round-arm bowling, the Manchester team, greatly discomfited, forfeited the match and skulked off home. Horrified by the chasm, possibly social as well as technical, this was absolutely the kind of incident that convinced the rising commercial men of the industrial areas that they must try and imitate their purported betters in such concerns.

Neville Cardus justly proclaimed A.N.Hornby 'the Squire of Lancashire', perhaps also recognising that, in a regional instance of a transformation that was happening all over the nation, 'Manchester Men' had become 'the Gentlemen of Lancashire'.

CRICKET'S PASTORAL IMAGE — THE PARK

A further factor in the development of this pastoral view of cricket and one which tended to assist the growth of club and by extension, county cricket, was the Victorian encouragement of the public park. In effect the park was one of the pleasant outcomes of the Public Health movement and the call for a more wholesome life-style for those existing among the filth and squalor of industrialised and urbanised Britain. Plainly, that argument was closely related to the 'Merrie England' vision. It was felt, in part wrongly, as it happens, that rural life had been healthier than its urban replacement, while the public park itself was a throwback, if not to medieval then to 18th century times. There was too, an urgency to offer some succour to youth. The median age of the early Victorian population was 25 compared with 39 today, and there were concerns about how to control such a youthful populace.

In 1834 a Select Committee of the House of Commons, scrutinising the subject of drunkenness, recommended 'the establishment by the joint aid of the government and the local authorities and residents on the spot, of public walks, or gardens, or open spaces for healthy and athletic exercise in the open air, in the immediate vicinity of every town, of a character and an extent adapted to its population.' Reforming MPs, like Joseph Hume and Robert Slaney, battered away at the bastions of lethargy and harsh frugality. Builders, in particular, opposed the unprofitable use of urban land for such purposes. One Manchester businessman argued against a park in the city, asserting that 'the proper park for a Sunday afternoon is a tastefully laid-out modern cemetery.' Perhaps the shades of cricketers playing in ancient churchyards cocked a ghostly ear. The seminal Public Health Act of 1848, however, provided some mild boost to the campaign for public parks.

It is worth noting that the two other main genres of park were not entirely ignored and aspects of them were included, but never to the point of dominance. One was the Italian baroque convention of a park as a dramatic civic focus, away from the urban slums, like Florence's Boboli Gardens. The other was the Indian 'Taj Mahal' model of the park as a cipher for paradise, 'an oasis of beauty blooming in an earthly desert'. The standard bandstand of the English park was a bow to the former and the 'botanical gardens' element, with colourful flowerbeds and maybe an aviary, was a curtsey to the latter dispensation.

Despite these additions, the 'park', in the English cultural lexicon, followed the Capability Brown (1716-83) and Humphrey Repton (1752-1818) fashion of the rural enclave, neatly landscaped. Unlike the Italian style, it was hidden from urban eyes by a surround of bushes and trees, normally with ornate gates at the entrance. In several cases the parks were estates bequeathed by or purchased from owners whose once countrified property had become surrounded by urban development. Within the heavy foliage of the outer fencing lay the 'Brownean' ring, a Macadamised path. Within this walkway was the grassland, sometimes with a boating lake included.

It was the perfect example of the Victorian belief in 'rational recreation' in the physical connotation of healthy but sedate exercise, like so much sporting and other approved activity, an attempt to lure young working people from the temptations of drink and idleness. These public walks came to be seen as 'the lungs of the city', although the helpful relationship of parks to the carbon cycle was later to be vigorously disputed. The social element was aptly exemplified by the Olympian announcement in *the Times* on the opening of the Regent's Park in 1841 about 'the redemption of the working class through recreation', for now workers would enjoy 'the liberty of taking a walk in the more plebeian portions of the park, provided they had a decent coat on'.

One enthusiast, Rev J.E.Clarke, claimed 'recreation is RE-creation, the creation anew of fresh strength.' Jacques Carré, a modern authority on the concept, has called the parks 'a spectacular manifestation of Victorian civic art' and 'a testing ground of the new urban ethos.' They were further acknowledgement of the potency of the Cobdenite type of local government council that tried, with exuberant vim if no little self-satisfaction, to redress some of the horrors of urban life.

The parks designers and their political allies gradually won the battle. Sir Joseph Paxton (1801-65), of Crystal Palace fame, and his protégés, worked hard. John Gibson designed Battersea Park and became Superintendent of London's parks, many of which – Victoria Park, Bethnel Green in 1845; Battersea in 1857 – had been in the royal gift; in 1900 a quarter of the capital's parks had been crown land. Edward Miller, responsible for parks in Halifax, Buxton and Preston, and Edward Vamp, who designed Southport's Hesketh Park, Liverpool's Stanley Park and Birkenhead Park, were two others. Industrialists and merchants subscribed to – sponsored would be the modern term – parks, for instance, in Sheffield, Middlesbrough, Saltaire and Glasgow, with Sir Robert Peel's philanthropic gift of £10,000 for Salford's Peel Park being the most well-known example.

It did not follow inexorably that the parks would be used for cricket. The Victorian gardening fixation went into overdrive with many a tree-lined avenue, ornamental lake, rosarium, arboretum or winter garden conservatory, with some parks mini-Crystal Palaces or Kews. Apart from this delight in flowerbeds in the Taj Mahal convention, these parks were often deemed to be 'public walks, fitted to the sedate promenade of the populace.' Reginald Hargreaves' thwarted rival, Lewis Carroll, mounted the most celebrated defence of walkers in both 1867 and 1879, when the Convocation of Oxford University moved to make The Parks the home of the university cricket club. He parodied Oliver Goldsmith's *The Deserted Village*, suggesting in his *The Deserted Parks* that this would rob poor people of their wholesome strolls: 'These round their walks their cheerful influence shed/These were thy charms – but all these charms are fled.' The Parks cricket ground, later to be regarded as the sublime haven of cricketing traditionalism, was viewed by Lewis Carroll and his allies as a modish, even revolutionary, innovation

But cricket, urbane and morally espoused by the middle classes, won out, in spite of the peril of the towering hook shot for the stately promenader or the precious flora. Jacques Carré explains that 'football was not often allowed and never encouraged, being considered rough and vulgar.' Later, of course, it would be, but cricket enjoyed the initial momentum. Socially and physically, it was the ideal compromise. Ingenious research, for instance, by N.L.Tranter on the citizenry of Stirling, suggests that, at this stage, while 75% of local footballers were from the artisan classes, club cricketers were more mixed socially, with as many as a third – above the national average – from clerical, professional and even landed ranks. It is also true that unregulated cricket forced authorities to amend by-laws and lay and rent pitches.

Parks cricket became a significant element. In 1860 it was said that the newly acquired Macclesfield Park staged as many as forty matches on a Saturday afternoon, when the mills closed. By 1908 the London County Council reserved 442 'park' pitches for 10,000 players and 30,000 fixtures. The sports historian Richard Holt tells of park pitches used serially, with match following match on the same day, with pre-breakfast starts to ensure everyone had a game. He mentions Liverpool's 89 municipal cricket pitches in 1930. It was not uncommon for a player to spend an innings fielding at cover point and square leg for alternate overs and forming a brotherly liaison with the third man-cum-long on of a different game. Most interesting, perhaps are the parks that provided venues for professional cricket, among them, over the seasons, Stanley Park, Blackpool, Wardown Park, Luton and Valentine's Park, Ilford.

All in all, the parks gave a substantial encouragement to the expansion of cricket in the towns of the nation. In their artificial way they echoed the 'romantic' Victorian view of escapism from the drudgery of the factory, the mill and the foundry. The parks were mock-rural enclaves in the urban environs, borrowing, like the county cricket clubs, from some largely unrealistic Arcadian memory trace.

English Literature underpinned this idyllic belief in the connection of cricket and 'Englishry'. Throughout the Victorian period, cricket is constantly used as a metaphor for serene, pastoral ease. George Meredith, described by his biographer, Siegfried Sassoon, as a vital writer of 'irrepressible energy and obtrusiveness', includes cricket scenes in one or two of his comedy romances, each of his novels written, in his own words, in 'a spirit not hostile to the sweetest song-fully poetic.' For example, the coach driver in his *The Adventures of Harry Richmond* (1871) extols cricket's virtues. 'Now cricket, he said, was a fine manly sport; it might kill a man, but it never meant mischief; foreigners themselves had a bit of an idea that it was the best game in the world, though it was a nice joke to see a foreigner playing at it . . . Now there's my notion of happiness . . . it comprises – count: lot's o' running; and that's good; just enough o' taking it easy; that's good . . . and you say good morning to the doctor and the parson for you're in health body and soul, and ne'er a parson'll make a better Christian of ye, that I'll swear'. No wonder that Harry and his companions on the coach 'talked of the ancient raptures of a first of May cricketing-day on a sunny green meadow, with an ocean of a day before us, and well-braced spirits for the match'.

And yet English top-class cricket had never really been – witness the London hegemony of Regency cricket – pastoral, and nor would it ever be, even if there were a sufficiency of village green cricket available to lend veracity to the image. Paradoxically, so-called county cricket would always be, and increasingly so, the creature of the industrial and commercial conurbations.

CHAPTER FIVE
EMERGING COUNTY

LEWIS'S SPLENDID CRICKET SUITS.

A Victorian advertisement for cricket 'suits'

A paradox lay at the core of top-class English domestic cricket. Cricket's rustic charm was only tenable, for any superior national manifestation, in heavily urbanised settings. So much is a commonsensical truism. Looking back over the decades it is evident that London, with some assistance from nearby enclaves like Hambledon, was the true begetter of cricket as a national diversion. As soon as one engages with paid players and paying customers, a catchment area of intense numbers is obviously required. It is for that reason that regular first-class county cricket, curiously enough, was a product of industrialism.

The social saga of the industrial revolution involved the interactive process of three chief elements. Steam-driven technology, demographic growth and increased urbanism spiralled, in a dizzying whirl of cause and effect, to create the first industrialised nation. During Queen Victoria's reign, from 1837 to 1901, the British population almost doubled from 24m to 41m, and, during that same period, the majority had turned from rural to urban in character, with a high proportion living in communities of over 100,000 people. New industrial techniques had caused the decline of domestic manufacture in favour of the factory formula, with mills, foundries and mines at the forefront of a process whereby workers gathered in high, not penny, numbers. By the last third of the century half the work-force was employed in heavy industry, with 200 employees the average size of the manufacturing unit.

The political scientist, Herman Finer, termed this phenomenon 'concentration', an admirably laconic word for the equation of more and more people cramped into bigger and bigger towns, where they packed into larger and larger factories or their equivalent. It was in these bustling urban areas that much county cricket took formal root, rather than in the broad farmlands of the old shires.

Thus the counties often based their headquarters, not in the ancient but often relatively soporific county town, but in the thriving industrial city. Hence London hosted Middlesex and Surrey, while Birmingham, Manchester, Bristol, Brighton (Hove), Southampton and Leeds or Sheffield, for examples, stood surety for Warwick, Lancaster, Gloucester, Lewes, Winchester and York. Essex, initially, focussed on Leyton, hopeful of providing an East London outlet for first-class cricket, imitative of Surrey to the south and Middlesex to the north of the capital, while Canterbury had the edge on Maidstone, the county town of Kent. Nottingham, with Trent Bridge just across the boundary river in the shire, was one of the few centres of first-class cricket that combined old-time county administrative headship with new-found industrial wealth, with Derby and Leicester lesser examples.

However, the allied and critical component in the rise and incidence of first-class cricket was the advent of the railway. The railways, from their inauguration in 1830 as a contributor to the public conveyance of passengers, were the *summum bonum* of the industrial revolution, and almost sacrilegiously adored by the Victorians. The railways were both the finest product and the chief progenitor of primary industrialism. By the time the formal county cricket competition had been launched in the 1890s, there were 20,000 miles of railway lines in the United Kingdom and some trains travelled at speeds above 50mph. Although road and coach improvements had benefited travellers from about the last quarter of the 18th century, even the flying coaches racing along Macadamised roads and through Turnpike Trusts, could not compete with the railway engine. The journey from London to Manchester may, by dint of improved highways, have been reduced from three days to 30 hours, but the train soon managed the journey in five hours. By 1844 there were already over 25m railway passengers a year and by the end of the century the annual figure had soared to 1600m. A once near immobilised nation was up and running, with, from as early as 1844, the 'parliamentary' train, at a penny a mile, making the system affordable to those on low incomes.

Almost single-handedly, the private railway companies, of which there were 28 in the 1870s, albeit under strict governmental regulation, changed the public perspective on time. Until this juncture, it had not mattered that clocks were kept differently up and down the country, often according to the movement of the sun, rather like 'lighting up' times today. For example, there was a six minute ten seconds difference between London and Leeds time. In 1840 the Great Western Railway standardised the clocks and staff watches on all its stations. Another firm blow was struck when the Lancashire and Yorkshire Railway persuaded the Manchester Corporation to align its town hall clock with 'London' time. The Greenwich Observatory, utilised by astronomers for its precision, was the natural institute to decide on standard or 'mean' time for the nation, and this aim was attained in 1880, with a world conference in Washington in 1884 agreeing that this should become the international yardstick.

A compelling factor was thus the prim regularity of the railway system, for, in spite of occasional dislocation, its accuracy was spellbinding. Of course the train was valued for carrying customers to or near cricket venues, swelling the crowds that gathered to watch the counties but its role was much more salient than that. The speed and regularity of the trains enabled the disparate and far-flung county clubs to construct quite complex fixture lists, in the knowledge that they would be able to fulfil their obligations travel-wise. Indeed, rail access became a major, if not exclusive, determinant of whether a county was regarded as first-class or not. A circular argument applies in some part, whereby the most populous districts were, of course, both the more likely to provide crowds for first-class games and to be furnished with the busiest railway stations. Nonetheless, this did not always work in reverse. There were well-populated locations where good cricket had been played, which, having been late in receiving the blessings of general rail linkage or even with that advantage, being still too distant from the mainstream, did not enjoy the advantages of first-class county cricket.

The pre-1890 county contests chiefly involved eight premier teams. These were Middlesex and Surrey in the London area, Kent and Sussex from the home counties, Gloucestershire to the southwest, and Yorkshire, Lancashire and Nottinghamshire from the north midlands. They were known to the erudite cricketing press as the Octarchy, in yet another back reference to medievalism in respect of the seven Anglo-Saxon kingdoms of the Heptarchy. The first phase of rail development might be described as an inverted capital T, with some calligraphical twirls at its extremities. One of its many benefits was to ensure the mainline octet could reach one another with some exactitude and dispatch. London was located at the junction of the reversed T, with the upright speeding northwards to connect with Leeds, Sheffield, Manchester and Nottingham. An eastern branch tracked out to Canterbury and to Brighton, while, to the west, the Great Western Railway brought Gloucestershire into the fray. Bristol, the seat of Gloucestershire cricket rather than the old county town of Gloucester and already a thriving manufacturing city, was the rail link, one that soon also had links with the north via Birmingham. Without the GWR it is doubtful that the genius of W.G.Grace would have been much noticed outside the southwest region. Paddington plays as important a part in the Grace saga as does Lord's.

That of course is not the whole of the story. After an ingenious investigation, Duncan McCleish, in 'Early Railways and Cricket' (*The*

Cricket Statistician, 141, 2008) demonstrates that leading towns in all English counties, bar Cornwall and Herefordshire, had rail connections with London before 1850. In passing, one should observe how amazingly brisk the railway builders had been in covering the nation so sufficiently in twenty years, so much so that the travelling Exhibition elevens were enabled to make use of the system in their later years. Why, he pertinently asks, did some and not other of these shires become first-class rather than minor counties? He draws the conclusion that these latter were often areas where cricket's organisers 'did not have the know-how, even the will', to form a stable and enterprising county club that might be ambitious for first-class status.

The London link is a valuable yardstick of railway access but it does not provide a ready insight into the network at large and the possibilities of say, a Leeds to Bristol journey. There may have also been a countervailing movement. People in counties close to London, like Hertfordshire, Buckinghamshire and Berkshire, may have found the railways useful for trips to Lord's and the Oval, leaving less call or demand for first-class cricket in their own backyard. The adjacency of Cheshire to Old Trafford is another example. Duncan McCleish's article included fastest journey times for his London-bound trains, but he reminds us that these were usually first or first/second class trains and that trains conveying third class passengers could be extremely slow. The fastest train journey from London to Carlisle in 1850 was over nine hours; there was not much chance of Cumberland forming and sustaining a major county club.

It was, obviously enough, the outlying regions that suffered the most. The northeast and the southwest, together with East Anglia were particular victims. A Norfolk club established in 1827, had prospered a little, with the legendary batsman Fuller Pilch its stalwart but his recruitment by Kent was instrumental in its collapse and the dilatory progress of the Eastern Counties Railway Company – and their trains – did 'cricket in East Anglia no favours'. Tyneside remained the largest conglomeration of the English population without access to county cricket, although decent cricket had been witnessed in those parts, while Duncan McCleish suggests that the slowness of creating rail links with Stoke-on-Trent may have impeded cricketing matters in Staffordshire.

Then there is the question of Wales and Scotland. Andrew Hignell, cricket's leading, possibly only geographer, and with a particular expertise in Welsh cricket, has argued cogently that the advent of railways in the Principality had a dramatic effect on the fixture lists of clubs like Chepstow, Neath, Llanelli and Bangor, which were able to utilise local lines to extend their activities. It is certain that this was the experience of many other areas. Although Cardiff and Swansea had rail connections with London as early as 1850, it was to be some decades before the varied elements were to come together and produce, in Glamorgan, the first and only Welsh first-class county.

Scotland had rail links with the south, although these were not quick journeys initially – and it should be recalled that Edinburgh and Glasgow, the centres of a major concourse of population, had been the foci of good cricket. W.G.Grace played in fourteen minor matches north of the border, principally in the two lowlands cities. It is something of a disparaging Sassenach sentiment to suspect the Scots of not being too favourably inclined towards cricket, but one must factor in Scotland's lack of access for major visitations. The more staccato rhythm of three day matches, with the need to make perhaps a longish trip for the next game, was different to the explorations of the Exhibition elevens. It is true that their matches, including some in Scotland, now included three day fixtures, but, of course, there were no 'return' matches. The pattern of home and away matches depended on a reliable rail service over a relatively constricted area.

All in all, it becomes apparent that the railways were the essential but not the sole determinant of the first-class county programme. Apart from rail connections, the cricketing kingdoms of the Octarchy were each housed within conclaves of sizeable population from which members and spectators could be attracted, and they assuredly had backing and leadership of adequate ambition.

THE TIME FACTOR

It is appropriate to note at this juncture the moving dial of the time factor in cricket itself. Until the beginning of the 19th century a two innings cricket match, great or small, was frequently negotiated in a day, with weather the usual culprit if this were not possible. In any event, games were, as far as possible, played out to the bitter end. The first recorded four day game, interrupted by weather, was Hampshire versus Kent, 15-18 August, 1774, at Broadhalfpenny Down. There was a commitment to completion.

When cricket first framed its laws in the 18th century, time was not considered. It was presumably taken for granted that a day was sufficient, although, for some big contests, the arrangers stipulated a longer time. Most other sports sought a regulatory framework in the last third of the 19th century and a realistic view was taken of the outcome of each game. Two general concepts were deployed. One was to have a strict time allocation and whichever team or performer had progressed most satisfactorily would be declared the winner. The football codes, hockey and other field-sports chose this route, where hitherto there had often been some latitude about time. Boxing is a helpful example. The Queensberry Rules of 1887 insisted on a timed round, usually of three minutes duration, a specified number of rounds and a points system to supplement the timed knock-out or stoppage. It was a dramatic turnaround from the earlier unabated fighting, broken only by intervals caused by knockdowns. The first rules for the FA Cup in 1871 stipulate a playing time of 90 minutes, suggesting that this was not an assumption that might be left unwritten.

The other option was to assess who performed better over a routine set of targets or the earliest accomplishment of a given aim; eighteen holes of golf; the best of five tennis sets; the heaviest scorer in a frame of snooker; fifteen points over a series of bowling ends; 21 points up at badminton; 501 at darts . . . and so forth. Intriguingly, the intensification grew over the years, partly in response to media demands. Thus the long drawn out weeks of the mid-20th century Joe Davis era of snooker championships became the sharper televised focus of the present hour of much fewer frames, with a single black ball decider in the event of a tie. The football penalty shoot-out, the tennis tiebreaker and golf's sudden death play-off are other instances. Even cricket would introduce a 'bowl-out' – several deliveries at undefended stumps – in one day knock-out ties spoilt by rain. These were to prove rather embarrassing, so infrequently were the wickets struck.

Over against such reductionism, cricket had tended initially to expand its time frame, until the five and even six day Test match was usual and even county cricket added a day to the traditional three of Victorian usage. It was not until the 1960s that the matter was addressed, with the somewhat synthetic response of limited overs tournaments. It is, of course, that endearing twin component of cricket – the defence of the targets as an attacking base for scoring – that makes timing difficult to estimate. Even with that second general alternative of a schedule of targets, the necessary time can be gauged within reasonable limits. The average golf round will consume three or so hours; on balance, the more competent the player and the fewer strokes required, the faster the completion of the round. No one is hitting the ball away from the hole, let alone being granted points for so doing. It is this open-endedness of cricket that defies the clock. A game could be as long as a piece of string. Cricket is alone among major sports in having, as well as a draw, a tie, endorsed by the 1947 code of laws, with the side batting second losing all its wickets with the overall scores even. Thus since 1948 there have been some thirty or so examples of what in football or rugby would be called draws. Gerald Brodribb calculated that, between 1864 and 1994, there had been 35,000 county games, of which 38% had been drawn, with, in the seasons after 1968, the proportion often topping 50%. In effect, these are uncompleted games or, to use Regency parlance, 'unfinished'. Occasionally, these games may prove to be thrilling cliff-hangers but essentially they have not been resolved.

The technical changes that produced higher scoring and longer games have been considered rather more by historians than the increased duration required for staging them. However, the issue of a sport that, at its highest level, now needed three days rather than one, and even then with a fair chance of its being 'unfinished', had a major impact. As the county clubs embarked on programmes of fixtures that involved a spectator and membership element, the arrangements required for, in essence, a series of eighteen hours contests became quite elaborate. The upkeep of an amenity and the recruitment of the human resources to cater for this was a relatively massive undertaking. It was only feasible, in practical and financial terms, for a limited number of counties.

The comparison with professional football is interesting, partially because there is a natural, and often useful tendency, among commentators to equate the eighteen clubs of the County Championship with the twenty clubs of the Premier League, the old First Division of the Football League. It is when one decides to compare the 92 clubs of the Premiership and the Football League with the eighteen of the County Championship that the perspective alters. In other words, it was possible for many more towns than in cricket to host a soccer team and help create a thriving network whereby, for example, a Tottenham Hotspur could rise through the ranks quickly from moderate origins to national fame.

Cricket has, by and large, failed to introduce that degree of flexibility into its processes, leaving the County Championship, almost from the onset, as a sacrosanct and aloof tournament. And one element that set it apart from much of the rest of cricket was the time that had to be allocated to offer any chance of completed games. Apart from the practicalities of county clubs contriving to play, at the peak of first-class county activity, thirty and more three-day games a summer, something that scarcely any non-first-class county club could dream of emulating, cricket became one of the rare sports where there was a totally different construct for its professional and recreational manifestations. Minor Counties often came to play two day games, but the ordinary clubs, the backbone of recreational cricket, just had a few hours on Saturday afternoon and evening for their game. It was as if professional golfers had to play a round of 54 holes or professional footballers for four and a half hours a game.

The advancing dominion of bat over ball had come about despite changes in bowling styles. Round arm bowling, although long, if not widely practised, before it was legalised, enjoyed but a short term of general usage. It had included the approach of, among others, William Clarke, whereby the ball was projected from shoulder height, rather like a darts throw from arm-pit level, while underarm bowling, of the length rather than the skittle alley trundle, had been maintained. Given the conservationist tenets of cricket, the shift to over arm bowling was swift. An incident, in which the Kent bowler, Ned Willsher was no-balled frequently at the Oval for raising his arm above shoulder level, initiated speedy processing. MCC, by the narrow margin of 27 votes to 20 at a meeting to debate the question, changed the law in 1864. It might be noted that MCC membership was very much smaller then than now; it was about 400 in mid 19th century.

In one sense, the rapidity of the reform, as opposed to the more long drawn nature of the round arm controversy, is understandable. Once the decision had been taken that 'bowling', as on a bowling green, could be adapted to something more akin, in normal language, to 'throwing', then the move of the arm from shoulder to side of the head, beyond which no further progress is possible, was predictable. It must have been hard for the umpire to judge whether actual release of the ball was just below or just above shoulder level. Now his task was that much easier. In effect, all possible styles, apart from the bent arm that cricketers deem 'throwing', were legitimate. W.G.Grace did extremely well as a chiefly round arm bowler, as did several 'lobsters', as the under arm bowlers came to be called. Under arm bowling was to be observed, albeit rarely, at club level certainly until the 1940s. A minor nuisance was the linguistic distortion of the actual word 'bowling', for the phrase 'over arm bowling' is a tortuous one.

As for others ways of stalling the advance of batsmanship, devices such as more or larger wickets, narrower bats and longer pitches (presumably to reduce the run rate; it could scarcely have assisted the bowler) were eschewed. The pitch, at 22 yards, a ploughing measure of a chain, equal to a tenth of a furlong or 'furrow-long', has remained an agricultural constant, another tiny tribute to cricket's treasured agrarian heritage.

SOCIAL CLASS

Where cricket continued to distinguish itself from other sports was in its capacity to embrace the class system. Other games found the social mix of paid and unpaid, or simply working and middle class, players distasteful and sought methods of avoiding such cross-class activity, the separation of the two rugby codes, union and league, being perhaps the most pronounced example. It was a social as much as, if not more so than, an economic issue. The Amateur Athletic Club, started by Oxbridge men in 1866, had a rule forbidding the membership of 'artisans and mechanics' and manual workers in general, and when the London Athletic Club decided in 1872 to admit tradesmen (that is, respectable, upper tier workers) 60 members resigned, with the support of *the Times*, anxious that there should be no pollution of gentlemen by the inclusion of 'outsiders, artisans, mechanics and suchlike troublesome persons.' To be absolutely clear, the term 'gentlemen amateurs' was deployed in athletics. When the professional controversy hit association football, W.H.Jupe, of the Birmingham Football Association, opined it was 'degrading for respectable men to play with professionals.'

Cricket, with a long tradition of masters and servants playing together and with a convention of professionals acting as groundsmen and net bowlers, avoided that degree of divisiveness, but the social chasm was more difficult to bridge than the economic one.

In truth, gentleman was a more exact word than amateur to describe the cricketing social division. By the end of the 17th century, and as a consequence of economic change, the gentry was sufficiently well established as a social order that their numbers may be quoted as some 20,000, that is, about one in every ten males in the population, over against the nobility of about 120. The distinction was between 'gentle' and 'simple', and, whilst both adjectives gathered new connotations, so that Simple Simon became a dullard instead of a prole, the former stayed the linguistic course more steadily. 'Noble' and 'ignoble' or 'churlish' played cricket together. At Hambledon we hear of 'players belonging to the club', as opposed to 'gentlemen members of the club'. The Exhibition elevens would sometimes include a gentleman, like Arthur Mynn or Nicholas Felix or W.G.Grace himself, who would do the socialising, make the speeches and greet local dignitaries. They were, of course, rewarded for their troubles. In county cricket the gentlemen of uncertain means would be found sinecure jobs, such as assistant secretary to the club, and healthy expenses.

The game was given away by the MCC inquiry in 1879 into 'the definition and qualification of amateur cricketers', which decreed a seasonal maximum of £50 for travel and accommodation expenses. Some of the run-of-the-mill professionals, in days when the top fees were £4 or £5 a match, inclusive of expenses and the 'no play, no pay' rule applied, might have settled for £50 for his summer's work. There were professionals who would die in squalid poverty, but there were some who prospered. It is fascinating to compare, for instance, the career of a noted shamateur, the majestic Archie Maclaren, his bungling, madcap business disasters hardly in keeping with his authoritative batting, with that of that highly competent professional, William Gunn of Nottinghamshire. A co-founder of the prosperous sports firm of Gunn and Moore, he died in 1921, leaving an estate worth £54,392. To be a gentleman one had to have polish as well as, even instead of, brass.

The novels of Anthony Trollope are a rich source for an understanding of the concept. Victoria Glendinning, his felicitous biographer, has described how 'gentlemen recognised one another by complex codes of dress, gesture, taste, use of language and shrewd references.' The novelist himself placidly concluded that 'the one great line of demarcation in the world was that which separated gentlemen from non-gentlemen.' In *The Last Chronicle of Barset* (1867) the wealthy Archdeacon Theophilus Grantly receives the impoverished (only one servant) vicar of St Ewold's, Josiah Crawley. Their children are to wed and the vicar's daughter has no fortune. The Archdeacon comforts his embarrassed inferior. "We stand', said he, 'on the only level ground on which such men can meet each other. We are both gentlemen'.' In *Rachel Ray* (1863), Anthony Trollope praises the Rev. Samuel Prong for his devotion, his intellect, his earnestness and tenacity, continuing, '. . . true in most things to the instincts of his calling – but deficient in one vital qualification for a clergyman for the Church of England; he was not a gentleman.' The author protests that Samuel Prong is not a liar nor a thief nor even ill-mannered: 'I am by no means prepared to define what I do mean, thinking, however, that most men and most women will understand me.'

That rather complacent tone, echoed by Trollope's readership, explains both how the gentleman – and, of course, the gentlewoman – was judged and why there was such a silent acceptance of the differing fashions by which gentlemen and players were remunerated.

COUNTY ORDER

The county as the only contender; its base in highly populated and rail accessible towns; the long three day contest among a severely limited group of teams; the maintenance of a middle class/working class compound in team selection – it was with this extraordinary compound of features that the County Championship stumbled rather than developed into conscious focus.

In playing terms, and in the years from the mid-1860s to 1890, Nottinghamshire were the undoubted leaders, their triumphs built around the professional prowess of John Jackson, Arthur Shrewsbury, Richard Daft, William Gunn and Alfred Shaw. The last-named is arguably the most successful bowler in history, taking a little over 2000 wickets at an average of 12 and, with his naturally round arm slow medium paced deliveries, conceding fewer runs than he bowled overs. The bedrock of professional cricket was the lace-making and hosiery trade of the region, which contrived to combine the advantages of industrialism with a certain flexibility of broken time. In the manner of Silas Marner, much of the work remained cottage-based, giving some leeway for men to take a day or two away to play cricket.

The harsh discipline of the factory was slower in arriving in these crafts and many professional cricketers mixed two trades more effortlessly than a Lancashire cotton spinner might have done. The Yorkshire woollen trades similarly had something of this flexibility. Moreover, it became the cultural mode to be a cricketer in such famed villages as Sutton-in-Ashfield, just as a Welsh child could scarcely have avoided the allure of choral singing. The fact that there were rewards to be had was a crucial aspect of this form of social emulation. It has been calculated that in the years from this point until the First World War as many as 400 Nottinghamshire born professionals would annually be plying their trade at home and abroad, as club professionals, school coaches and so forth. It was, unusually, 1889 before the amateur ethos fully gained its authority at Trent Bridge, when J.A.Dixon became Nottinghamshire's first non-professional captain.

Nottinghamshire, like Yorkshire, were happy to pick teams of native birth, whereas Surrey and Lancashire, areas of a more swirling cosmopolitanism, were content to seek professionals from outside their immediate terrain. The argument about birthright became one of the motivating factors in a more structured approach to county cricket. There had long been a non-formal acceptance that either birth or established residence should be the criteria for eligibility, with some latitude for amateurs in terms of the family residence. The real bones of contention had become poaching and excess mobility among the jobbing professionals, especially as the county competition evolved into something more regularised. It was the professional who shopped around who was the irritant, not, for example, Yorkshire's autocratic titan, Lord Hawke, who, to the delight of critics of Yorkist chauvinism, was born in Lincolnshire. 'Importation', as it was known in the football world, was the fault. Professionals sought games and payments where they could. Roger Iddison, for instance, contrived to play for Lancashire, Cheshire, the United North of England XI, of which he was the principal organiser, and the United Yorkshire XI.

In 1873 the Surrey club inaugurated a series of what proved to be keenly contested meetings with other county representatives. It was finally agreed that no player, paid or unpaid, should play for more than one county a season, the choice, either by birth or residence, to be made at the commencement of the summer. Somewhat grudgingly – its members were not too happy about the amateur escape hatch of the parental home – MCC gave its approval to these measures, which, for many years served as the base of county qualification. Given the emphasis placed, over the years, on the importance of county birth-right, it is proper to recall that its official introduction, far from being an evocation of local loyalist sentiment, was the strict application of the then commonly used employment practice. It was a severe contract of 'master and servant' – the term was freely utilised with regard to both football and cricket professionalism. Such authoritarian practice was the equivalent of what county committeemen would have understood both in their own businesses and homes.

MCC also experimented vainly with a cup competition, offered to six counties, with ties played on neutral grounds. It was in 1873, the year after the first FA Cup competition had been successfully staged, but, apart from one disastrous match between Kent and Sussex on a perilous Lord's pitch, the scheme came to nought and the knock-out idea was shelved for a conservative ninety years. Many felt that there was enough cricket already and – a second modern-sounding fear – that gambling would be re-introduced.

The seeming standoff between the counties and MCC has been interpreted by historians of a pseudo-Marxist predilection as the rivalry of progressive bourgeois counties versus retrogressive aristocratic MCC. A search of the backgrounds of both groups does not quite support this notion, and torpor at Lord's, where playing standards had declined and over which the Oval's successes loomed, may be a more telling explanation.

It was a short-lived interlude. The counties, without any structure, needed the authoritative accolade of MCC and MCC needed a boost in its fortunes. The role of mentor to the counties was an excellent investment. H.A.Perkins became secretary of MCC in 1876 and he energetically and drastically overhauled the membership, introduced other reforms, and, critically, negotiated the agreement that Middlesex should play home matches at Lord's. A reasonably amicable coalition resulted as between the leading counties and MCC. The county secretaries met annually at Lord's to agree next season's fixture list and perhaps settle other quandaries.

When MCC approved the county proposals on player eligibility, it insisted that this applied to all counties. This included even some Scottish shires that were convivially endeavouring to sustain Caledonian cricket. MCC had no wish to be dragged into the ceaseless bickering over first-class status, preferring to leave that to the divination of the press. The Octarchy were free of this burden, except when they played one of the smaller fry; it was more to do with the few county clubs that flirted on the fringes. A fixture of three days duration was one sign but it was not a foolproof one. One suspects that another reason for MCC's reluctance to be involved with county jurisdiction had been this very controversy about first-class categorisation.

In 1882 the county secretaries began to meet annually and formally, before, in 1887, establishing the County Cricket Council. This was the belated response to calls in the press in the early 1860s for a cricket 'parliament', although the council was seen as a complement to, not a substitute for, MCC. Lord Harris, the powerful ruler of Kent and a potent Lord's' figure, took the chair, with the elite octet and twelve other counties represented. It was resolved to decide on player qualification, albeit with MCC as the final adjudicator.

The discussions, while of value, were marred by the acidic rivalry that seems to consume so much sporting action, the chief causes of bitterness the continued accusations about poaching and irate arguments about bowlers accused of throwing.

Nonetheless, the Council valiantly seized the nettle of classification. In 1890 a special sub-committee meeting of the Council agreed a modish system of three eight-strong divisions, with promotion and relegation, an idea promulgated by Charles Pardon, the perky editor of *Wisden*. Obviously, the success of the Football League, inaugurated in 1888/89, was an influence. Surprisingly, the major part – the actual classification – caused few squabbles; it was the minor point – the complicated oversight of promotion and relegation – that undermined this logical plan. As well as an order of merit, determined on the then current practice of subtracting wins from losses and ignoring draws, there was to be a 'qualifying series' of home and away matches for the top and bottom teams of each division. Furthermore, and critically, there was the matter of what constituted a requisite number and brand of fixtures.

The secretaries of the second-class counties met and wondered aloud whether the new procedure might be a 'sham'. They put forward amendments at the annual meeting of the Council in 1890, which had to confirm or otherwise the plan and, suddenly and unhappily, the house of cards collapsed. Fixtures were the main anxiety. In W.G.Grace's words, the majority forcefully 'declined to pledge themselves to any classification scheme that would compel them to play more matches than they wished to' or to 'the compulsion of a county to play another'. In some chaos and frustration, the Council itself came to 'an abrupt and unlooked for termination.'

In a matter of months the aspiration of a logical programme for all the combatant counties was denied and with it the destruction of a controlling body for the counties. Fixtures had proved to be the bugbear but plainly, without some parity of fixtures – ideally, the home and away routine of the Football League – it was difficult to calculate tables of merit. To labour a point, the requirement for all counties to find the necessary resources to engage in a bespoke series of three day games was the logistical problem. Not for the first or last time did cricket take a backward step. The counties had failed to order their own house, and, since that time, no method of automatic entry to or exit from the sacred grove of the first-class championship has been devised.

In sorrowful despair, the counties turned again to the newly revivified MCC to take control of this aspect. W.S.Gilbert modestly claimed to recognise only two pieces of music. One was *God Save the Queen* and the other wasn't. MCC, as advised by the county officials, took the same simplistic line. In 1894, after long deliberation, it judged that there was 'no need for further sub-division' and that, just as one cannot be 'a bit pregnant', one was or was not wholly first-class. Mystically and without published yardsticks, MCC proceeded to arbitrate on what could be regarded, for the compilation of averages, as a first-class fixture, including as mentioned in the last chapter, the rising competence of the two universities, the touring Australians, and on occasion, some other elevens of standing, as for instance, for major Festival matches. MCC could propose and it could dispose.

This muted and baffling solution did help resolve the conundrum of the county competition. Hampshire and Derbyshire had wandered in and out of the running in chequered fashion and neither was, at this point, regarded as first-class. It was a thriving Somerset that next broke into the first-class register in 1891, while the official accolade of MCC was proffered Leicestershire, Essex, Warwickshire and a redeemed Derbyshire in 1894. Oddly, they were not allowed into the Championship until 1895, where a recomposed Hampshire joined them. It was a huge leap from eight to fourteen in so short a time. All did reasonably well but it would be sometime before any of them challenged for the title. However, no first-class county ever perished from herein on and fell from grace into second-grade degradation, so that Topsy-like, the County Championship 'just growed', possibly to its own detriment and to that of English cricket.

In the meanwhile, the second tier of counties started their own competition in 1889, to witness it being rather weakened by the removal of their strongest brethren in the early 1890s. In 1895 the Minor Counties Association was formed and although there were occasional games between first and second-class counties, there would never again be any prescribed channel for changing membership between the two groups. Perhaps some were content – Norfolk has been cited as a sample of this cheery spirit – to avoid the solemn and unrelenting road of the first-class circuit.

As for the county championship, it was officially instituted in 1890, when the county representatives actually agreed that it existed and determined a method of deciding the result. Hitherto, the press had utilised several modes, such as fewest defeats or most wins or an amalgam of the two, with draws regarded, with typical Victorian manliness, as hardly worth the bother, while, in 1888, an unofficial points concept was tried. To give some flavour of the confusion, when W.G.Grace included in his published memoirs of 1899, the champions for the 1870s, he conflicts with the *Wisden* roster in six of the ten years. As ever, the great variation in the number and quality of fixtures played was the basic puzzle. Some order was introduced in 1894 when a plus point for a win and a minus point for a loss were awarded, with the proportion of points to finished matches providing the final tally. Draws still had no part in the calculation.

1895 was the first season of MCC official classification of counties, the first year when the competition was extended to fourteen counties and the first time a logically constituted decision-making technique was employed. For the purist, 1895 might be thereby judged the first summer in which an official and comprehensive county competition had been organised. A resurgent Surrey, with Bobby Abel the prolific batsman and George Lohmann the lethal bowler, were the worthy winners and the leading team of that epoch. The expansion of first-class county games was naturally extravagant. These rose from 31 in 1873 to 72 in 1892, then there was a near doubling again to 131, an average of 19 matches per county, in the significant year of 1895.

In 1904 MCC tried to bring some semblance of order to the embarrassments and arguments that beset its relations with the counties and the counties' squabblings and suspicions among themselves. An Advisory County Cricket Committee, with a delegate from each first-class county, was established under the auspices of MCC and with MCC's representative as its chairman. It served the purpose fitfully until 1969.

The county cricket system received an unexpected and indirect political boost from the 1888 County Councils Act. In the wake of the 1884 Parliamentary Reform Act, which gave the franchise to the rural householder, there was an administrative need to bring some more democratic order and bureaucratic rationale to the shires, still chiefly ruled through the quarter sessions by non-elected magisterial oligarchies of the landowners and the gentry. The statute was enacted under the premiership of Lord Salisbury, last mentioned in these annals as the victim of Etonian bullying. The staunchest and most strictly principled of Conservatives, with a wily streak as a political operator, he succeeded in producing a situation very favourable to traditional Toryism. The old shire boundaries were retained, which was a great relief to the county cricket clubs, while the major towns, some 61 of them, were severed away from the counties under the oxymoronic title of 'county boroughs'. Given that, in oversimplified electoral terms, there was an urban/Liberal-rural/Conservative split, this had the right-wing benefit of both swamping the non-county boroughs within the Tory shires and cutting off from the counties the often radical political leadership of their large towns and cities. In consequence, there were contests in only a minority of counties when elections were first held, the bulk of the new councillors were the old guard of the ancient regime and in 28 counties the previous chairman of the magistrates or the Lord Lieutenant were appointed chairmen of their county councils.

Lord Salisbury was a quiet expert in the art of giving a reactionary twist to a much sought for and apparently Liberal measure. This was almost certainly viewed with satisfaction by the chairmen of the county cricket clubs, encouraged to see this acknowledgment and reinforcement for the shire principle. The downside for Lord Salisbury, apart from the virtual loss of any Tory representation in Wales, was the progressive fire of the new London County Council. The prime minister moved to trim its reddish sails in 1899, when the London Government Act created the outer ring of 28 mainly Conservative boroughs, a hefty reduction of the LCC's ambit of authority. One consequence of the creation of a London 'county' was the move to run, from 1899 to 1905, a London county cricket club at Crystal Palace under the tutelage of a veteran W.G.Grace. It was an erratic if genial venture and although some of its fixtures were declared first-class, it never really aspired to join the county championship. There was enough high-grade cricket at and around London to satisfy most tastes by this point, and the Crystal Palace authorities discovered there was 'no partisan nucleus' around which to build. They also discovered, doubtless to W.G.Grace's chagrin, that the provision of a lawn tennis facility was more profitable.

Although, inevitably, several of the counties had their headquarters located in one or other of the new county boroughs, their committees and officials were able to look with some complacency over the passing scene. The curious compromise of the 1888 act underpinned the traditional strength of the county. It occurred at a point when the cricketing county clubs were resolving critical issues of their own, with, as in the case of the collapse of the originally accepted three-tier system, an unadventurous outcome. It left the leading group of fourteen county clubs, along with the two universities and MCC, in an inviolable position as the sole protagonists of major domestic cricket. It did so, providentially and exactly, as the golden age of cricket dawned. They would be indispensable players in the glorious sunshine of that proud era, their supremacy never again to be seriously challenged for a hundred years.

Chapter Six
SETTING SAIL

New South Wales v Victoria at Sydney, 1857

The golden age of cricket was not solely of an English provenance, at least from a geographical viewpoint. The English scene overlapped with the first vivid flourish of Australian cricket and was marked by some splendid cross-oceanic exchanges, while South Africa, the West Indies and India were other regions where cricket was played to a reasonable standard. That said, the protagonists continued to be, on the whole, Anglo-Saxon by origin and breeding. As Charles Tennyson wrote, in *Victorian Studies* (vol 2 no 3 1959) the English-man was the world's 'games master', carrying his cultural luggage with him. The poet, Horace, sang accurately in his lines, 'they change their climate, not their souls, who push across the sea.'

Acknowledging that it is believed forms of cricket had been engaged in on the continent in pre-modern times, it is perhaps safer to announce that signs of a recognisable English version of cricket had been spotted overseas by the commencement of the 18th century. Until quite late in the 19th century almost all of these sightings involve Englishmen abroad in their varied roles as sailors, soldiers and settlers. The earliest seems to have been when a party from three naval vessels included 'krickett' among their recreations in 1676, when they enjoyed a picnic at Aleppo, a base for the Levant Company in what is now Syria. It is listed among several pastimes in a diary entry describing the occasion and as is common for that time, we do not know precisely what the picnickers actually did. A reference to cricket in a coded diary in Virginia in 1709 was recently re-transcribed as the game 'old-two-cat', further testimony to the confusion about the lineage of games from a time when play was localised and incidental.

North America

Nonetheless, it is to North America that one must turn for the first formal development of English cricket outside the British Isles. However counterintuitive that might seem to today's cricket-lover, for whom the American understanding of cricket is regarded jokily, North America was of course, the first 'Empire', the first region to be properly settled by the British and thus opened to the cultural values of the motherland. It is a fact made clear in the critically acclaimed novel, *Netherland*, published in 2008 and written by Joseph O'Neill. It includes a major dimension of cricket in present-day New York, supported by the cricketing protagonist's claim that 'cricket was the first modern team sport in America. It came before baseball and football. Cricket has been played in New York since the 1770s.'

It is certainly true that there was a spread of cricket clubs throughout the colonies and the coming of independence in 1783 had no visible effect on these activities in the newly founded USA. This despite the fact that some objected to the notion of having an American 'President' on the patriotic grounds that English cricket clubs had such figureheads. Continued British rule in Canada required the presence of the military, partly to keep a careful eye on the now independent colonies. New York and Toronto thus became the chief American centres by the early 19th century and from 1840 the St George's club, New York, and the Toronto club, formed by George A.Barber in 1827, played occasional fixtures. Beginning in 1844, these were labelled United States and Canada, thereby allowing for the freak suggestion that North America was the site of the first international cricket, indeed, in the absence of other formalised field sports, the first international team sports encounters.

While St George's initially fielded one or two from Philadelphia and Toronto similarly enlisted some assistance, this was basically an augmented club fixture. It suffered from the desire of cricket-lovers and newspapermen to lavish extravagant titles on their rather more mundane arrangements. Not for the first time in cricket history did its practitioners confuse the issue in this colourful manner. The fixture was sustained until 1912, with Philadelphia more or less standing proxy for the United States.

The Philadelphia area had, by the 1850s, taken over the leadership of American cricket, a position that was to be unchanged for many years, while, over the rest of the century, a number of English professionals found work in the United States and in particular, at the Philadelphian clubs. In 1859 a strong professional team, captained by the Nottinghamshire favourite, George Parr, travelled to North America and played matches on both side of the border. They played and won five games against XXIIs and a further three exhibition matches during a two month tour. They were well received, although chilly October weather marred the last two fixtures somewhat. It is right to underline the import of this journey. It was the first time a major overseas cricket tour had been undertaken, a mighty portent for the future.

The American Civil War of 1861-64 proved to be more damaging to cricket's chances than the American War of Independence. Apart from the short-term effect of preventing any substantive cricket exchanges, it heralded the dawn of a more in-built nationalism, suited to the surge of European migration into the USA and the need to forge a new nationhood from the polyglot elements this represented. Baseball came to the fore. There was a scholarly dispute between the American school, vowing allegiance to Abner Doubleday, a hero of Gettysburg, who apparently developed the game at Coopersville in 1839 from the American pastime of old cat, and the Anglo-Saxon school, clinging to the notion that early colonists brought over a version of rounders from the southwest of England.

Whatever the case, in 1865, with the civil war scarcely over, a National Convention of 91 clubs was established. Although cricket tours to North America were resumed some of the zest had gone and baseball was in the ascendant. The American and Canadian version of football evolved from British origins, basically on college fields, and the USA Intercollegiate Football Association was formed in 1876. In 1891 the Rev. James A. Naismith, of the International YMCA Training School, managed the rare feat of actually inventing a game from scratch, when he created basketball, which fast became popular. In Canada, French settlers borrowed the North American indigenous game of 'baggataway' and called it, after the stick shaped like a bishop's crosier, lacrosse. This was about 1840, and 'baggataway' is yet further evidence of the ubiquitous nature of 'play'. Then the Canadians started the Ontario Ice Hockey Association, the central authority for that sport, in 1887. Lacrosse and ice hockey deposed cricket from its hopeful throne of top sport in Canadian eyes.

Especially in the USA, but with some ramifications in Canada, the pattern emerges of a region eager to internalise and modernise its sports, almost as though there was a deliberate turning of the back on Europe. Cricket did persist in the United States but it never recovered any degree of truly national identity. Its silver days were the couple of decades or so before 1914 when Philadelphian cricket and cricketers bloomed in spectacular fashion. Possibly the nostalgic memory of Philadelphia's golden age in the 18th century, when it flourished as a major port and as a leading educational and political centre, acted as some bulwark against the overwhelming demands of the brash new American code of nationalism, leaving its cricketers to bask in that sentimental glow. Their leading light was J.Barton King, far and away the best American-born cricketer, and a fast bowler of considerable venom.

Then there was decline. In spite of the help of a handful of English professionals, the Philadelphian teams were usually all-amateur, and while there was some enthusiasm in both Canada and the USA for the big games, a spectator and financial base was not to be developed. Baseball, College football, basketball and lawn tennis won out. Where cricket continued, it was often an expatriate activity of a socialising kind, typified by the jolly diversions of the Sussex and England batsman-cum-film actor, Sir Cecil Aubrey Smith. Somehow the tinsel sheen of his Hollywood team, starring Boris Karloff, David Niven and Errol Flynn, aptly epitomised the condition of American cricket after the First World War.

AUSTRALASIA

The link between North America and Australia concerns the requirement of the British to seek elsewhere, after the loss of the American colonies, for the disposal of surplus population, notably the criminally disposed section. It was in the May of 1787 that eleven ships with a human cargo of a thousand convicts and assorted settlers, set sail from Portsmouth for Australia, led by Arthur Phillip, first governor of the new settlement. They may well have turned to cricket for diversion but the first recorded testimony is a newspaper reference of 1804, which describes the crew of HMS Calcutta at cricketing play. Thereafter it appears that the British army and the New South Wales army corps maintained an interest in cricket and slowly if sporadically and intermittently, clubs were formed. Distance, as we discovered in examining early English cricket, lends enchantment to the rules. For many years, Australian cricketers earned five for a hit that cleared the ropes and six for one that cleared the ground, while the luck of the toss was courteously replaced by yielding first innings to one's visitors. Given the rugged terrain and conditions, the slow arrival from England of equipment, and the usual intrusion of gambling, quarrelling and other unhelpful features, the spread of cricket was both extensive and wondrous. Nevertheless, it was, at bottom, recognisable cricket.

In 1851 at Launceston, what was then regarded as the first intercolonial match – and later recognised as the first first-class fixture to take place in Australia – ended in a three wicket victory for Van Diemen's Land (Tasmania from 1855) over Victoria. It should be added that there was no Tasmanian cricket body as such. It was the Launceston club officials who were the hosts and selectors, but they did include Hobart players in the eleven. As for the Victorians, they were mainly from the powerful Melbourne and East Melbourne (Abbotsford CC until 1860) clubs. Indeed, Chris Harte, the Australian cricket historian, believes some of their games should have been declared first-class. On the other hand, another knowledgeable Australian expert, Jack Pollard, throws cold water on the 1851 claim, asserting firmly that the 1856 match between New South Wales and Victoria in Melbourne is a juster choice of that first Australian first-class fixture on the grounds of the standards of the participants.

Once again we run into the quandary of writing history backwards, in the sense of prescribing labels, such as 'first-class' – and 'Test match' will shortly provide a further illustration – after the events. As it was, from that opening inter-colonial game in 1851 to the advent of the Sheffield Shield Competition in 1892, there were 153 listed first-class matches on Australian soil, 76 of them of an inter-colonial character and several of the rest involving English touring teams.

One distinctive aspect of the Australian situation was the status of its separate colonies. Victoria and Queensland, for instance, devolved from New South Wales in 1851 and 1859 respectively, whilst Tasmania, South Australia and Western Australia each had a separate being. This was to have many repercussions in the story of Australian cricket. In this respect, Australia resembled the original thirteen colonies of the United States, each of which had separately withdrawn from crown control to participate in the 1776 rebellion against the British king in parliament and each of whom had separately ratified the draft American Constitution, when victory had been secured. Then, later, there were the nine southern states which had felt they had the legal right, each separately, to secede from the union to form the Confederacy in 1861. Each Australian region was similarly a colony in its own right.

Another distinctive aspect of Australian life, by contrast, differed from the American practice. Where the Americans tried to cook a new mix in the boiling cauldron of its varied ethnic and cultural ingredients, eschewing much that was starkly British, the Australian settlers were English to the core. They out-Heroded Herod. Their Anglophilia knew few bounds, as, in the manner of many expatriate groups, they sought, as in this case, to be more English than the English. In schooling there was a series of 'little Rugbys'; in journalism there was a Melbourne *Punch*; in leisure there was a Hyde Park; in cricket there was a Marylebone CC. They were anxious to mimic and then surpass their English models and ancestors – and cricket was the ideal medium for that sort of contest.

The timing of the Australian settlement is crucial. North America had been settled by the British before cricket had become a sport of national and well-organised pretensions. This is another reason why the previously argued point, that formal or official cricket was of a later vintage than some commentators would plead, is of more than academic importance. The North American migrants probably carried across the Atlantic the *bric-a-brac* of umpteen half-formed diversions – the fully developed versions of a few national sports arrived much later and were faced with different attitudes. Association and rugby football, no less than cricket, eventually lost out to sprightly competitors cast in the new American mould and Canada was also much influenced by this.

The Australian migrants transmitted fully-fledged English sports into a fully-fledged English community with cricket the leading one among them, for cricket, in the critical second half of the 19th century was at its cultural height in the UK. Australia was the first all-English overseas settlement where, in effect, proper cricket arrived with the incomers. This is a very compelling point when one ponders why Australia so readily became, and was to remain, England's chief rival in the emerging cricketing world.

The 'Englishness' of Australia in this its infancy cannot be denied. It was the most fervent base of what was called 'the New Imperialism'. Australians valiantly crossed the seas to fight on the British side in the Boer War and the two World Wars. In the 1914-1918 War, 400,000 troops, almost a tenth of the population and almost half the active adult male population, made the long journey to Europe, of whom, appallingly, 80,000 were killed and 200,000 wounded. That was their solemn testimony to the English heritage. Cricket was the happier recreational emblem of that same impulse.

Less vociferously, New Zealand demonstrated some of the same Anglicised characteristics. 1840 was the date of the first emigrations from the old country – and it did not take long for cricket to be played in Auckland and Wellington, while the Otago CC was established in 1848. The provincial structure of New Zealand was, like the colonial administrations of Australia or the English county system, a useful tool for raising the standards of club cricket, and some one-day provincial games of a sketchy inter-provincial nature were played from 1860. In 1864 Otago engaged nearby Canterbury in a three-day fixture and this is regarded as New Zealand's first first-class game.

Just as the Australian schools were to give polish to some of their leading cricketers, so was the contribution of J.P.Firth, headmaster of Wellington College towards the end of the 19th century, instrumental in giving succour to the rather ailing roots of New Zealand cricket. That emulation of the English public school had also been witnessed in Canada, where George A.Barber, sometimes labelled 'the father of Canadian cricket', had taught and coached at the Upper Canada College. New Zealand had, however, neither the population nor the social sinews to raise its cricket standards to any world-class heights until the years between the two World Wars. In the interim, the rugby codes solidified their hold as the country's national sports. For all that, New Zealand was to remain perhaps the most Anglicised part of the British Empire with cricket a never insignificant aspect.

Another parallel between the British colonisation of North America and that of the Antipodes was the subjection of the indigenous races, their relegation to an inferior and separate existence and often, as in the case of the Tasman native, extermination. In spite of a rather circus-like Aboriginal tour of England in 1868 that was not taken as seriously as it should have been on either side of the oceans, neither that group nor the Maori people figured much more influentially in cricket that the Amerindians in the United States and Canada. However, in varying degrees and for differing reasons, British settlement in the other three principle regions of cricket development took a different, if never wholly tolerant, route, with the relationship with the native inhabitants a decisive factor.

WEST INDIES AND SOUTH AFRICA

The basic situation in the West Indies was as straightforward as it was gruesome. The sparse populations of Carib and Arawak Indians certainly succumbed wholesale to brutality and disease but, of course, the influx of African slaves arrived to provide a huge labour force. It is rare to find an area such as the West Indies where both the overseeing and overseen races are, in historic time, newcomers, with scarcely a trace of inhabitants of pre-Columbus vintage. Even after the emancipation of the slaves in 1833, the division of labour was maintained as more of a caste than a class system. There was, unlike in Australia and New Zealand, few signs of an expatriate British working class.

The plantocracy reigned supreme and aided by army personnel, played cricket, the first buds of the game observed and recorded in Barbados about 1806. There was an intriguing correspondence with the manner in which the ancient British estates had raised teams of master and servants. The black West Indian workers were used, like their rural predecessors in 18th century England, to bowl and field, exhausting occupations in that climate, and thus they gradually joined in the cricket proper, so much so that a few professionals gingerly emerged by the end of the 19th century. Again, the construction of public school equivalents for the sons of planters, colonial officers and other well-to-do British immigrants was a source of cricketing inspiration with, as a prime example, Harrison College, Barbados, where the England cricketer and administrator, Pelham Warner, was schooled before he went to Rugby. Jamaica boasted Kingston College, Jamaica College and St George's College, while there was Queen's Royal College in Demerara.

The far-flung locations of the islands discouraged much cricketing fraternisation among them. It was 1865 when Georgetown CC, with other representatives from Demerara (which is now part of Guyana) clubs, travelled to Barbados and played the first first-class match in the West Indies at Bridgetown at the Garrison Savannah ground. The teams were all white. Trinidad, where black players were more resolutely coming to the fore, made up a threesome from later in the decade, while Jamaica, set hundreds of miles from the more easterly islands, played its first top-class cricket in the mid-1890s. .

South Africa was a slightly more complicated case. The Cape Town littoral had been colonised by the Dutch in the 17th century and was only occupied by the British in 1795. After some seesawing of possession, British control was accepted and agreed by the London

Convention of 1814. A rejection of the more liberal ethics of the British, in particular, the wish to sustain slavery, led to 'the Great Trek' eastward of the Dutch settlers to found the republics of the the Orange River Colony and Transvaal. Natal was annexed to the British Cape Colony in 1844 and became a separate colony in 1856, to which, following the British victory in the Zulu wars, Zululand was added. Thus there were two pairings of Anglicised and 'Dutchified' colonies, all four of them heavily dependent on indigenous African labour.

Predictably, the first recorded cricket is military, dating from 1808 in the Cape of Good Hope but with travel across and around a harsh terrain a lengthy business, the standard basis of club cricket was slow in evolving. Dale College, King William's Town, in the Cape Colony, emulated some of colonial schools elsewhere in acting as a nursery for cricketers and by the 1850s, the Diocesan College, the South African College and the Port Elizabeth Academy added to this educational tributary for cricket.

However, it required the enormous boost of the South African gold rush and the development of mining, especially for diamonds, in the last decades of the 19th century to lift both the economic and population levels of the four colonies. Only then did the mushrooming cities of Johannesburg, Cape Town, Port Elizabeth and a score of supporting townships have the wherewithal to maintain fully-fledged cricket clubs of growing stature. With the Boers largely indifferent and the black population discouraged from playing the white man's game, the hitherto small English contingent had struggled to make much of a fist of cricket until the entire country was galvanised by those commercial and demographic events.

INDIA

India, of the three non-Antipodean areas of major cricketing concern, was the most complex example. The British conquests in North America, the West Indies, South Africa and Australasia were at the expense of relatively small groups of indigenous tribes who were, at least by the yardstick of European practice, unsophisticated. It became normal to term these 'discoveries' (of land already settled by humankind) as the introduction of 'civilisation' to these peoples, although their treatment by the European invaders scarcely affirmed the ordinary canons of civilised behaviour. The position in India, where intricate and rich patterns of life had long been extant, where large populations – for example, in Bombay in mid-19th century, there were 7000 Europeans as against 650,000 Indians – were definitively layered by social category, and where political rulership and religious belief was mature and elaborate, was quite different.

From the 17th century the East India Company had established thriving trading settlements on the subcontinent and it was, as in Canada, the commercial rivalry of the French, as well as the antagonism of some of the Indian princes, that precipitated the string of events by which, in 1784, the chartered company was taken over by the British government. Slowly, suzerainty was extended over the whole of the region. Although the relationship was uneasy – witness the Indian Mutiny of 1857/8, dubbed by some Indian historians as 'the First War of Indian Independence' – there was a necessary rubbing along of the brusque incomers' administration with the long established principalities.

Cricket had, inevitably, been played by the officers of the East India Company and by visiting naval and military personnel during the Hanoverian period and there was a Calcutta cricket club, playing at Eden gardens, from as early as 1792. The English occupiers were not settled residents, as in Australia or South Africa, where new Anglo-Saxon towns emerged. Although they might have served long years in the Raj, they remained essentially visitors. Their consolation in self-appointed exile was the social club, borrowing strongly from the 18th century English model that was already serving English cricket so well. The Calcutta club, like many another, provided an escapist oasis in an alien desert, the locus not only for cricket but also for a range of general social activity.

Military references then proliferate during the early 19th century, including the games of the 97th Regiment in Ceylon, the first mention of cricket in what would later be Sri Lanka. Elsewhere, and although indigenous peoples might watch their self-appointed superiors at play or, in the case of the West Indies, involve them initially, almost as supernumeraries, there had been no spontaneous delight in cricket except among British expatriates. Indeed, there was a conscious exclusion of the indigenous people, for cricket was a crucial element in the social retreat and respite from the daily chore of reigning over these very subject races.

The Indians were not subjugated in the same way as native races elsewhere in the British Empire. They retained much autonomy and sufficient of them enjoyed a high-class social life and could adopt English practices, if so they wished. In 1848 Bombay's Parsees or Parsis, devotees of the Zoroastrian creed, formed the Oriental cricket club, replaced after two years by the Young Zoroastrian club. This establishment of a wholly indigenous club is a significant landmark in cricket's history. Others – thirty or so Parsi clubs were formed over the next twenty years - followed suit, braving the scorn of the British and the difficulty of obtaining or fashioning implements.

Eventually, in 1870, one of the Parsi teams, the deliciously named Mars CC played and lost against the 95th Regiment XI. It was the first-ever game between an English eleven and one that had arisen solely from and organised by men of a non-British heritage. Hindu (1877) and Mohammedan (1883) clubs were formed in Bombay, and others were established in cities like Madras. In 1877 the Bombay Gymkhana, a composite of sporting interests, played cricket against the Parsi team and despite several arguments about the shared usage of the available space with European polo adherents, that fixture was occasionally renewed thereafter.

It is no coincidence that the Parsis, who themselves had been driven from Persia by the onset of Islam and settled on India's western coast, were the Indian race that found commonest cause with the incoming British. They were heavily involved in commerce and took appointments in the legal and administrative services. They were quick to adopt English fashions and habits and their young sons had imitated the British soldiers at cricket from the 1830s. It was on the 'maidan', the open ground outside the fortified walls of Bombay, that Indians first played cricket. It is worth adding – with a glance back to earlier references to the universalism of 'play' – that Indian youngsters, like young people everywhere, played games, among them 'gilly danda', in which, in a manner reminiscent of some old English pastimes, a curved twig was struck as far as possible by a stick about a metre long.

Interestingly, the Indian film, made by Ashutosh Gowariker in 2001, *Lagaan;Once upon a Time in India*, refers to gilly danda. Set in 1893, it symbolises the colonial struggle through a challenge match between Captain Russell's 'ferenghees' and Bhuvan's motley villagers of Champaner in the Central Province, with 'laagan' or tax the basis of the wager. Bhuvan is caught off the last ball by the obnoxious Captain Russell – but he realises that he is standing behind the boundary line and the locals win. Despite its inordinate length, it has claims to being the best film produced with cricket as its salient motif, but fascinatingly, it depicts the gradual adoption of cricket by the Indians as a means, quite literally, of taking on the English at their own game.

Then in 1870, there was the launch of Rajkumar College, Rajkot. Its principal, Chester Macnaghten, a Cambridge graduate, built a public school for the sons of the Indian aristocracy, with cricket an important part of the curriculum. His most distinguished alumnus proved to be Prince Ranjitsinhji. Where the Canadians, the Australians, the South Africans and the West Indians had erected cricket-playing schools almost exclusively for the sons of English residents, here was the model applied to an indigenous people or at least, the upper crust of that people. It was a mark both of the distinctive nature of the Anglo-Indian settlement and of the first breakthrough for cricket as a game separated at last in some fashion from its tenacious English roots.

It was a not too common illustration of assimilation. Mihir Bose, in his excellent *History of Indian Cricket,* quotes the magazine *Cricket Chat* in 1886: 'anything that can tend to promote an assimilation of tastes and habits of the English and the native subjects of our Queen-Empress cannot fail to conduce to the solidity of the British Empire,' It would be hard going – it would be 1926 before the English deigned actually to play at the Hindu club in Poona – but for some Indians it was the pragmatic way ahead. The hope was that one might, through adoptions of 'Englishry' such as cricket, tread upwards to acceptance, parity and even independence.

OVERSEAS

Cricket, chiefly courtesy of the British army, was played at many imperial outposts, from Gibraltar to Singapore, during this seminal era. Peter Wynne-Thomas, among others, has shown that cricket was played in every single British colony, normally by British residents or visiting sailors and soldiers, but it was in the few regions reviewed above where the game became most deeply entrenched. These were the areas from which the only Test-match playing nations of the 21st century evolved. It is at this rather arbitrary juncture in the last third of the 19th century that the next move in the process began to happen. This was the start of the elaborate criss-cross of cricket tours over the oceans that did so much to encourage the spread of cricket and its decisive improvement. Most of them were to and from England, with cricket gaining a fortunate benefit in the location of much global cricket in the southern hemisphere. This meant that English cricketers were free to coach in or tour round these southerly regions during their off-season while conversely, overseas teams were enabled to visit Britain in summer time. Cricketers were edging towards their destiny as the progenitors of international sport.

North America may have suffered a little from this meteorological disbenefit but its cricketers led the way. We have already observed George Parr's team visiting the region in 1859, and this was the model for many of the forthcoming trips, that is, they were commercial ventures based on professional cricketers. Several groups crossed the Atlantic, for example, in 1868 and 1872, with W.G.Grace a dominant figure during that second instance. It was sometimes the practice for both the English professionals – Alfred Shaw's tour in 1881 - and the Australian tourists – in 1882, with the quick bowler F.R. Spofforth in his fierce pomp – to include North America in their itinerary when visiting Australia and England respectively. In the 1880s there were tours too and from North America and the West Indies, while there were one or two not very substantial trips by the Canadians to Britain. The strong Philadelphian teams paid five successful visits to England, the last in 1908, whilst the succulent cherry on their fruity cake was their defeat of the Australians in 1893. In all, there were seventeen tours of assorted English teams to the USA and Canada before 1914, but thereafter the pace slackened, never to be restored.

Thwarted by the intercession of the American Civil War, business minds turned attention from America to Australia. In 1861/62 H.H.Stephenson led the first group of English professionals to

Australia, followed by George Parr's touring party in 1863/64, all of these fixtures being against odds. In 1873/74 W.G.Grace was included among the tourists and made an even greater impact than he had in North America. When James Lillywhite's tourists visited in 1876/77, they played the first eleven a side game in Australia, against New South Wales in Sydney. The Australians were beginning to benefit from the tuition of English coaches, such as Jesse Hide, especially noted for his knowledge of ground preparation, Charles Lawrence and Willian Caffyn, who had gone as tourists but remained behind as tutors. The 1887/88 winter found two English troupes in Australia, a reminder that such trips were organised primarily for business reasons. The unprofitability of this confused arrangement spelled the end of out-and-out professional touring, which had, in essence, been the old-style Exhibition elevens across the seas. Henceforward, visiting English teams tended to be more representative outfits.

Conversely, the Australians now felt of sufficient strength to undertake trips to Britain. These began in 1878, with Fred Spofforth the 'demon' bowler and Charles Bannerman the commanding batsman. MCC, and, indeed, English professionals, were concerned with their 'amateur' appellation, for they received £20 a match expenses, where the English 'pro's' earned only £5 or so for their endeavours. MCC, perhaps already conscious of the ethical cartwheels turned to accommodate the English shamateurs, W.G.Grace principally amongst them, decided to refer to the Australians as 'honorary amateurs'. The tour was marked by the sensational match in which the visitors defeated MCC at Lord's by nine wickets in a single day in which 105 runs fell for 31 wickets. Interest was aroused and the Australians came to the British Isles with lucrative effect, every two summers until 1890.

New Zealand had been included in these exchanges. George Parr's 1863/64 team conducted the first English visitation, while the New Zealanders had to wait until 1877/78 to welcome its first Australian side, D.W.Gregory's tourists as part of their journey to the UK. A representative New Zealand team did not reciprocate until, in the 1898/99 season, they played in Australia, but it was to be 1927 before New Zealand, captained by T.C.Lowry, travelled to England.

The West Indies and the United States began a series of exchanges as early as 1886, but the significant breakthrough in the Caribbean was in the winter of 1894/95, when the Middlesex amateur, R.Slade Lucas, led a well-balanced non-professional party to the West Indies, where they found pretty lively opposition on most of the islands. This was the beginning of a number of such tours, with the amateur cricketers taking the opportunity of a pleasing holiday excursion. The first return trip was in 1900, with Pelham Warner's brother, Aucher Warner, leading a party that included two black professionals, who, predictably, took a large majority of the wickets on what proved to be a difficult tour. Learie Constantine's father, L.S.Constantine, was enabled to take the trip only by dint of public fund-raising.

It was in 1888/89 that an English team, arranged by Major R.G. Warton, who had seen service in the colony, and with C.Aubrey Smith its skipper, toured South Africa and played twice against a representative South African eleven. Another journey was made in 1891/92, with W.W.Read in charge of a team that included a Malay XVI among its fixtures – it would be many years before England was again to play a non-white side. In 1894 the South Africans travelled for the first time to England, albeit without their best quick bowler, Krom Hendricks, a Cape Coloured. These exchanges fell into a settled pattern, with the South African contribution rated by the English, if not always for cricketing reasons, second only to the Australians. As well as being a little more accessible, South Africa concentrated on an all-white amateur approach. Indian cricket, of course, was wholly indigenous in being and West Indian cricket was ever more reliant on professionals of African or East Indian race.

It may be instructive to pause a moment over the political background to the South African cricketing position. Richard Parry, in a detailed and informative piece in *Cricket Lore* (vol II ii), explains how William Milton, the senior administrator of Western Province CC., 'the MCC of the Cape Colony', in particular, and nascent South African cricket in general, was also Cecil Rhodes' parliamentary private secretary when the famed imperialist was the Cape's premier. Cecil Rhodes, who also had a controlling interest in the thriving diamond, gold and allied developments, was convinced that union under the British standard was the precondition for the economic progress of a region suddenly booming with industrial possibilities. He recognised the ideological impact of cricket, first, as a way of keeping the area in the eye of the British establishment and, second, acting as a cultural forerunner of political unification. Hence he took a directly personal interest in encouraging the 1894 tour, during which Herbert Castens' South Africans recorded their first ever win as a combined team, when they dramatically defeated MCC at Lord's.

Furthermore, the exclusion of Krom Hendricks was determined at the highest level, for Cecil Rhodes, with William Milton's support, was intent on forcing through a labour policy that would have made such an invitation harmful. They were faced with a major labour problem, as the demands grew for railway building – the Rand to Port Elizabeth line was opened in 1894, the model for replacing ox carts and mule wagons with modern transport links – for mining in the Rand and around Kimberley and for work on white-owned farms. It was Cecil Rhodes' systematic policy to deny the franchise to existing and migrant non-white workers, in association with a successful attempt to drive them out of peasant subsistence agriculture and into paid employment in the mines and on the large farms. The 1894 Glen Grey Act, drafted by William Milton, embodied requirements in respect of taxation, tenure and voting that formed the basis of a segregated labour policy. The informal distinction between 'white' and 'coloured' was formalised in what was a blueprint for 'the economic basis of Apartheid.' With his sensitivity to the import of political tokenism, Cecil Rhodes could not risk fouling his message by permitting a non-white cricketer to play for South Africa.

That insight into the beginnings of both South African cricket and politics serves as a reminder to those who seek to 'keep politics out of sport' that the entanglement of the one with the other began as soon as sport adopted national and other political apparel and apparatus.

As for India, Lord Harris, the gruff and pompous autocrat of Kentish and English cricket, transferred his authoritarian skills thereto in 1890 as Governor of Bombay. He persuaded that other draconian peer, Lord Hawke, the doyen of Yorkshire cricket, to take a team out to India in the winter of 1892/93. It enjoyed a rather higher profile than G.F.Vernon's side, which had toured in 1889/90 and had been the first English team to visit the subcontinent. The Parsi Gentlemen made a much-delayed visit to England in 1886 and again in 1888. It was 1909 before, again after one or two deferrals, All-India toured the UK. Finally, it was in 1882/83 that the Hon. Ivo Bligh's tourists, on route for Australia, stopped off to play a couple of matches in Ceylon, the first MCC, that is, England team so to do.

Thus by the turn of the century a regular configuration of oceanic comings and goings may be traced. Such journeys would have been much less possible without the invention of the steamship, the device that did for international cricket what the railways had done for English county cricket. The first sea-going steamship had been the American *Phoenix,* which plied along the eastern seaboard of the USA from 1809. In Britain, steamships were developed for the Irish and continental crossings. The first rudimentary Atlantic crossings began in 1819 and from 1834 transatlantic journeys of some fifteen days became regular and common. At much the same time steam travel to India became a reality, while the opening of the Suez Canal in 1869 cut the journeys down noticeably. Late Victorian cricket trips to Australia took about eight weeks.

Although these sea voyages were more regularised and speedy, they were not without their discomforts, while internal travel in hinterlands like those of Australia, South Africa and India was often rigorous. Those who undertook them, either to follow their cricket-ing trade or to bask in the glory and occasional pleasure of so doing, were undoubtedly pioneers of genuine toughness.

The victory of steam over sail was as prompt and as rapid as that of rail over coach. The proportion of oceanic sail to steam tonnage changed from a mid 19th century ratio of five to one to an Edward-ian ratio of one to eight. It was advantageous that Britain built two-thirds of the ships launched and that its mercantile fleet was four times bigger than that of its nearest rival, Germany. These were the ships that sustained and protected the colonies and in so doing, they ensured that a cricketing empire evolved within those greater imperial bounds.

The conception of the New Imperialism ineluctably fashioned the framework within which both domestic and international cricket thrived. The question must next be asked as to how this came to be so compelling a force and so persuasive an idea.

Chapter Seven
IMPERIAL WAY

The 1860 Victorian eleven

'Tis the King of Anglo-Saxon Games – the Type of Our
   Strength Confessed;
Where the Charms of Perils Bravely Dared Inspires each
   Manly Breast.'

Thus ran *The Cricketer's Song*, first sung in 1859. That was the same
year that Charles Darwin published his momentous *The Origin of
Species* and Samuel Smiles produced his best-selling collection of

biographies, *Self-help,* hagiographical accounts of diligent enterprise. 'The spirit of self-help', he unctuously wrote, 'is the root of all genuine growth in the individual . . . the true source of national vigour and strength.' Each of these books illustrated an aspect of the ambience in which cricket flourished at home and abroad.

EARNEST PROGRESS

It was a bracing atmosphere that, among all classes, engendered a confident spirit and a serious view about England's global responsibility. So many strands were woven into that Union Jack of a design. There was the patriotic sense of imperial mission, enlivened by a spurious and racially inclined view of Social Darwinism. The competitive instincts of the Victorians were also enticed by the concept of examinations, whether at school and university or for professional purpose, most famously, and not without hot dispute, in the civil service. James Booth, a foremost promoter of exams, said that they led to promotion 'by competition rather than conspiracy'. Adam Smith had earlier averred that 'rivalship and emulation render excellency', while, in a characteristic phrase, Jeremy Bentham hailed examinations as a means of 'maximising aptitude'. Whatever the truth of the evolutionary theory of natural selection, one may instantly spot why it struck a chord in the Victorian psyche and even perhaps why a Victorian was the first to understand and identify it.

There was an assured awareness of the inevitability of progress and a staunch belief in self-improvement. Seriousness was all. Writing in 2003, the literary critic Andrew Sanders concluded that 'earnestness was the quality the mid-Victorians adulated above all others.' There was, critically, the extremely strong underpinning of a particular interpretation and practice of the Christian religion along these solemnly respectable lines. And cricket was at once the emblem and cultural custom of this steadfastly English compound.

The English national character, against the affirming background of the industrial revolution and its urbanised context, underwent a profound alteration between the last decades of the 18th century and mid 19th century. Nationality is, in the historian Benedict Arnold's evocative adjective, 'imagined'. That is, it is the mask worn by a race in accordance with the dictates of social conditions and fashions. It

is not, as some people fondly believe of national and regional characteristics, in the blood. No genetic design could explain the swiftness
of the change in English behaviour and attitudes on the platform of
industrialism. Swiftly, there was a switch from the aggression, even
bloodthirstiness, and brutality of those early times to the civility,
even sentimentality, and orderliness of the Victorian era.

Correlli Barnett has, in several books, and while endorsing the
profundity of this change in national values, bemoaned its political effect. He has argued that a Victorian 'ethical' foreign policy, as
opposed to the 'expedient' and 'opportunist' hard-headedness of
Hanoverian stratagems, eventually helped wreck British chances of
forthright foreign domination, while the rather distasteful view of
industry that complemented this more religious stance did, in his
view, little good for the nation's economic efficiency.

Whatever the truth of that explanation, it was not all good news on
the social front. Candour and bluntness were swapped for hypocrisy
and prudishness, yet for all the censoriousness of Victorian society,
civil behaviour was remarkably improved. The scaffold provides a
macabre measure. From an annual average of over 500 executions
about 1815, the number dropped to less than fifty by 1840, a tribute
both to more lenient sentencing and to a fall in crime. In the last
half of the century the *per capita* crime rate, proportionate to the
population, fell dramatically by a half. The 'new police' forces may
have assisted but the willing acceptance of their activities by the
reputable sections of the populace was a major contributory feature.
Community disciplines, in the home, the street, the work-place, the
school, the church and elsewhere, were strongly evident. While often
suffocating and narrow-minded, they did ensure that civil disorder
was, if not entirely suppressed, then largely avoided.

One effect of this was that the historical phenomenon of 'the crowd',
so decisive a player in 18th and early 19th century political and allied
events, was feared no longer. This was to be an important element in
the development of spectator sport, in that thousands might assemble for a great cricket match with just a couple of policemen on patrol
without any cause for anxiety. As we shall later observe, the mood
changed again, or rather, returned to its Hanoverian belligerence,
after the 1960s – and the crowd was dreaded once more.

The cultural historian, Jeffrey Richards, offers an eloquently simple explanation. In the ceaseless struggle for supremacy, the 'respectable' component had temporarily subdued the 'rough' component. It did not of course, obliterate it. One may find many signs of boisterous disorder in late 19th and early 20th century Britain, just as there were many refined examples of what was called 'decency' in the earlier period. It is a relative distinction but, for the present, the social temperature was comparatively low and cool.

One of the engines of change has already been identified, to wit, the delight in 'Chivalry', as a part of the pseudo-medieval fantasy of the Victorian mentality, and the emergence of the prototype English gentleman of Trollopean styling. It offers a colourful example of the change in national character. Jules Verne's Phileas Fogg, resolved to travel *Round the World in Eighty Days* (1873), is one illustration of this self-controlled, infinitely courteous, quietly determined pattern. So many contributed to the vogue. Thomas Carlyle, another with a preference for the medieval condition, asserted the call for the 'great man' in his 1840 lecture series *On Heroes, Hero-worship and the Heroic in History*, while Cardinal Newman's – a high Anglican, then Roman churchman, who played for Harrow in their first match with Winchester – appeal for the 'just soul' was, in part, another paradigm of the ideal English gentleman.

Evangelical Duty

The other powerful engine of change was religious, a switch from the somewhat casual and easygoing fashions of the 18th to the earnestness of purpose of the 19th century. Its advance probably played a part in the temporary decline of cricket in early 19th century England, described in chapter three. Only when cricket became as respectable as its host society could it be fully absorbed therein.

In her truly great novel, *Middlemarch* (published in 1871/72, but set in the early 1830s) George Eliot, within the compass of her comprehensive dissection of a whole society, wrote of one family, the Vincys, who 'had the readiness to enjoy the rejection of all anxiety, and the belief in life as a merry lot, which made a house exceptional in most county towns at that time, when Evangelicalism had cast a certain suspicion as of plague-infection over the few amusements which survived in the provinces.'

Although formally, it had a narrower interpretation, 'Evangelicalism' serves as a general descriptor of this type of abstentious Puritanism and its attendant trait of vigour of action. From the high serenity of Cardinal Newman's or Thomas Arnold's view of the virtuous Christian gentleman, through the ranks of the 'low' churchmen of the Anglican community to the potency of Methodism and the brisk energies of the nonconformist creeds, the message of duty and responsibility, however constricted the ambit, was urged. The dogma of 'respectability' enshrined within each of these creeds as the outward sign of inward grace was the perfect ethic for industrial and urban life.

It embraced the restlessly energetic boss, the likes of John Thornton, the hard-headed, clear-sighted mill owner of Mrs Gaskell's novel, *North and South* (1854/55, and, incidentally, the only classic novel to share its title with a famous cricket fixture) and the hardworking if deferential artisan, such as Stephen Blackpool, the extremely upright, blamelessly virtuous mill-worker in Charles Dickens' *Hard Times* (1854, arriving contemporaneously with *North and South*) That moral link between the two classes was to be a social cement of enduring quality. Matthew Arnold said of the diligent working class that they were 'at one in spirit with the industrial middle class.' Plainly, this soldered the bond between the gentleman and the professional cricketer. Matthew Arnold, sensing what he called the 'Philistinism' of this bourgeois sentiment, apostrophised it by reference to the acerbic step-father in Charles Dickens' *David Copperfield* (1849/50) when he wrote of 'Murdstonian drive in business and the Murdstonian in religion.'

It was all in the active and not the passive mood. Thomas Carlyle, the pundit of that age, thundered the instruction, 'descend from speculation and the safe pulpit, down into the rough market-place and say what can be done.' The 'Muscular Christianity' we encountered on our visits to the Victorian public schools is ample proof of the force of this social-cum-theological credo. In fact, the public school was the powerhouse of this transformation, even, so felt its protagonists, this purification, of society, its fuel a pungent mix of 'chivalry' and 'evangelicalism'. For not only did its alumni go forth as teachers, clerics, soldiers, businessmen, landowners and officials to carry the message to the British people *in situ,* they also were the crack corps ready and willing to convey the word and the deed far across the oceans.

ETHNIC RESPONSIBILITY

The demographic and economic shocks of the primary industrial era contrived to boost the concept of empire, in part as source of raw materials and market for finished products, in part for settlement of excess population. Despite the loss of the American Colonies, Britain benefited from the solid base of its 18th century triumphs in India, Canada and Australasia, as well as its sustained control of many Caribbean settlements. Strong in naval and military authority, strong in industrial thrust, Britain maintained its interest as 'the scramble for colonies' was hectically pursued in the later 19th century. By the death of Queen Victoria in 1901, British realms covered a quarter of the globe and encompassed a quarter of the world's population, no less than 700m people. Trade and flag sailed and marched, not so much one behind the other, as side-by-side, accompanied by another army of missionaries, colonial officers, educators, farmers and others. Millions of that vast host of 700m were, in 1901, of British stock. The connections with the homeland, itself housing a population of 41m, were close and manifold.

The ideological stock in trade of this vast concourse was precisely the same, unsurprisingly, as that which prevailed in the overseeing nation. As well as the urgent necessity, as it was perceived, to exploit the economic resources of the colonial regions and to defend them from possible takeover by rival countries, there was a coupled mission to import into these lands a cultural accommodation of Victorian English branding. It is the customary stance of exiles to conjure up an idealised vision of what they have abandoned and, throughout the Empire, the migrants, whether as settlers or colonial apparatchiks, went to some lengths to out-vie the English in their 'Englishry'. Similarly, there were areas, India and the West Indies among them, where some of the indigenous people were not indisposed to imitating the invader.

The classical education of the public school trainees had been taught of the glories of the Roman Empire, just as they had learned too, of conveying the benefits of Christianity to those who had not yet had an opportunity to accept the righteous faith. The publication of Charles Darwin's *On the Origin of Species*, while leading, as everyone knows, to widespread controversy, also had the dubious effect of strengthening the case of racial superiority upon which much of the plea of 'the White Man's Burden' rested. The bogus notion, one heartily contested by 'Darwin's Bulldog', T.H.Huxley, of 'Social Darwinism', alongside Herbert Spencer's coinage of the 'survival of the fittest' and Francis Galton's invention of the term 'eugenics', thus played a part in pressing the claim of the Englishman to take the onus of spreading 'civilisation' to all parts of the planet. Thus did these mangled versions of ancient classicism and modern biology back the middle class English buoyant sense of supremacy, constantly reminding them that they had a duty as well as an ability to rule over a vast acreage of land and a vast number of souls.

Cricket was inextricably entangled in this rather jumbled batch of imperatives. Robert Ensor, an authoritative voice on late Victorian scholarship, offered, among many insights, two of relevance to this discussion. One was about the Victorian gift of sport to the rest of the world. He wrote that, 'the development of organised games on any reckoning must stand among England's leading contributions to world culture'. It was, he concluded, an age of 'games-dominated Tory Imperialism'. One was about the depth of religiosity in British society at that time. He described it as one of the most genuinely religious societies the world had known. In 1840 it was said that 'we do not believe that in the world there is a community so virtuous, so religious and so sober-minded as the middle classes of England.' One might contrast the Battle of Waterloo in 1815, when the Duke of Wellington chased 'methodistical' interfering padres from around the camp fires, where sat boisterously scornful men captained by coolly unbelieving officers, to the Battle of the Somme in 1916, before which thousands, officers and men, voluntarily attended church parades and during which men died clutching prayer books and bibles.

It was, inevitably, a very English kind of religiosity. A Disraeli devotee who became poet laureate in 1896, Alfred Austin, smarmily intoned 'who dies for England, sleeps with God', a sentiment not too far distanced from the aspiration of the suicidal terrorist.

It was, naturally, suffused with manliness. Interestingly, a mistaken rumour spread widely that, upon his arrest in 1895 for homosexual practices, Oscar Wilde had been holding a copy of *The Yellow Book*. This was an *avant-garde* aesthetic quarterly to which writers and artists such as Aubrey Beardsley, Max Beerbohm, Henry James, Edmund Gosse and Walter Sickert contributed. It was suspected of a *fin de siecle* sickliness by the solid and durable English middle class, although another contributor, Evelyn Sharp, sister of the folklorist Cecil Sharp and herself a pioneering feminist, wrote that this shocking periodical contained 'not enough impropriety to cover a sixpence.' Nonetheless, such was the taint of association that the supposed Wildean connection destroyed *The Yellow Book*, which was forced to cease publication in 1897, having only been launched in 1894. Evelyn Sharp tells how, at this same time, a London daily newspaper 'started a shilling cricket fund to which panic-stricken citizens hastened to contribute lest their sexual normality should be doubted – the connection was subtle but felt at the time to be real – the idea gained ground that *The Yellow Book* had stood in some way or another for everything that was the antithesis of cricket.'

Pagan Obsession

Cricket was, then, at the time of its great flowering, the bright token of Muscular Christianity, valued for its moral worth. School songs and hymns were riddled with cricket references: 'and be faithful to the willow as your fathers were of yore' . . . ' Sermons and homilies were dressed in cricketing garb. If the Church of England was, in the old phrase, the Conservative Party at prayer, cricket was the Church of England at play.

The historian Professor L.C.S.Seaman has written, 'just as free-masons refer to God as the Great Architect of the Universe, young cricketers were taught to think of Him as 'the one great scorer' and almost to regard the Straight Bat as second in religious symbolism to the Cross of Jesus.' Benny Green argued that 'this marriage between Holy Writ and the Laws of Cricket was solemnised at the public schools . . . a typically English compromise between a religious mani-festation and an instrument of policy, a vaporous hinterland where ethics and biceps merge into a third entity, an exquisite refinement of that other Victorian concept, the White Man's Burden.'

Gerald Howat has cited the words of the interestingly named Rev Thomas Waugh from his *The Cricket Field of the Christian Life* (1894). The rhetoric is finely sustained and the extravagant end-piece may give the grandiose taste of this extravagant dish:

'And when 'time' is called you will 'bring out your bat', your conscience will say 'well done' and those who have cheered and helped will say 'a good man! Thank God for such an innings.' Aye, when on the resurrection morning you come out of the pavilion robed like your glorious Captain-King, your joy will be as full as you hear the captain and 'the innumerable company of angels' greet you with the words, 'well played, sir'.'

However eccentrically demented the cricket buff of today may seem, he or she appears almost indifferent compared with the devotees of the late Victorian age. It is essential for a grasp of the obsessive nature of cricket in that dimension of Victorian life to comprehend the depth of that adoration. It is difficult, on occasion, to decide which is the figure of speech and which the reality. It is now that the search for myths begins, with, for instance, the adoption of Hambledon as 'the cradle of cricket', the Bethlehem, if you will. W.G.Grace, another interesting name, arises from the obscurity of the west country, a bearded Mosaic figure, travelling the world with the message. Now too, is the time when the statisticians and archivist begin to pore in massive detail over the minutest records, treating them with a Rabbinical meticulousness. Cricket historians, like Rowland Bowen, have been quick to catalogue the instances of cricket journals and annuals appearing in various parts of the world, almost seeing them as the counterpart for the Anglican church magazine or the *Catholic Herald*. Not for nothing did *Wisden*, first published in 1864, become known as 'the Cricketer's Bible'.

Beyond W.G.Grace a secular gallery of saints emerged and the feats of these grand apostles were commemorated in paintings, photographs, porcelain, embroideries and many other fashions, creating, along with antique implements and the like, a mass of relics and memorabilia to be found in the several museums and private collections that still venerate, if not quite with Victorian avidity, 'the holy game'.

The outrage from the later faithful when the marketeers, late in the 20th century, introduced coloured costumes for cricketers is instructive. The use of virginal white for cricket had been acceptable for barely 130 years before which coloured clothing, including some team uniforms akin to football, had been the norm. In 1798 MCC had played in azure coats and nankeen breeches, Hambledon had donned sky blue coats, and the All-England XI had worn white shirts with pink spots, all more in keeping with today's 'pyjama' costumes. The varsity 'blues' themselves actually wore dark or light blue shirts, while Rugby School cricketers sustained the coloured shirt until 1962. It was between 1880 and 1895 that the regular use of white shirts and white sweaters, became common

The wide-scale adoption of the hue of purity – was it conscious or unconscious? – is quite dramatic. The druidic umpires; clad in long white robes, processed forth from the sacristy of the pavilion to the altar of the wickets, the acolytes following. The umpires made ready to indulge in their range of mystic signs, like priests genuflecting and crossing themselves at benediction. From school to country there were the pseudo-religious trappings with colours and caps to mark the confirmation and ordination of cricketers along with a suitable selection of blazers and ties and badges and with silver cups and chalices as if borrowed from the communion table. I Zingari led the way with colours – gaily pigmented ribbons round white bowlers – and the universities were among the first to adopt the distinctive blazer that was to become commonplace in schools and clubs generally. The Oxford University blazer was introduced in 1863.

Cricket, by this point in the 19th century, was the major sect within the comprehensive creed of Athleticism, its ethic a bastardised take on Pauline doctrine. Its adherents were willing to 'fight the good fight' and 'run the straight race' of manly and sporting values, with the Epistle to the Corinthians lending its title to their endeavours. The cult penetrated the culture. The language quickly became littered with cricketing usages of a moral thrust, like 'playing a straight bat' or 'it's not cricket'. 'Stumped' for perplexed, even, later, 'crucified' for routed, became common conversational slang.

Lord's is the only major English cricket ground that does not have a geographic – if one includes the rather outmoded Kennington Oval

– flavour. With comic irony, Lord's is sometimes referred to as the 'Mecca' of cricket, but one wonders why it was not eventually named after the Marylebone club of which it is the headquarters. Was there something attractive in the heavy duty religious inference, the destination of believers who made 'pilgrimages; thither, as they might to – hence the 1934 *Manchester Guardian* headline, when England won the Test match, 'Miracle at Lord's', with an overt side glance at Lourdes. (Or the House of Lords – during World War II a prisoner of war in Italian hands received a message from Sir Pelham Warner saying he had been made a member of 'Lord's', and was instantly treated as a possible political hostage, the Italians assuming he had been elevated to the peerage).

Of course, other sports mimicked cricket and assumed dubious theological words for arenas, like 'temple' or 'shrine', but cricket was the formative game in this regard and the most complete in range. The Long Room at Lord's adopted hallowed proportions, the pavilion the repository for the treasures of the game, a veritable St Peter's in the walled domain of a cricketing Vatican City, a wall that now bears the iconic text 'play up, play up and play the game'. Male Chauvinism may have left its dread mark on all formal religious observance and there was something of that in the barring of women, until recently, from the sacred purlieus of the Lord's pavilion. One is reminded of Betty Marsden's agonised revue query when peeresses were first created – 'where in Hades are 'the ladies' in the Lords'. Cricket was, according to Lord Harris, writing in *the Times* on the occasion of his 80th birthday in 1931, 'a moral lesson in itself and the classroom is God's air and sunshine'. Lest it be thought that these comparisons border on the fantastical, let it be remembered that one man's conviction is another man's superstition.

The term 'cricket-lovers' is not an idle one. As one studies the annals of the time, it does become difficult to judge which was the metaphor for the other, Christianity or the mock-Christian, the near pagan worship, of cricket.

ENGLISH EXCLUSIVITY

It was, therefore, with some zealotry that the cricketing missionaries voyaged the length and breadth of the earth and made cricket 'the chief spiritual export' of the imperialists. As we have witnessed, they did so with earnestness and gusto. It was, nonetheless at this serious juncture, that the intellectual clutter, this muddle of competing themes, arrested the progress of cricket. For central to the imperial, the Christian and the nationalistic themes was the exclusivity of the English. Cricket was certainly taken to the colonies – but it was principally for English settlers or English temporary residents. By the end of the 19th century and apart from a relative minority of Indian middle class and West Indian working class enthusiasts, cricket was still restricted to the English elite.

Moreover, so special was cricket that little or no effort was made to involve either the young men of other European races either on the continent itself or among European stock in the so-called 'informal empire' of South America and other locales where the British were trading and working. It is true that in such places clubs started by British residents included cricket on their recreational agenda. It is also probably true that, even where the English tried to persuade others to join them, there was little interest shown in the artful intricacies of the game.

The reverse is true, of course, of association football. Its advent as a formalised game was later; not only public school old boys but others, railway engineers, electricians and so on, were engaged in the pastime; it was decidedly simpler and possibly more adjacent in style to the games already played; it did not carry the emotional and spiritual baggage of cricket and the British were probably keener to enlist non-British aid for soccer. It is true that both football codes had a strong relationship with several of the strands of Athleticism discussed here. Many common factors attended their birth and growth. But they never emulated, perhaps never quite strove to emulate, the mystique of cricket.

The upshot was that football was energetically pursued outside and cricket inside the British Empire, with the alternate making precious little impact in either set of regions. No former British colony has ever won the football world cup, and England has only managed it once; only former British colonies, and not even England, have won the world cricket cup.

This stifling exclusiveness was expressed in self-admiration of the English and contempt for the foreign character, with cricket often used over a lengthy period as a prime example. In 1833, John Mitford, in a piece in *The Gentleman's Magazine*, asserted that 'cricket is the pride and privilege of the Englishman alone. Into his noble and favourite amusement no other people ever pretend to penetrate.' The cricket archivist Rev. James Pycroft wrote in 1851 that 'the game of cricket, philosophically considered, is a standing 'panegyric' on the English character; none but an orderly and sensible race of people would so amuse themselves.' In 1927, the editor of *Field*, Sir Theodore Cook, wrote of a cricketing code 'drawn from the deep-seated instincts of the English race – the instincts of sportsmanship and fair play.' These three quotes cover a century of complacent racial discrimination. For all Lord Harris tried to encourage cricket in India, it remained his view, in 1921, that 'it is in the matter of patience that the Indian will never be the equivalent of the Englishman.' In 1939 C.B.Fry dismissed the Maori as 'equally undevoted to work or to worry'. Keith Sandiford cites the *Athletic News* in 1900, with its view that West Indian 'men of colour', apart from being unable to cope with chilly summers in England, would never 'hope to bring the same amount of intelligence to his game' as the English masters.

It is said that the some of the few black West Indians included in the 1900 tour of England were so enraptured by the fierce hitting of Gilbert Jessop that they flung themselves down on the grass roaring with mirth. That behaviour was perhaps, whilst unsophisticated, at least preferable to niggling tantrums and slowed down over rates, but inevitably, it was interpreted as testimony to the nature of the black West Indian. To the despair of advocates of racial temperament, a generation or two later found that their descendants had, without benefit of abrupt genetic change or miraculous blood transfusion, attuned themselves to the demand of top-class cricket and created a lethal professional cricketing outfit.

Neville Cardus began his *English Cricket*, published in 1945, 'none except the people of England or of English-speaking countries has excelled at cricket. Its rules and its general legal system tell of the English compromise between individual freedom and corporate responsibility . . . it somehow holds the mirror up to English nature.'

The examples are prolific, but one that forcibly catches the mood is a couplet included in Gerald Brodribb's anthology of cricketing verse, viz.

> No German, Frenchman or Fiji will ever master cricket,
>   sir,
> Because they haven't got the pluck to stand before the
>   wicket, sir.

It is only just to insist that this ethnic bigotry was common among all Europeans and European settlers. In his story, *Victory*, published in 1915 and set in the Far East, Joseph Conrad, spoke of Ricardo, an adventurer and Schomberg, a hotel keeper: 'Both of these men thought of native life as a mere play of the shadows. A play of shadows the dominant race could walk through unaffected and disregarded in the pursuit of its incomprehensible aims and needs.' It might even be argued that the English version was more benign than some, with the added layer of a sense of sombre duty possibly tempering the excesses of some other brands of European colonisation.

This ideological edifice was supported by a vast literary foundation. Those whom Keith Sandiford termed in a telling phrase 'the eloquent evangelists of imperial expansion' ranged from historians, like Sir John Seeley in his *Expansion of England* (1883) to a host of novelists, among them Rider Haggard and John Buchan, later Baron Tweedsmuir, who became Governor-General of Canada in 1935. Rudyard Kipling's *The White Man's Burden* (1889) was, of course, the title that became the mantra. It was an Australian, W.H.Fitchett, headmaster of a Methodist Ladies College, who wrote the best-selling *Deeds that Won the Empire*. It sold 750,000 copies in a nation only 4m strong, and apart from its own success throughout the English-speaking world it became the model for many, many similar titles.

Older, much older readers, may recall the flags that flew and the bands that played on 24 May, Queen Victoria's birthday and thus Empire Day. Certainly until the days of the Second World War it was widely celebrated throughout the dominions and colonies, especially in schools, where there were plays and songs and other festivities. The author has a 1930s memory of playing the role of Cecil Rhodes, a white handkerchief stuck in the back of his hat to protect his juvenile neck from the merciless Mancunian sun. Imperialism was a very real concept.

For four or five generations, for close on a hundred years, these public school 'English' mores were transmitted to the majority of the nation's youth through the medium of schoolboy literature. In the wake of Tom Brown, there were scores of authors, many of them self-confessed 'Muscular Christians', penning boarding school stories, usually with cricket as an element. At their heart lay the doctrine of 'sportsmanship', a bluff, hearty credo of constant friendship and of giving and taking knocks without complaint or telling tales.

With Thomas Hughes' blueprint to hand, the schoolboy story frequently ended with a cricket match. One illustration of this theme is *David Blaize* (1915) by E.F.Benson. Adam's House plays Tovey's House at Marchester School and David Blaize joins his bosom companion, Frank Maddox, in a partnership that swings the match in favour of Adam's. The use of a batting stand to signify close friendship was a standard component: 'Maddox paused. 'Best of all the days I've had at school, David', he said. 'Same here, ' said David.

The books were heavily supplemented by periodicals. *The Boy's Own Paper* was launched by the Religious Tract Society in 1879 and holds the record for the longest running juvenile magazine ever. By the 1890s its print run was 665,000 weekly, with an estimated readership of 2m. Aimed at those seeking something 'manly' to read as an antidote to the bloodthirsty 'penny-dreadfuls' that had flooded the market, *BOP* was joined by *Chum* and *The Captain*. It has been authoritatively stated that *BOP* 'became a prime vehicle of the public school ethos', with its many cricket-studded school yarns. Talbot Baines Reed, his creed one of 'cheerful Puritanism', serialised in *BOP* the seminal tale of *The Fifth Form at St Dominic's* (1881/82; first published in book form in 1887, its last reprint was 1971). With its 'what rot' slang and stolen exam paper subplot, it really set out the devices of the post-Tom Brown tale, with close friends Oliver Greenfield and Horace Wraysford ensuring the 'School' defeat the 'Sixth Form' in an enthralling encounter on the school cricket field.

The Captain serialised P.G.Wodehouse's *Mike* (published in book from in 1909) and the author – who took 7 for 50 for Dulwich College against Tonbridge in 1899 – claimed it was his best book, not least because it recaptured, he said, 'the ring of a ball on a cricket bat, the green of a pitch, the white of flannels and the sound of schoolboy cheers', as Mike Jackson leads Sedleigh School to unlikely triumph against his old school, Wrykyn.

Although these periodicals endured, they were rather superseded by *The Gem* (1907) and *The Magnet* (1908), which brought years of school stories to a large youthful audience. Frank Richards, one of the twenty-five pseudonyms of Charles Hamilton, is reputed to have been the most prolific writer ever, weighing in with 60/70m words, the equivalent of a thousand full-length novels, within which he created 125 fictitious schools, most of them hosting a cricket match or two. An admirer of Talbot Baines Reed, he, too, took his role as inculcator of good form and English gentlemanliness with considerable seriousness. His most noted creation was the Greyfriars of Billy Bunter, the greedy and cowardly anti-hero, and Harry Wharton's Famous Five, another gloss on schoolboy friendships. A fascinating article by J.F.Burrell, *Cricket at Greyfriars* (*Journal of the Cricket Society*, Spring 1983) reveals the import of the game in that establishment and points out that Bunter's initials are 'W.G'.

The Gem and *The Magnet*, were, in turn, overtaken in popularity after World War I by 'comics' from D.C.Thompson and Co.Ltd. By the 1930s it was reckoned that 75% of teenage boys were reading one or more of *The Adventure, The Rover, The Wizard, The Skipper* and *The Hotspur*. All contained school and/or cricket themes among their ripping yarns, with 'Empire' allusions equally common. In *The Adventure* there was Bill Simpson, 'The Wolf of Kabul', whose local militant associate was Chung, armed with 'clicky ba', with which trusty cricketing implement he pressed home the link between the laws of cricket and imperial rule. From 1933 to 1958, *The Hotspur* ran 1155 tales of Red Circle School, where, unlike Greyfriars, the boys actually grew up and left, many of them, such as Dead-wide Dick Doyle and Cripple Dick Archer, trailing cricketing glories.

Among all the hundreds of endorsements of the appeal and influence of this vast and long-lasting literature, none is more poignant than that of Robert Roberts in his evocative account of his childhood in the slums of Edwardian Salford: 'with nothing in our own school that called for love and allegiance, Greyfriars became for some of us our true *alma mater* to whom we felt bound by a dreamlike loyalty'.

He writes of rushing at dawn, with other newspaper delivery boys, to the station in order to tear open the packets and avidly feast on the latest edition of *The Magnet*. Wryly, like most working class children, he left school at twelve, a year younger than Harry Wharton when he arrived at Greyfriars.

The penetration of these values and their points of cricketing reference, had a marked effect on the youth of the country at large. Schoolboy literature undoubtedly helped to indoctrinate millions in the belief that cricket made manifest a swathe of fine virtues. It was about excitement, surely, but it encompassed much else in terms of close fellowship, character-building, the qualities of dependability and disciplined team-work and the opportunity of experiencing leadership.

The consistent use of the cricket match as the end-piece, with friends sharing in some triumph acknowledged with an understated sensibility, exemplifies a further dimension in the discussion. There was substantial continental comment about the inhibiting English practice of removing the children of its upper middle and upper classes from home and the gentle solace of womankind and incarcerating them within boarding schools. The baffling sight of English aristocrats and well-to-do gentlemen cavorting at cricket and other sports, sometimes before the gaze of lowly paying customers, was puzzling to many from abroad and was sometimes explained in terms of an immaturity resultant on this stultifying habit. A literary instance occurs in Tolstoy's *Anna Karenin,* written and published 1874/76, Anna and Vronsky, her lover, enjoy a sophisticated and luxurious existence, surrounded by the then fashionable accessories of English furnishings and artefacts. These include the new-fangled accoutrements of lawn tennis. Anna's sister-in-law, the more old-fashioned Dolly is shocked by 'the unnaturalness altogether of grown-up people playing a child's game in the absence of children.'

The concentrated density of this school experience together with indoctrination of millions more through the vicarious perusal of schoolboy literature, was compelling. In the eyes of some British as well as continental observers, it so arrested the emotional, intellectual and even physiological development of pupils to the point where 'permanent adolescence' was the consequence, with adult games-playing one of its symptoms. This was sometimes directly confused with homosexuality, even, on occasion, paedophilia or sado-masochism For all those practices – for some of those who rushed to send a shilling to the not-*The Yellow Book* 'cricket fund' mentioned by Evelyn Sharp may have been protesting too much - should not be disregarded, it was not quite that. It was possibly more asexual. E.F.Benson, author of *David Blaize* and a Marlborough pupil soberly claimed, 'in many ways boys are a sex quite apart from male and female'; they were eager in adult life to recapture 'more of some quality that is inseparable from the wonder and sunset of boyhood.' Like so many other authors, he carefully described chaste but deeply felt friendships, as symbolised by the batting partnership, and he, like many of his fellow writers, often used the analogue of David and Jonathan, their love being 'wonderful, passing the love of women.'

The hypothesis of 'perpetual adolescence' was most lucidly delineated by Cyril Connolly, an Old Etonian, in *Enemies of Promise* (1939). He conceptualised the notion of *puer aeternus*, 'the eternal boy' – 'their glories and disappointments are so intense as to dominate their lives and arrest their development. From this it results that the greater part of the ruling class remains adolescent, school-minded, self-conscious, cowardly, sentimental, and, in the last analysis, homosexual.' Jeffrey Richards has suggested that, through the public school as 'the powerhouse of the nation' – maybe with the help of all that schoolboy literature – these Romanticist values, like strict regimes, hero worship and sports, attached themselves to the whole of Victorian society. The attachment, Platonic and passionate, of Alfred, Lord Tennyson and Arthur Hallam is often quoted as a real-life example of this kind.

It is certainly intriguing to spot the boy-men in the writers of schoolboy literature – there are tinges of this to be found in Thomas Hughes, Talbot Baines Reed, Frank Richards and P.G.Wodehouse, described by J.B.Priestley as 'a brilliant, *super de luxe* schoolboy' – and Bertie Wooster, himself the subject of a magical series of schoolboy-man stories.

It is at the high point of the imperial way, just before the Great War, that the two leading texts on a refusal to grow up were devised.

J.M.Barrie, something of a permanent child himself in his quaint if relatively innocuous delight in children, wrote *Peter Pan* in 1904, while, in 1908, Sir Robert Baden-Powell published the ambiguously-titled *Scouting for Boys*. One of the latter's biographers dubbed him 'a perennially singing schoolboy', who called his closest friend 'the boy' and named his only son after Peter Pan. Both were keen cricketers. James Barrie ran his own social team, the Allahakbarries, and said that his bowling was so slow that he could run and fetch the ball back if he didn't like the initial delivery.

It is uncanny how many famed English adventurers, warriors and heroes of the era may be described as 'eternal boys'. As one revisionist biography followed another, the many secondary schools that had sedulously named their houses after Gordon of Khartoum, Cecil Rhodes, Kitchener, Captain Scott or T.E.Lawrence wriggled in some discomfort. Each had seeming flaws of character that could be interpreted as fixated adolescence. It overlapped into the later decades. Nigel Hamilton, the biographer of Field Marshal Montgomery, suggests that the soldier was 'a repressed gay'. The evidence presented of his 'aberrant' marriage and his deep affection for young men might also fulfil the terms of Cyril Connolly's speculation about 'eternal boyhood'.

That class of English youth did not obey the Pauline injunction to 'put away childish things'. They clung to their cricket. It almost reaches the point where the Christian thesis was upended. Schooldays were indeed the happiest, that other Eden, after which came the stern business of dutiful toil as soldier or missionary or colonial officer. Paradise came before the mortal journey.

Where Tom Jones had become Tom Brown, Tom Brown now became Peter Pan.

The fallacious justification was often made and is still sometimes utilised that cricket was a training ground for 'the battle of life' and that, for example, the captaincy of a cricket team somehow prepared one to be an infantry subaltern. Cricket is a game that is a vehicle by and upon which character traits are exhibited and maybe reinforced. Thus the youth whose makeup and background are predilections that he might be a decent cricket skipper or regimental officer are the same. The one does not produce the other. 'Transfer of training' of this direct fashion is not a tenable concept, for character-building is a much more complicated, cyclic process.

Inevitably, nothing went entirely to plan. The ideal was often sullied, as high aims usually are, by deviant or hypocritical behaviour. This was often treated with prefectorial lack of fuss, *in extremis,* exile or the pistol on the desk. When W.R.Gilbert, who was W.G.Grace's cousin, was found stealing from the clothes hung in cricket dressing rooms, the matter was hushed up and he was ushered out of the country across the seas to Canada. P.C.Wren could hardly have bettered this Beau Geste scenario. And when Rowland Bowen prepared to publish the sad little tale in 1970, MCC suggested he should let sleeping dogs lie.

This whole complex interfaces of the imperial Victorian ethos is beautifully encapsulated in Sir Henry Newbolt's oft-cited poem, *Vitai Lampada,* wherein the ex-schoolboy rallies the ranks when 'the Gatling's jammed and the colonel's dead', just as he had responded to the cry of 'play up, play up and play the game', when, 'with ten to win and the last man in' on 'a bumpy pitch and a blinding light', that same slogan had worked the oracle.

It is a startling conceit, whatever its hollowness of sentiment. Nonetheless, one should at the last, not forget that other Victorian affection, the avaricious love of money and the Forsyte-like zeal for business. Thus to another verse, Grantland Rice's quatrain, *Alumnus Football:*

> *For when the One Great Scorer comes*
> *To write against your name,*
> *He marks not that you won or lost*
> *But how you played the game.*

Yes, it is yet another attempt to relate cricket and Christianity, with the parallel of the divine ledger, the book of judgement, and the scorebook, for no game is so diligently logged as is cricket, so much so that, from a well-kept scorebook, it is practically possible to follow an unseen game ball by ball, just as the omniscient God never misses a human act. But there is a third parallel. The scorebook was squarely based on the accounting ledger, with its double entry bookkeeping of runs credited to the batsmen and runs debited against the bowler, with all audited and found correct by not one but two scorers.

The scorer, scratching away on a high stool, could well be Newman Noggs or Bob Crachitt or Mr Wemmick or Tim Linkinwater or any of a score of Dickensian clerks in a Victorian counting office, keeping their ink-stained check on the money. Victorian commercial and banking men took Samuel Smiles' dogma of self-help very seriously. Published in 1859, the same year as Samuel Smiles' *Self-help*, Grantland Rice's verse unconsciously parades three Victorian obsessions; religion, cash and cricket.

W.G.Grace, 'the Great Cricketer' as his Lord's gates entitle him, was an adept in the last two of that trinity of manias.

Good suburban club cricket has for over a hundred and fifty years formed the core of English cricket. Two examples are Bury St Edmunds CC (top) and Basingstoke and North Hants CC, playing, as they have since 1865, on the May's Bounty ground (bottom).

CHAPTER EIGHT
AMAZING GRACE

'The Great Cricketer'

The eight days beginning Friday 11 August 1876 mark a great watershed in the craft of cricket. On that day and the next W.G.Grace scored 344 for MCC against Kent at Canterbury, this being the first triple century in first-class cricket. On the Sunday he travelled through London to Bristol, where, on Monday, he scored 177 for Gloucestershire against Nottinghamshire. His 8 for 69 in his opponents' second innings secured a handsome victory. Yorkshire then visited Bristol and 'the big 'un', as the professionals gruffly nicknamed him, batted through Thursday and into Friday, amassing 318 runs. It was the first 300 in the County Championship. W.G.Grace had scored 839, average 419.5, and made a hundred runs on each of five days. Indeed, in his only ten first-class innings that August he assembled 1,278 runs, perhaps the most intensely concentrated thousand runs ever collected. In that eight day period he batted for seventeen and a half hours and gave, it is said, only two chances. Twenty-five bowlers were deployed against him as he hit two sevens, four sixes, four fives and 103 fours.

'THE GREAT CRICKETER'

Few other sportsmen have ever proved themselves so pre-eminent in their craft in such a brief spell. It was if Tiger Woods had suddenly begun to navigate golf courses in scorecards of regular fifties. It changed the face of cricket.

Born 1848, W.G.Grace played his first club match, aged nine, in 1857, and his last, aged 66, in 1914, thereby playing in each of 58 seasons. In first-class cricket he made 54,211 runs at an average of 39.46, including 124 centuries – he was of course, the first to reach a hundred hundreds. It must not be forgotten that he took 2808 wickets (he was the first to reach 2000 victims) at an average of a little over 18, took 876 catches and stumped five. He never suffered the ignominy of a 'pair' in first-class cricket. It has also been identified that he made 46,837 runs and took 4695 wickets in minor cricket, many of those games being against odds. It was one long colossal performance and the statistics suggest that W.G.Grace was, throughout his career, just about half as successful again as his nearest rivals. In terms of his indefatigable energy, it should not be forgotten that, in his early days of few official boundaries, many of those 100,000 or so runs, as those 'sevens' indicate, were 'all run'. He was an aggressive batsman, asserting, 'I don't like blocking; you only get three'. The Prebendary A.P.Wickham, the Somerset wicket keeper during W.G.'s hundredth hundred at Bristol in 1895, when he score 288 in five and a half hours, counted only four balls that passed the 47 year old's bat.

'Ecce Homo', announced the Vulgate: 'Behold the Man'. W.G.Grace personified the creation of modern cricket and led the inauguration of much of what we now perceive as international sport. By train in England and by steamboat across the seas, he became the first famous international sportsman. He did so at a time when, for example, it is doubtful whether statesmen such as Abraham Lincoln or Bismarck would have understood the concept of international sport, so much was it in its infancy.

As for his domestic influence, his elegant modern biographer, Simon Rae, makes no bones about Grace's part in the switch of power in the 1870s from what the Lord's establishment regarded as impertinent professional intrusion 'firmly and irreversibly back to the amateur citadel'. Simon Rae continues, 'The single most important factor in this turn-around was the emergence of Grace himself as a player of unprecedented ability, and his decision to nail his colours to the MCC mast.' He was one of the most easily recognised figures of his epoch and he remains one of the most readily recognised of Victorian personages. He is a genuine historical personality in that he made a dramatic contemporary impact and then bequeathed a fulsome cultural heritage. He remains one of the very few, in terms of popular culture, to whom the over-employed term, 'icon' may realistically be applied.

Ranjitsinhji, albeit probably ghosted by C.B.Fry, wrote that Grace 'revolutionised cricket', turning it from 'an accomplishment into a science', while, noting his intense pragmatism, making 'utility the criterion of style'. By the exuberance of his success he also revolutionised cricket as a social habit, changing it finally and irrevocably from a casual players' diversion into a crucial part of the entertainment industry. In so doing he was very much the man who came with the hour. Amid sportsmen, he was the one who approached nearest to reflecting Thomas Carlyle's Victorian eulogies of the heroic figure, the one who seizes history by the throat and makes it. He was, as Norman Birkett splendidly wrote, 'the great Englishman playing the great English game on English fields.' When the gates were raised to commemorate him at Lord's, Sir Stanley Jackson did not prevaricate with the indefinite article when he phrased the telling epitaph, 'the Great Cricketer'.

C.L.R.James' *Beyond the Boundary,* first published in 1963, and one of very few books about cricket to stand proudly in its own right as a genuine and major classic, stresses the importance of W.G.Grace purely as a historical character. Writing of Grace's completion of a hundred centuries in 1895, he asserts; 'Never since the days of the Olympic champions of Greece has the sporting world known such enthusiasm and never since . . . On what other occasion, sporting or non-sporting, was there ever such enthusiasm, such an unforced sense of community, of the universal merged in the individual? At the end of a war? A victorious election? With its fears, its hatreds, its violent passions? Scrutinise the list of popular celebrations, the unofficial ones; that is to say, those not organised from above. I have heard of no other that approached this celebration of W.G.'s hundredth century. If this is not social history, what is?'

W.G.Grace tumbled headlong between the two stools of Victorian social classification. He was a gentleman who could not afford, economically, to play full-time cricket. He was an amateur who could not afford, socially, to play as a professional. However, with his talent his major credential, supported by a formidable personality, he claimed the best of both worlds. He enjoyed the social perquisites of the amateur, while earning monies beyond the dreams of the professional cricketer's avarice. The writer's own rough calculations suggest that, by stratagems direct and indirect, he earned from cricket, and apart from the proceeds of his truncated medical career, something in the region of £120/150,000 between 1870 and 1910, an amount that would be worth two or three millions today. He left £10,000 in his will, a tidy fortune for 1915. By way of perspective, Mrs Beeton's *Household Management*, first published as a separate volume in 1861, suggested that an annual income of £1000 should secure a household of five servants. Thus he earnestly satisfied one of the leading Victorian tenets in his steadfast pursuit of lucre. Although denied the England captaincy for many years, and never honoured at all by the nation, presumably because of his mixed categorisation, that other Victorian trait, hypocritical cant, drew a veil over his outrageous shamateurism.

Perhaps the analogue of the scorebook and the accounting ledger occurred to him, although, his not being an imaginative man, it is unlikely. He was in fact, the perfect example of 'permanent adolescence'. Coming from a cricketing family, his brothers and he formed the core of the successful Gloucestershire side of the time. It should be observed that the district where the family dwelt and worked provided the source of about a million tons of coal a year. It was not just a countrified area, but also another localised example of the correspondence of cricket and industry. It was the coal pits and the secondary manufactures of Bristol, like soaps, chocolate and tobacco, that attracted the road and rail builders to the thriving city and its environs. W.G.Grace's base was urban and commercial more that it was rural and agrarian.

With a strong affection for Martha Grace, his dominant mama, he made a low-key marriage, with a whiff of family arrangement about it, to Agnes Nicholls, his cousin. That was the first and last of his relationships with women. A.A.Thomson describes Agnes as 'sweet, gentle, womanly and sympathetic'; they had much-loved children two of whom sadly pre-deceased them, but one looks in vain at home for the passion that he brought to cricket. On his famous – and sponsored – honeymoon tour of Australia, the far from ardent Grace deserted his young bride in favour of hunting kangaroo, rabbit, quail, pigeon and plover. Modern coaches who have anxieties about the presence on tours of wives and partners would not have had to worry about Grace. That is not to suggest it was a riven marriage; rather was it one in the middle class Victorian mould of comfortable convenience, especially for the male.

The orthodox Freudian view might be that lots of sexual energy was thus sublimated into soldiering, trading, evangelising, empire build-ing . . . and cricketing. Like many Victorians, Grace brought untold gusto to his activities. His friends, Colonel Trevor and the big-hitting Gilbert Jessop, bore witness to a typical day in W.G.Grace's later years. Up at six; 45 holes of golf, a hearty dinner, then curling at the Prince's ice-skating club until the small hours – not forgetting that, because of his endeavours in that field, he was fondly known as 'the Father of Bowls'. So many characteristics point to attenuated boyhood. The apparent lack of interest in women, the reluctance to learn as exemplified by the gruellingly prolonged nature of his medi-cal studies and the resourcefully 'boy scout' character of his medical practice, these are of a piece with the concept. His contemporary Clifford Bax wrote candidly, 'he is a case of arrested development and remained, intellectually, always at the age of sixteen.' One friend described him as 'just a big schoolboy in everything he did' and another called him 'a great big baby'. His ghost writer, Arthur Porritt, said he had 'the simple faith of the child . . . he was a big grownup boy, just what a man who only lived when he was in the open air might be expected to be.' He even, amusingly, had the typical schoolboy's distaste of hygiene. 'Monkey' Hornby's cold baths made him 'shudder', while Viscount Cobham's aristocratic opinion was that Grace's was 'one of the dirtiest necks I ever kept wicket behind'.

In a generous but percipient judgement, the cricket writer Bernard Darwin wrote of his 'schoolboy's love for elementary and boisterous jokes, his distaste for learning, his desperate and undisguised keenness, his guilelessness and guile, his occasional pettishness and pettiness and his endless power of recovering his good spirits'. Unluckily, the boylike personality in the adult frame, as in F.Anstey's 1882 highly perceptive novel, *Vive Versa*, in which the Bultitudes, father and son, exchange bodies but not personalities, is fraught with hazard. Plainly, W.G.Grace bullied and cheated and dogmatically insisted on his own way, traits which commentators, through the lens of passing time, have sometimes observed as roguish geniality. For his 1997 biography Robert Low unearthed the tale of Grace assaulting an insolent youth with a cricket stump in 1889 and coming close to being faced with criminal charges, another horrid sample perhaps, of the immature child in the giant's carcass.

He was as sports-obsessed as possibly only a middle class Victorian boy could have been. When he played cricket there was a total abnegation of other matters. Arthur Porritt tried for a year 'in absolute despair' to grind something usable for his reminiscences from 'this singularly inarticulate man'. Asked about how he felt when making a big score, Grace replied curtly, 'no time for feeling with the next ball to be bowled'. Others found him equally obdurate on such topics. Lord Charles Russell said of Grace as a cricketer that 'he puts every muscle into it from the sole of his foot to the crown of his head'. It was an exercise in total concentration. Modern sports coaches speak of athletes being in the 'zone'. W.G.Grace was able, hour after hour, day after day, even after a night spent with a difficult maternity case, sometimes from March practice until October fixtures, season after season, to locate himself in that 'zone' of trance-like self-absorption.

What the always thoughtful sports journalist David Foot has called the 'emotional immaturity' of W.G.Grace may then, have been the key to his focussed batting, bowling and fielding. That very obsessive fixation is, from one angle, immature. The mature mind might have doubts or questions to raise or even think of something else. It is the single-mindedness that counts. Whether it was facing the Mahdi in Sudan or the Turks in the Western Desert . . . or the Australians at the Oval . . . W.G.Grace, like General Gordon or Lawrence of Arabia, never for a second doubted his one awesome gift.

THE QUESTIONABLE TEST

W.G.Grace was of course, a dominant figure in some of the earliest Test matches on both sides of the oceans. Or was he? It perhaps depends on the nomenclature, for gradually, there was a blurring of the descriptors 'test' and 'international'. It all adds up to further evidence of the cricket establishment's desire to backdate events in its history.

Earlier references to the mix of 'important', 'great' and 'first-class' matches have been made. In fact, it was 1947 before there was eventual and tardy agreement by the Imperial Cricket Conference (ICC) as to what constituted a first-class match. Gerald Brodribb suggests it is no cause for surprise: 'it should be remembered that it was not until the (MCC) 1884 code that any attempt was made to define the game at all. Up to then no mention had been made of how the game was played, the number of players concerned, or what constituted victory.'

The 1947 compact resolved that a first-class match was one of three or more days between teams of eleven players 'officially judged first-class', and that the status of such sides lay in the jurisdiction of the governing body of each country. It followed that a country had to have a governing body recognised for this purpose by the international administration and as regards players, it left the system open to the old quandary of the theatrical profession – you couldn't work on the stage without an Equity card and you couldn't obtain an Equity card until you had worked on the stage. However, it was retrospectively from this base that the full list of first-class matches was assembled. Because cricket is so intricate a compound of individual and collective attainment, statisticians are loath to ignore noble personal deeds that may have preceded official announcements about the status of teams. For instance, whether one begins an analysis of the county championship from 1895, 1890, 1864 or even before, visibly affects the official county averages of dozens of players.

Some of the same problem may have influenced the authorities' view of international cricket, although the sentiment of lengthy heritage, so much a part of the cricketing cult, must have had considerable sway.

The word 'test', with a lower case 't', was first used to indicate 'tests of relative strength' during the 1861/62 trip to Australia, organised by the caterers Felix Spiers and Christopher Pond, who were busily providing refreshments for the gold-miners and who, incidentally, had also toyed with the idea of a Charles Dickens lecture tour down under. Mainly comprising Surrey professionals and led by H.H.Stephenson, the tourists undertook these 'tests' of strength against Victoria, Tasmania and a combined Victoria and New South Wales side. Played against odds of up to twenty-two opponents, they could not be regarded as first-class matches anymore than international matches. The term then seems to have lapsed in much of its usage and it would be twenty or so years before it was in broader circulation.

What came to be regarded as the first 'Test' match – and it was only in the 1890s that the sporting press began to log a list of Test matches – took place in March at Melbourne during the visit of the English tourists of 1876/77. W.G.Grace, with whom few would pick an argument either on grounds of experience or temperament, described the match, which the Australians won by 45 runs, as when 'an Australian eleven for the first time beat an eleven of England'. The distinctions are sensible. The indefinite article is prominent. The teams were even-handed as to personnel but they did not constitute 'the' eleven, simply because there was no practical or legislative way in which either side could make the claim to be representative. Indeed, the individual colonial associations were noisily opposed to the fixture.

What had happened was that, following their near-victorious drawn encounter with the New South Wales eleven – making that match the first first-class game between an English and an overseas team – the visiting organiser, James Lillywhite, had asked his friend, John Conway, very much his Australian counterpart in these affairs, to raise a more representative eleven. This he effectively did, by recruiting both New South Wales and Victoria players. It might be added that, of the eleven, four were born in England, one in Ireland, one in India and only five in Australia, but it would be over-pedantic to introduce the question of birth qualification. Furthermore, as the talented Australian historian Bernard Whimpress reminds us, in his fascinating *The Official MCC Ashes Treasures* (2009), 'regional loyalties divided the combination which had two sets of selectors from New South Wales and Victoria, and did not practise together before the game', one group going through their preparatory paces in the morning and the other in the afternoon. Frank Allen, of Victoria, 'preferred to attend an agricultural show in his home town' rather than play in what he evidently did not regard as an historic fixture, while Fred Spofforth would not play because Billy Murdoch was not keeping wicket.

The English were still feeling the effects of seasickness in consequence of a rough return crossing from New Zealand, but they rallied to win a return fixture, with accusations of deceit from the betting fraternity in the belief that the tourists had thrown the first meeting to extend the odds. In the new year of 1879 the next English team, more of a missionary outing, with Lord Harris leading a bunch of mainly aristocratic amateurs, played what became known as the third test match, although it was actually billed as 'the Gentlemen of England (with Ulyett and Emmett) versus the Australian XI'.

Next, the Australians, backed by the two chief colonial associations, visited England in 1880 and played one test. It was at the Oval, although its centenary memorial match was played, to the chagrin of the Surrey faithful, at Lord's. There was much trouble over fixtures, with many counties already over-committed and no chance of a representative game at Lord's. Lord Harris, whose hauteur had been ruffled by the so-called 'Sydney Riot' during the previous winter, when there had been serious crowd troubles during one of the tourists' matches, tried to insist that the Australians 'admit that their trip is one of pleasure and that they are only accepting expenses'. The Australians politely declined. In the event, it was the progressively thinking Charles Alcock, the farsighted and highly competent Surrey secretary, who organised such a fixture for early September at the Oval and he even managed to persuade Lord Harris to pick, on Surrey's behalf, the side that, powered by W.G.Grace scoringEngland's first ever century, won by five wickets.

Possibly the downside of Alcock's smart initiative was that it created the precedent of the county responsible for the venue choosing and inviting the players. It was scarcely a device of national stature and it endured for some decades. It gave rise to county authorities – Yorkshire's Lord Hawke would seem to have been an instance – showing prejudice in favour of playing men from one's own county or, alternatively, not playing them, so that the county would not be weakened.

This is an argument about the legitimacy, not the efficiency, of the selectors. Archie MacLaren, when captaining one of the first officially chosen English teams in 1902, is said to have stood in the dressing room, surrounded by abashed selectees, as he clutched the team-sheet in anguish and expostulated on the mediocrity of the performers gifted to him. 'My God, look what they've gimme', he groaned, 'do they think we're playing the blind asylum.'

For their part, the Australian associations grew restive at the trans-oceanic comings and goings, believing that they robbed the colonial and club sides of support. Chris Harte, the Australian cricket historian, cites a New South Wales report that bemoaned 'the refusal of members of returned teams to take part in the inter-colonial contests has shorn these matches of much of their wonted interest . . . the inter-colonial matches were a matter of first importance and one to which all others should be subservient.'

These small 't' test matches remained infrequent. There were only 134 between 1877 and 1914 and the number had only risen to 274 by 1939. Thereafter the trickle became a river – the centenary test in Melbourne in 1977, and won, remarkably by the home team by the same 45 run margin as in 1877, was the 803rd in the whole sequence of Test matches and the 225th in the Anglo-Australian series. Then the river became a torrent. It took eleven years for the first 29 tests to be played. Now more than 29 tests are staged each year. It used to be said that, somewhere on the planet, there was always a production of Gilbert and Sullivan's *The Mikado* in performance. These days one begins to feel the same about five-day and limited overs internationals.

In the meanwhile, South Africa joined the fray. They had played eleven tests by 1905, eight against under-strength English teams, the first in 1889/90 and three against the 1902 Australians returning home via the Cape. Curiously, South Africa was the first of the three test-playing countries to establish an explicit national agency, the South Africa Cricket Association, formed in 1890. Predictably, it was for white cricket only. The struggling non-white cricketers created the South African Coloured Cricket Board in 1897 and, later, the South African Independent Cricket Board in 1926. On the English tour of South Africa in 1891/92 a game was played against a South African non-white team but the English amateurs refused to take part.

This touches on the merging of 'test' and 'international'. It was acceptable that, if the experts wanted to apply the term 'test' to English and Victorian elevens in even-handed contest – and, pre-sumably, by projection, to an Australian eleven fixture in England with, say, Yorkshire . . . but confusion arose when Tests assumed their capital 'T' and became synonymous with internationals. The uncertainty was of two kinds. One involved the geopolitical issue of whether the area in question was a nation. The second raised the constitutional subject of whether or not the nation, if such it was, hosted a readily recognised national cricket body to organise such international games, pick the teams and so forth. Without these two prerequisites, it was arguable that the expression 'inter-national', a word coined apparently by the Utilitarian philosopher, Jeremy Bentham, could not justly be applied.

Although South Africa might have had a national cricketing agency, at least for its European minority, its political constituency was indeterminate, as the 1895/96 tourists discovered when their cheery jaunt was caught up in the events involving the notorious Jameson Raid and a posse of Boer guerrillas confronted them. Technically, it was 1910 before the quartet of autonomous colonies, Cape Colony,

Transvaal, Natal and the Orange River Colony, later the Orange Free State, became a unified polity, albeit still under the British flag. By that point South Africa had played in 24 'international' matches.

Australia too, was, in respect of international law, a loose conglomeration of separate colonies, cricket being – rather like some sports, such as rugby union, on the present island of Ireland – one of few collobarative activities. The point was underlined at the Colonial Conference held in London in 1897 to celebrate Queen Victoria's Diamond Jubilee. Whereas Canada, which had enjoyed dominion status since 1867, sent a single national delegation, each of the Australian colonies dispatched its own representatives, for each had distinct administrative links with the Mother Country.

In 1892 and with the nationalistic tide flowing in Australia, three of the colonies formed the Australasian Cricket Council but amidst warring factionalism, it had collapsed by 1900. However, on the stroke of midnight 1st January 1901, the Commonwealth of Australia Act of 1900 came into force and the existing six colonies became, in the American connotation, 'states'. Provincialism, as the Americans found when the 'states-rights' issue led to secession and internecine warfare, was not too easily quelled. It took a tough, wheeler-dealing solicitor, William McElhone, to negotiate the formation, not without many alarums and excursions, of a new Australian Board of Control, which met for the first time in Melbourne in 1905. It reflected its South African equivalent, of course, by being solely European in membership and purpose.

Typical of the 'states-rights' poser was the fact that the Council began with just New South Wales and Victoria as authentic originals, with Queensland joining a few months later. South Australia switched from observer to member status in 1906, Tasmania enlisted in 1907 and Western Australia became a member in 1914, after the outbreak of the Great War. MCC, keen to see the establishment of some form of reconciliation of Australian squabbling in such a body, actually went so far as to decline to support the sending of an English team to the Antipodes in 1906/07 'until the Board is entirely representative of Australian cricket'.

MCC settled for an almost complete set. The Sydney Test of December 1907 was the first when the home team had been selected by such a Board and ostensibly without the usual exhibitions of player power and inter-colonial rivalry that, inevitably, simmered beneath the surface. MCC being a private club, it may be thought that there was something of kettle calling pan sooty black about this attitude. However, steps had been taken to regularise the position in England. MCC had slowly been building, as was earlier noted, its power and prestige in its controls of county and allied matters. In 1898 the outworn device of the relevant county committee acting as national selector was abandoned and MCC, with general agreement, took over another task as the MCC Board of Control. This completed MCC's takeover of English cricket. The Board's membership was six MCC and six county representatives and they picked the selection panel for Tests. In 1899, the first summer of five Tests, MCC chose all five elevens, as opposed to just the one for the Lord's Test. There was then much confusion over the selection of players for the 1901/02 tour of Australia and MCC thenceforward took complete responsibility, even unto labelling 'England' as 'MCC' when abroad. 1903/04 is the date of the first official MCC tour, one in which Pelham Warner was the captain and Lord Hawke the manager.

Thus the first Anglo-Australian Test match in which both teams were selected by two nationally acknowledged bodies representing two sovereign states was in 1907 at Sydney. It was the 96th listed 'Test' match; it was the 77th in the Australia/England canon and the 93rd played by England, who had played sixteen matches against purported South African 'national' teams. Australia and South Africa had played out the remaining three games of the 96 arranged. To be really niggling, that is, to be patient until the Australian Council had achieved perfect representation with the inclusion of Western Australia, then one would ideally have to await the 1920 Sydney Test, the 95th in the Anglo-Australian series, the 107th that Australia had been engaged in, and the 135th all told.

Of the other two main contenders, New Zealand established its Cricket Council quite early in 1894, with the West Indies forming a Board of Control more tardily in 1927. Politically, New Zealand, which until 1841 had been conjoined with New South Wales, moved from separate colonial to dominion status in 1907. The political position of the West Indies was and remains convoluted by the fact that these were a set of colonies that, in the post-war settlement, proceeded to become a series of independent states. From the stance of international law, the West Indies now is a multinational rather than a national team. India, where the game came to be dominated by the indigenous population, formed a Board of Control for Cricket in 1927. Geopolitically, it remained just an enormously large colony until, in 1947, it was partitioned into the two independent polities of India and Pakistan.

THE IMPERIAL ORDER

However, neither New Zealand nor the West Indies, let alone India, was considered for membership or Test status when the Imperial Cricket Conference was inaugurated in 1909. The first meeting of the Conference was prompted by the idea of a triangular Test tournament, the only one of which took place in 1912 in England and fell a little flat. It was South Africa, in particular, its leading sponsor, Abe Bailey, who was keen on the idea of the threesome meeting and playing. South Africa was still weaker than the other two and the notion of a quasi-legal togetherness obviously appealed to the South Africans as a means of holding on to their tentative third ranking. It was a also a move in line with what was previously observed of the South African yearning to present a bold political front in British eyes. The Earl of Chesterfield, President of MCC, chaired the first meeting, and Francis Lacey, the competent if rather chilly Secretary of MCC was present, along with five other delegates.

Apart from the absence of New Zealand, the West Indies and India from the ICC, there was of course, no room for, say, Philadelphia, where cricket was still something of a force. It was an Imperial, not an International, Conference, and, true to form, an all-white assembly. It would be 1925 before New Zealand, the West Indies and India were welcomed to its counsels. The inaugural Test match for each of those countries was 1928 for the West Indies, 1930 for New Zealand and 1932 for India. The three ICC originals had played 172 so-called Test matches before anyone else had a look in.

A word in season is required about Ranji's part in the Indian aspect of all this. Prince Ranjitsinhji, the Jam Sahib of Nawanagar, was very much the Prince Charming of the Raj. He was, as Mario Rodrigues' hard-headed political biography presses, a 'role model of propriety', opposing, along with many others of his princely caste, the popular aspirations of the Indian people. He was a marvellous Sussex and England batsman, but he was not an Indian cricketer *per se*, and advised his talented nephew, Duleepsinhji, not to play for India. Resolute in his defence of British Imperialism, he was reluctant to encourage cricket in India, perhaps conscious, between the wars, of its likely appeal to insurgent nationalists. He would certainly have objected to India having an independent, a non-British, voice in any Imperial forum, such as the ICC.

Other sports developed neater patterns. In England the Football League, something of an equivalent of the County Championship, began life in the 1888/89 season, and has complete continuity and no preceding baggage. The Football Association, which had assembled itself in 1863 and immediately issued standard laws, first organised the FA Challenge Cup competition over the winter of 1871/72, before selecting a side in 1872 to play the first official international match against Scotland, aka Queen's Park, in Glasgow in 1872. Such was the rapid development of 'association' football that national associations, often with similar league and cup tournaments, arose quickly, so much so that it was only 41 years after the formation of the FA that a world body was started. This was the Federation Internationale de Football Associations or FIFA, an agency that first met in Paris in 1904, five years before the inaugural ICC meeting and by 1914 FIFA had twelve members.

However, if one follows the geopolitical route, in respect of either cricket or football, the curious case of 'England', not alone a sovereign state, might raise an academic eyebrow or two. True enough, the Celtic fringe has furnished 'England' with some useful cricket players but it is not legally, a nation-state. One notes with interest that the West Indian 'nations' compete separately in the world of football, where the UK still contrives to field four teams.

It is true, as has been already mentioned in the previous chapter, that expatriate Englishmen tried to start cricket as well as football clubs when in European and South American countries. In 1889 Alfred Edwards gathered together the British and Swiss merchants who started the Milan Cricket and Football Club, later to be more famously known as AC Milan. There were plenty of other examples in South America as well as in Europe. Once the local people became more involved, the cricketing elements tended to evaporate and football made flourishing progress. Now football was the fashion. This was the epoch of industrialism and high finance when British engineers and other craftsmen, together with merchants and bankers were very active both in Europe and South America.

Very importantly, the English considered cricket to be a sublimely and inclusively Anglo-Saxon sport. All in all, and at the risk of some oversimplification, soldiers, missionaries, teachers and colonial officers carried cricket to the imperial lands in the late 18th and early 19th centuries, while tradesmen and businessmen conveyed football to Europe and South America in the late 19th and early 20th centuries.

THE GOLDEN AGE

In the meanwhile cricket was basking in its 'Golden Age', intrinsically the era from the 1880s to the beginning of the First World War. The mystique of the Ashes arose in 1882, when, after the truly inventive Charles Alcock – an even greater influence on football as Secretary of the FA than he was on cricket – had arranged another test at the Oval, the Australians won a gripping contest in which the 'Demon' Spofforth took fourteen wickets. A journalist, Reginald Brooks, composed the obituary notice for the *Sporting Times* 'in Affectionate Memory of English Cricket which died at the Oval on 29th August 1882 . . .' The following winter the English team, this time invited over by the Melbourne CC, won the rubber and their captain, Hon. Ivo Bligh, was presented with the urn containing, it was alleged, cremated bails. That enduring legend further emphasised the religiosity of the sport, with its sacrificial aroma of the burnt offering.

On that note, Mike Selvey, the former England bowler and current cricket journalist, heralded the 2009 'Ashes' series with the fascinating yarn of Reginald Brooks' contribution, along with Anthony Trollope and others, to the campaign to legalise cremation. Had the charred bails been a corpse, it would have been unlawful and Reginald Brooks was making the rather macabre satirical point. Contemporary readers may well have understood that intention, given the recent newsworthiness of the cremation debate. Cremation only became legal at the turn of the century but in yet another small way, there was an interface of cricket, society and its tribal and religious rites of passage.

The intensity of emotion evoked by cricket probably contributed to the yearning to trace its lineage back into the ancient mists of time, with the litany of Test matches to the fore. In 1894 the Australian, C.P.Moody, published his *Australian Cricket and Cricketers, 1856 to 1893/94,* It included a summary roster of inter-colonial and purported international matches and it appears to have been accepted without undue quibbling as the official list of Test matches up to that date between England and Australia. It was as simple and as cockeyed as that. Longevity lends lustre to the saga. It did mean, however, that cricket's peak was scaled amid an untidy mess of often unsupportable interpretations about its past.

Nevertheless, the late Victorians and Edwardians in both England and Australia had genuine grounds for regarding their cricketing period with pardonable pride. Just as the football professionals were emulating and overtaking their amateur counterparts, there was a luxurious flowering of talent among the amateur or rather, with W.G.Grace as the most exotic bloom, 'gentleman' cricketers, giving them a degree of parity with the professionals they had not enjoyed for some decades. This confident realisation of what was felt to be the ideal of cricket certainly helped to polish the sheen of the Golden Age.

Apart from the late flowering – his famed Indian Summer of 1895 brought him 2346 runs at an average of 51 – of W.G.Grace, the differing gifts of the silky Prince Ranjitsinhji and his Sussex colleague, C.B.Fry, an all-round sportsman of undiminished assurance and hauteur, were on show. The appropriately imperious Archie MacLaren, the wristy Reginald Spooner, the haughty F.S.Jackson and the powerful Gilbert Jessop were four other majestic figures, while the Australians could turn to such talents as Billy Murdoch, Warwick Armstrong, Clem Hill and the immortal Vic Trumper. Australia's Arthur Mailey, first-rate spinner and able journalist, said that when, as a young man, he bowled Vic Trumper, he felt as if he had 'shot a dove.'

Records tumbled. In 1895 Archie MacLaren made 424 for Lancashire against Somerset at Taunton and he still remains the only player born in Great Britain to have scored a quadruple hundred. Even this monumental effort was overshadowed, at least numerically, by an occasion in 1899, when the thirteen year old A.E.J.Collins, of Clifton College, *alma mater* of W.G.Grace's sons and the site of several of his own outings, broke the world record for the highest innings. It was a junior house match between Clark's House and North Town House. Young Arthur Collins won the toss, elected to bat, opened the batting and batted through for an unbeaten 628 out of 836. A beleaguered North Town could only manage 148 in their two innings, in which Collins took 11 for 63, leaving the victors with a comfortable margin of 688 runs. It broke the record of 485, scored by A.E.Stoddart, the Middlesex and England star, in a club match for the prestigious Hampstead club against the aptly named Stoics in 1886.

The house match took several late afternoons with Collins batting, in instalments, for seven hours. There were the usual cries of it being a contrived event and it is true that the huge and excitable national coverage did Clifton College little harm by way of advertisement but what of the educational content of the exercise? What of the adverse effect of all this for the other twenty-one boys involved? Taken at face value as part of an educational experience, it was tediously ludicrous. Any self-respecting teacher, conscious of the needs of child development, would have had a quiet word with master Collins, after an hour or two, on the subject of cricketing *hari kari*.

But this was a Victorian public school. In 1898 580 Cliftonians were serving in the army and a 1901 survey showed that Clifton had more Old Boys in the Indian service than any other school. Sir Henry Newbolt himself was a Cliftonian, whose *Vitai Lampada* was published in that same year of 1899. Sir Henry wrote, 'there were very few members of the school who would not have bartered away all chance of intellectual distinction for a place in the cricket eleven or the football fifteen'. As for poor Collins, who was born in India, the son of a judge and apparently a most modest and unassuming young man, he became a lieutenant in the Royal Engineers and was killed in action in the November of 1914, leaving a young widow to mourn him.

The whole unhealthy charade acts as a sad emblem of the hold cricket had on this dimension of English society and of how it was of such dominance in its day-by-day thinking and attitudes.

It is understandable, not least given this degree of commitment to cricket, that the Gentlemen could match the Players at this stage, for, in the Edwardian era, they typically contributed five or six to the Test team and about half the players in the County Championship. A third of the amateurs were varsity blues. They were overwhelmingly former public schoolboys from families who could bankroll their summer jaunts.

For the professional cadre, especially in the more manual toil of bowling, was also very strong. J.T.Tyldesley was the pre-1914 batsman who was paid the compliment of it being said he batted with the panache of a gentleman, while the two Yorkshire all-round stalwarts, Wilfred Rhodes and George Hirst, enjoyed tremendous success, ensuring the White Rose county's superlative results in that period. In 1906 George Hirst completed for the only time the double double of 2385 runs and 218 wickets. Surrey's George Lohmann was another exceptional bowler and another Surrey professional, Tom Hayward, gathered together the long-standing record aggregate of 3518 runs for the 1906 season. The Oval also witnessed the arrival of the young Jack Hobbs, beginning his superb career that was to bestride the gulf of World War I and with all but 200 first-class centuries, leave him remembered as one of the finest opening bats ever.

Some commentators claim that England's 1902 eleven, a resplendent compound of mainly amateur batsmen and mainly professional bowlers, was their strongest ever. 'Familiar in his mouth as household words' were A.C.MacLaren, C.B.Fry, K.S.Ranjitsinhji, Hon.F.S. Jackson, J.T.Tyldesley, A.F.A.Lilley, the wicket-keeper, G.H.Hirst, G.L.Jessop, L.C.Braund, W.H.Lockwood and W.Rhodes.

Regarded as one of the best bowlers of all time, despite his finding first-class cricket less profitable than league cricket, Sydney Barnes was another name to conjure with. He took 189 wickets in 27 Tests at an average cost of 16.43, including 9 for 103 against South Africa at Johannesburg during the 1913/14 tour. A man of fierce independence, he did not take kindly to being underpaid or ordered about by bristling authority. Selected practically from league cricket to tour Australia in 1903/04, he soon showed his mettle. His captain, Archie MacLaren, had soon become disillusioned with Barnes' lack of deference. As the leaky tub heaved and strained in the swirling storm during the crossing to New Zealand, the composed MacLaren reassured a terrified young amateur with the consoling remark that 'if we drown, then that bugger, Barnes, will drown with us'.

One ambitious professional who was not deterred by the perils of the ocean was the tenacious Billy Midwinter, who was born in St Briavels in the Forest of Dean before emigrating to Australia as a child, with his miner father keen to swap coal for gold. He developed all-round cricketing skills and took 5 for 28 for Australia in the English first innings of that first Test match in 1877. The ever watchful W.G.Grace noted his Gloucestershire birth qualification and he became one of the county's first regular professionals, for hitherto Gloucestershire, if one discounts the high expenses and other perquisites claimed by the Grace brothers and one or two others, had remained largely an amateur outfit. Although Billy Midwinter is recalled by cricket quiz buffs as the only cricketer to have played for Australia versus England and England versus Australia, the important precedent he created was that of being the first mainstream trans-oceanic commuter. From 1880 to 1882 he played six full seasons, three in Australia, mainly for Victoria, and three in England, chiefly for Gloucestershire. In that 36 months period he spent the equivalent of twelve of them aboard ships. It was a resolute enterprise of far reaching consequence.

On the whole, the professionals were deferential. Apart from an altercation – it hardly amounted to strike action – by five players demanding £20 instead of £10 as their pay for playing in the 1896 Oval Test match, there were few labour problems. Their complaint had much to do with the expenses and earnings of the English amateurs and the Australians. Shameful although that was, most cricket professionals realised what, in modern righteous concern about the iniquities of the gentleman/player divide, is forgotten, that by and large, the reasonably successful cricket 'pro' earned more money and enjoyed a less exacting life-style than the majority of those in the manual classes from which most of them sprang.

The gap was not immense but it was worthwhile. In the last years before the outbreak of the First World War, at a point when there were some 200 paid county players, the well-established professional might have earned an annual sum of up to £275, inclusive of a small winter retainer, out of which travel and subsistence had to be met. The agricultural labourer might have earned little more than £50, the urban manual worker £90 and the coal miner £140 a year. Provided the allure of alcohol could be evaded, it was, for the day, reasonable. It placed the cricket professional above something like 80% of the work force in respect of income, pushing him by that valuation close to the ranks of the lower middle classes. Meanwhile, shamateurism remained rife. For example, the Surrey accounts show sums of £100 or more paid to the gentlemanly W.W.Read for 'good cricket' plus suitable match expenses.

Of course the professionals remained unrepentantly working class but of the superior sort. To take the by no means idle comparison of the army, they were non-commissioned officers rather than privates in relation to the commissioned officers of their amateur overseers. Another parallel might be the rich household, in terms of the senior servant group, like Gordon Jackson's Hudson, butler to the lordly Bellamy family in television's *Upstairs, Downstairs* series. Like him, like the grizzled sergeant major, like Wilfred Rhodes at Yorkshire, they may even have been more attached to and defensive of the equivalent of blue blood family or regimental honour than their supposed betters. Dependable and complacent, as many of them were, aware and proud, like any other artisan tradesman, of their prowess in their craft, they formed an essential part of the cricketing pattern of the Golden Age.

The crowds, invariably well-behaved, that assembled to admire these joint groups of upper and middle class men, many of them on wholesome expenses, and working class men, many of them on decent wages, comprised the same two sorts. Many of the former were subscribing members in the pavilion and many of the latter paid their sixpence or shilling for a place on the terraces. They reflected the 'integrated culture', that solid casting of respectability across the sober-sided middle and aspiring working classes that Matthew Arnold noted. They shared the same experiences at differing prices and from separate angles. Other examples include the paid and free pews in the same church or chapel, the expensive and cheap ends or districts of the seaside holiday resort, the saloon and public bars of the hostelry, the stalls or circle and gallery of the theatre, and the 'class' divisions of the train.

Culturally, the family novel, as popularised in serial form by Charles Dickens, exemplified this phenomenon both in thrust and form. It penetrated deep into society, with group readings in settings ranging from middle-class households to the 600 Mechanic' Institutes that had sprung up by mid-19th century. During the reign of Queen Victoria 42,000 novels, penned by 3,500 authors, were published, many of them enjoying, astonishingly, both popular and critical acclaim. Moreover, they often had cross-class romantic plots to match, as did the other signal expositions of Victorian culture. As well as Pip and Estella in Charles Dickens' *Great Expectations* or Eugene Wrayburn and Lizzie Hexam in his *Our Mutual Friend*, there was a similar crossing of the social tracks in pantomime, another lovingly shared diversion of the age, with Cinderella finding romance with Prince Charming or, the reverse example, Aladdin winning the hand of the Princess Balroubadour. Following suit, the Gilbert and Sullivan comic operas likewise found their love interest, for example, in the affection of the captain's daughter, Josephine, for the ordinary seaman, Ralph Rackstraw, in *HMS Pinafore* or the devotion of Mabel, the major-general's daughter, for the reformed brigand, Fredric, in *The Pirates of Penzance*.

W.S.Gilbert spoke often in culinary metaphor of how the Savoyard operas were deliberately composed to cater for 'the gastronomic mean'. Rather, for instance, than 'tripe and onions' for the working-class customers in the pit and 'sweetbread and truffles' for the middle-class theatre-goers in the stalls, he provided 'a plain leg of mutton and boiled potatoes' as 'the most stable fare for all'. Cricket was thus the sporting equivalent of the Savoy Theatre's 'a plain leg of mutton and boiled potatoes.' So it would remain, until the 1950s, when the collective leisure of this bonding of reasonably waged worker and salaried professional or businessman fragmented.

The attendances were variable, ranging from the large hosts at the major grounds for major games to somewhat derisory and scattered gatherings at some of the lowly county grounds or even at the big arenas when unfashionable opponents were in town. Accurate figures are hard to find, but Tony Laughton, biographer of Albert Craig, 'the Surrey Poet', has examined county accounts and reports for the early years of the 20th century. These suggest that match attendances at this time, not including subscribing members, averaged 4500 for Sussex, 7000 for Essex, 8000 for Middlesex, 10,500 for Kent, 12,000 for Surrey and 17,000 for all-conquering Yorkshire.

Of course, such figures have to be divided by three to obtain some idea of daily paying attendances. It is this that makes comparisons with the Football League difficult. By the Edwardian period First Division gates averaged 15,000 a match, where a cricketing county may have had 12,000 for a game but only a thousand or two on Monday and Tuesday after a healthy gate on the Saturday. Averages also hide the gamut of, say, Surrey, capable of drawing a bank holiday crowd of well over 30,000 against Nottinghamshire – that closely contested duel drew a record 72,565 over three days in 1892 – and yet only attracting a thousand or so, and gate money maybe under £50, for a mid-week day against a less glorious foe.

For obvious reasons, the grounds in the large cities attracted the largest crowds, and descriptions of them have sometimes given a misleading impression about the popularity of county cricket. Nonetheless, it was the first of the team sports to build a customer base, peaking around 1900, when 209 first-class games were scheduled in the British Isles, bringing in through the gate and through the attendance of county members, a clientele of a very approximate 1.5m people. Only at this juncture was the spreading might of the Football League beginning to overtake this kind of yearly support.

Below the level of the top-class game cricket was in a wholesome and reassuring position. The suburban cricket club, several of them of reasonable wealth and standing, and the typical village club were in fine shape, while in mimicry of the football phenomenon, the league concept caught hold. This was a feature of the industrial areas, compact communities capable of producing high attendances for a Saturday afternoon's sport. The first to be founded was the Birmingham and District League (1889), quickly followed by, amongst others, the North-east Lancashire League (1890, later just the Lancashire League), the North Staffordshire and District League (1890), the South-east Lancashire League (1892, much better known later as the Central Lancashire League), plus several across the broad acres of Yorkshire, including the expansive endeavours of the Yorkshire Council. Professionals were employed in the leagues and it is small wonder that Sydney Barnes, paid £8 for a Saturday's outing by Church in Lancashire, plus collections for good perform-ances, as opposed to about half as much for a week's arduous toil for Lancashire, was reluctant to submit himself too readily to the travails of first-class cricket.

By this time the other major cricketing regions had each built an edifice, especially imposing in Australia, of competitive club and provincial cricket. The Sheffield Shield tournament, inaugurated for the Australian states in 1892/93, and the Currie Cup, the similar contest for the South African provinces, established in 1889/90, were the acme of the solid cricketing structure in each of those countries. The former was named after Lord Sheffield, President of the Sussex club and the sponsor of the 1891/92 tour of Australia, while the latter was donated by Sir Donald Currie, politician and shipping magnate, initially for the then colony that prospered best against the English tourists on tour in 1889/90.

Both in England and in its vast overseas Empire, cricket flourished and was revered. Sir Pelham Warner, both judge and scribe of cricket, wrote that cricket had become 'more than a game. It is an institution, a passion, one might say almost a religion.'

But, to match Sir Pelham in his deployment of the cliché, Nemesis was just around the corner.

CHAPTER NINE
PETRIFACTION

A tranquil rural cricketing scene

The First World War is possibly the most significant episode in the history of cricket. That is true for a wholly negative reason. The 1914-18 War abruptly stopped cricket in its tracks. It was cricket's equivalent of the Fall of the Roman Empire, the collapse of a great institution, but one still able to cast influential shadows.

THE EFFECTS OF WORLD WAR I

The general shock in 1914 to the English national psyche was of a different kind to that suffered at the onset of the Second World War.

It was the first major war embracing Britain in Western Europe for a century, since, in fact, the battle of Waterloo in 1815, a few days before which the Duke of Richmond, whose wife gave the famed ball on the battle's eve, had disported himself at cricket just outside Brussels. All other British conflicts had been non-continental or colonial ones, with the relatively short Crimean War located off the Black Sea ranking as the nearest of such hostilities to these islands.

World War II was less of a surprise, with some historians regarding the 1914-1945 era as one long phase of warring. Only twenty-one cricket seasons separated the two conflicts and there had been constant worries about the possible onset of another major war. The elegantly talented Kent player, Frank Woolley, won eighteen Test caps before the first war, in which he served as a naval coxswain, before earning 46 more caps after the war and then appearing in charity matches in World War II.

Moreover, the second war was conducted at a different tempo. It encompassed everyone, with the blackout, the blitz, the rationing and the direction of labour, but it was sporadic in its perils. There were intervals of quietude – the 'phoney war' to begin with, the build up to D-Day in 1944 – amid the horrors. Sometimes these were on a short timescale. The Middlesex and England star, Bill Edrich, would heroically risk his life as a Coastal Command pilot one day and turn out at Lord's in a charity match the next.

The impact of World War I was more immediate, with Belgian refugees flooding instantly into the country and then with the carnage of trench warfare pursued with a lunatic constancy. The mood soon changed from happy and glorious to bleak and anxious. Those who, in acidic minds, merited 'the white feather' were scorned and maltreated, whereas the 60,000 conscientious objectors of World War II were shown more tolerance. In 1914 net practice was stopped at the Oval because the players were 'being jeered at by men off the trams cars' as they rattled by the ground.

The slaughter was unyielding. Over 900,000 British and British Empire service personnel were killed, compared with 373,000 in the longer second conflict, plus, for it was total war, some 93,000 civilian dead, most of them victims of bombing. There were little more than a thousand fatal British civilian casualties in the earlier war. Two-fifths of the 5m mobilised, volunteers and conscripts, in the first war were either killed or wounded. 6% of British males aged 15-49 died. Although fierce fighting occurred in many areas, from Northern Italy and the Dardenelles to the Palestine and Mesopotamia, the national focus tended to be on the trenches of the Western Front, stretching from Belgium to the Swiss border, and on the relentless daily record of dead and wounded soldiers.

What Benny Green, always an imaginative observer of cricket, called the 'hysterical idiocy' of the Great War accounted for the lives of well over 2000 promising cricketers. It was warfare designed to, in Siegfried Sassoon's grim phrase, 'speed glum heroes up the line to death', even if, according to revisionist historians, the design did not arise solely from the failures of 'the butchers and bunglers' in command. Rather was it, in this view, the prevailing conditions of armaments and allied factors that led inexorably to such heavy casualties on both sides. John Arlott explained why the slim *Wisdens* of the time seemed to have rarity value.

Grieving parents bought them to cling to as a memorial. The 1917 *Wisden*, for example, has 60 sombre pages registering the deaths of 400 such young men. Often it was but a brief obituary, sometimes no more than name, rank, regiment, date and place of death, and school or college represented at cricket. Bereaved families cherished such tiny notices. Peter Wynne-Thomas has calculated that one in every eleven first-class cricketers of 1900/1914 vintage lay dead, among them the gifted Kent left hand spin bowler, Colin Blythe.

This long and unexpected nightmare, affecting practically every family in Britain, was numbing and traumatic. Well-to-do youth had been nurtured in the concept of cricket being part of the preparation for the battle of life. The battle had arrived with a dreadful vengeance. The challenge was mounted for those 'who were playing their games in the fields of France'. It is important to recall the seriousness with which cricket was regarded. It was immensely important. Cricket came to a standstill with a shuddering halt, not because it was trivial, but because it was significant. It was not a question of mixing business with pleasure. It was a question of mixing two businesses, one of war and one of cricket. There was no room for two such solemn commitments and one, cricket – apart from some league cricket to entertain weary war-workers and limited programmes of schools cricket – had to be sacrificed. MCC maintained a fixture list for old or 'medically unfit for service' men to play against the public schools, where, of course, the practice of staying on until aged nineteen or even twenty, had been halted. But there were only about thirty such games a season, compared with the normal number of not much less than 200.

MCC ordered the counties not to organise games with each other, an instruction sedulously obeyed. There was a little easing of the sanctions in 1917, with one or two charity matches planned, and there was some desultory military cricket. Robert Graves wrote of how the officers played the sergeants at Vermelles in France, barely three quarters of a mile from the German positions. They played with a splintered piece of rafter for a bat, a knotted rag ball and, for wickets, a birdcage containing, with Pythonesque flourish, a dead parrot. Generally however it was regarded as unseemly to enjoy cricket when, every day, families or streets, sometimes whole villages or townships, were hearing harrowing news. Abroad, Australia and South Africa had little or no organised cricket after 1915, although there was some cricket in New Zealand, whilst India was not as affected as the other countries.

In the August of 1914 W.G.Grace wrote, not to *the Times*, as some accounts have suggested, but, much more appositely, to *the Sportsman*. In the only overtly political act of his life, he implored young men to stop playing cricket: 'I think the time has arrived when the county cricket season should be closed, for it is not fitting at a time like this that able-bodied men should be playing cricket day by day, and pleasure-seekers look on'. Thus did the incarnation of cricket, the man whose life was solely dedicated to its promotion, pull down the shutters on the game he loved and adorned. He died in 1915, his personal passing marking the demise of cricket.

Cricketers like Captain Archie MacLaren and Captain Gilbert Jessop acted as recruiting officers. In his *World of Cricket* magazine, the former intemperately referred to Kaiser William as 'that crowned madman' with 'an insane lust for power' and in a later issue, as 'the hog in armour'. It was in that fervid atmosphere that schoolboys laid down their bats and picked up their service revolvers.

Recall how those dead 2000 and more young cricketers had spent their happiest hours at school. These had been the afternoons in the nets or on the cricket square, with the grumpy ex-professional cricketer coach insistent on orthodoxy, paralleled by the afternoons on the barrack square, with the bellicose ex-army NCO drill instructor, as adamantly intent on military discipline. The latter ensured that many of his officer cadets would head straight for commissions and likely death or vicious injury. With regular chapel having lauded both cricketing and soldiering, off went those schoolboy and Oxbridge subalterns to glory, a generation destined to perish in mud or to survive irrevocably scarred.

There had been warnings. Well-placed individuals, after the manner of John Buchan's hero, Richard Hannay, of *The Thirty-nine Steps* fame, had warned of the German threat. Events like the sinking of the *Titanic* in 1912, a doomed liner that, with its social hierarchy ranging from plutocratic first-class to mundane steerage, was a floating microcosm of society, were seen as symbols of a shattered society. In fact, the retrospective view of the expansively prosperous Edwardian era was never more than a half-truth. There was the peaking of militant action by the Suffragettes in the pre-war years, Edward Carson's 'Tory Rebellion' on behalf of the exemption of Ulster from Irish Home Rule, which brought the Emerald Isle to the brink of civil war in 1914, and the now scarcely recalled threat of a virulent general strike by a 4m strong trades union movement in the summer of 1914. George Dangerfield's elegiac study, *The Strange Death of Liberal England* (1935) indicates how close Britain came to some form of revolution at that juncture. The war was the antidote to rebellion and the war's survivors would only remember the serenity.

The poet laureate of Imperialism, Rudyard Kipling, no less, had come, with sharp intelligence, to view the public school attitude to games as unhelpful and he blamed some of the military failures of the Boer War thereon. In *The Islanders*, written in 1902, he had famously chided:

> *Then ye returned to your trinkets; then ye contented your souls*
> *With the flannelled fools at the wicket and the muddied oafs at the goals.*

The flannelled fools in authority took a dim view of this heresy, rather blaming the 'sloppiness' of English youth, with the nationalistic poet Norman Gale backing that approach with such lines as, 'female men are thick as thieves, with croquet, ping pong and the rest.' He moaned of 'cricket gone to rust', and evinced little wonder that foreigners might 'humble England in the dust.' Of course, as was previously suggested, the superficial concept of 'transfer of training', with its tacit implication that the eager cricketing schoolboy would automatically emerge as a brilliant army commander, is no longer accepted; at least, one hopes it isn't. It is now believed that the Duke of Wellington was much too pragmatic a soldier to have made such a daft remark as the one about the Battle of Waterloo being won on the playing fields of Eton.

The stark contrast between the sunny polish of the greensward and the grimy carnage of Flanders could not have been more emphatic. Siegfried Sassoon's poem, *Attack*, told of 'Lines of grey, muttering faces, masked with fear./They leave their trenches, going over the top.' That scene was a considerable distance from the charming Flower Show Match in his *Memoirs of a Fox-hunting Man* (1928), his Edwardian recollection of the part-autobiographical George, on holiday from Ballboro' School. George was 'an awkward overgrown boy, fielding anxiously at mid on', for Butley against Rotherdene, scoring the winning run in the last over with one wicket left and as the Butley village band plays *The Soldiers of the Queen*, with all well with the world. Then, abruptly, in Kipling's haunting phrase, 'your English summer's done.'

It was said that A.E.Housman's unrelenting themes of lost youth, parted friends and futile death 'struck a powerful chord with a nation that was losing an entire generation of young men in the trenches.' His *The Shropshire Lad*, suddenly popular during and after the war, includes the lines:

> *Now in Maytime to the wicket*
> *Out I march with bat and pad:*
> *See the son of grief at cricket*
> *Trying to be glad.*

The yawning gap of the four wartime seasons in such 'a land of lost content' was more psychologically than chronologically traumatic.

At the war's end cricket was not so much revived as mummified. Many cricketers and, more importantly, many of those who ran cricket's affairs, fought the war to return to the Never Land of Hove, Canterbury and Worcester, to preserve what they cherished from the past. The Victorians, for all their cultural flirtations with medievalism, were mighty believers in progress. The formulators of the theory of evolution, they would have had no truck with such a halting approach. Their post-1918 descendants, paralysed by the bloodbath of the Great War and understandably so, looked back where their forefathers would have looked forward. They looked back in yearning. The mood was more about salvage than production.

The ache for the idyllic past was such that alteration was tantamount to blasphemy. Traditionalism replaced progressivism. The Victorian English game of cricket was played from memory, a constant, haunting celebration of a lost world. It was a trance rather than a coma. There was nothing ugly or distressing about it. It was akin to the lovely 'dead-pale' Lady of Shalott, of Tennyson's mournful poem, floating down the stream 'till her blood was frozen over.' Another literary image might be that of John Galsworthy's *The Forsyte Saga*, first published in complete form in 1922. Each 'Man of Property' was a brother-in-arms of cricket's empire-builders, thrusting, accumulative and a little too smugly complacent. The First World War shattered most of them, making wry play with their veritable absence of 'foresight'. In cricket, as in life at large, the next generation's establishment was to spend much of the 20th century endeavouring to cling to dated illusions.

Gone was the bustle and invention of the assured Victorians, with, in cricket, the 'over arm' revolution, the to-ing and fro-ing of the County Championship, the imperial spread of cricket, the adaptation to the calls of a spectator sport and other stratagems. Not all of it, in cricket or elsewhere, had been beneficial but at least it was movement. The post-1918 cricketing contingent turned its back on the thesis of creative progress and opted to conserve cricket, as it existed at the point of the Armageddon of 1914.

Conservation and Atrophy in the Inter-wars Years

In fairness to cricket and its organisers, the nation was in a condition of atrophy, enduring two inter-wars decades of what their meditative historian, David Thompson, concisely termed 'incorrigible *immobilisme.*' Reeling under the gruesome remembrance of the war, then bludgeoned by the Great Depression, Britain bunkered down, everyone pretending – there were, of course, valiant exceptions – that nothing nasty was happening in the continental woodsheds of Russia, Germany, Spain and Italy. There was a gloomy overlay of religious Puritanism in all creeds, defined by the American writer, H.L.Mencken, as being motivated by 'the haunting fear that somewhere, someone is trying to enjoy himself'. George Orwell spoke of 'England's deep, deep sleep'.

There were pressures on family life. The admiration of the large, sprawling brood of Victorian times had given way to the custom of having small families. In a more corporate economic clime, the need for parents to beget children as a small labour force for the family trade or business had declined, while a more humane practice of child care, in the belief that one should attempt to do more for a few than less for many children, had developed. There were material ends as well, part of the growing suburban cult, with, in those decades, 3m privately owned houses added to the very small amount of owner-occupation – only about 5% of households – in 1914, and the whole approach betokened by Gracie Fields' song, 'You've got to keep up with the Jones'. The motor car was a spectacular instance of new suburban living. The car began as a luxury product, a horseless replacement for the very few private coaches, with the rich man's liveried coachman becoming his uniformed chauffeur. The homely vision of Henry Ford triumphed – and the cheaper car became within the reach of the many. The 90,000 private cars of 1914 became the 2m of 1939, as, in a percipient comment, 'the garage replaced the nursery' – with the 'Baby' Austin of particular interest to historians with psychoanalytical inclinations.

The birth rate dropped by an alarming half from 30 births for every thousand of the population, a figure that had been roughly maintained throughout the 19th century, to 15, and pessimistic commentators spoke of empty streets and depopulation. The average age at which people married and the natural fertility levels were unchanged, and yet contraception was still at a low ebb. The social historian has to fall back on abstinence as a major factor in between-wars life – 'he has on his hands', declared the great historian, A.J.P.Taylor, 'a frustrated people'. It was one of those rare eras when there is a gap between the biological imperatives and the social determinants. In consequence, prudishness and prurience reigned over an inward-looking community of sober respectability.

This was reflected in the enervating inertia of government during this time. There was little memorable or definitive done politically, with only the rather tame General Strike of 1926 and the rather over-egged 1936 Abdication crisis, when Edward VIII forfeited the crown, to colour the monotone. Alan Bennett caught this mood with fastidious precision in his first play, *Forty Years On*, wherein the England of the 1920s and 1930s was reduced to the sort of boarding school, repressed and insulated, that had nurtured all those subalterns. One could imagine Stanley Baldwin as the avuncular headmaster and George V as the distant chairman of governors. George V hated abroad as much as he loved philately and shooting. 'Amsterdam, Rotterdam, and all the other dams', he grouchily exclaimed, 'damned if I'll go.'

Luckily, it was a more opportune moment to embark on preservation than most. Possibly it might be argued that it was the best of times for cricket to take stock. Some would urge, with a Thomas Macaulay-like Whig Interpretation of Cricket History, that cricket had progressed to the ideal end and was trapped in aspic at that moment precisely because it had been perfected. However, in human affairs, especially institutional ones, pausing and seizing up are all too often synonymous. Stalemate can be deadly. A military comparison might be the American army, bogged down in the Ardennes campaign during the winter of 1944/45. That was when there were the most desertions, not when the troops were either advancing or retreating.

The force of this traditionalism is evidenced in three key areas. These are the techniques of cricket, the expansion of cricket and the constitution of cricket.

First, the apparatus of cricket appeared, to all extents and purposes, to have been assembled and perfected by this time. The code of laws as issued in 1884 was not revised until 1947, mainly to incorporate and clarify the various notes of interpretation that had been appended, rather than to encompass any major developments. The dominion of over arm bowling had been achieved and with it, the varied types of spin, swing and other styles, among them the googly, sometimes called the 'bosie', after its protagonist, Bertie Bosanquet, who developed the mysterious delivery from about 1892. A panoply of batting strokes, allowing for forward and back and off and on side performance, had evolved and was hardly added to in the post-war years. In fielding it was to be the numbers competent rather than the degree of competency that altered. Fine specialist fielders –George Hirst at mid off, Lancashire's Vernon Royle, 'the police-man', at cover point, George Lohmann or Len Braund of Somerset at slip, are examples – were not uncommon, although there were probably many more passengers pre-1914 in the fielding compartment. Wicket keeping, even with much less adequate equipment than would be enjoyed later, was at a high level; witness England's Herbert Strudwick or Australia's J.M.Blackham.

From among several themes, boundaries might be selected as a salutary example. Field games had tended to be boundless or, at least moderated only by severe natural obstacles. In cricket runs had originally all been run out. The phrase 'fielding in the country', in use quite late in the 20th century, was not deployed idly. Even when the primitive football pitch was marked out, there was a chase for loose balls, the winner who secured the 'touch down' returned it to the 'touch' line to throw in, hence the rather archaic use of touch-line and touch-judge, although the 'touch-down' behind the goals in the rugby codes remains a vestige of that old regime.

As games became public spectacles such expansiveness became inconvenient. Where they remained essentially private it did not much matter. Lacrosse and, until its relatively recent entry into sports theatre with large crowds gathering, golf were free from any such artificial restraints. In early modern cricket, the tents that were put up around the field for public use acted as a form of boundary, with the ball declared 'dead' if it reached the marquee line. Sometimes they were known as 'booth-balls'. The crowd were expected to part, Red Sea style, to allow the true flow of the ball, as is sometimes seen at golf today when a shot is mis-hit off the fairway and into the rough. Sometimes the host was so packed that this was difficult, while there were also certain partisan acts of interference to both moving ball and pursuing fielder. Furthermore, there was a health and safety factor for the spectators. W.G.Grace reports the case of the energetic 'Monkey' Hornby rushing full pelt into the crowd and injuring a respectable old gentleman. It was incidents like this that, according to Grace who recalled his early hits at Lord's being 'all run', led to reforms.

According to Gerald Brodribb, it became common by 1870 for boundary lines of flags or ropes to be constructed and by the 1880s there was a regular boundary line at Lord's. It was in the 1884 code that the first mention of boundaries was included. The rubric read, 'the umpires shall arrange boundaries where necessary and allowance to be made for them.' This was a guideline. It was only required when needed, that is, the alternative of an open terrain was fine, even preferable. What the 1947 code termed the 'customary allowances' normally became four and six but there was still some argument over the latter as to whether a sixer was over the boundary line or out of the ground. Although the 1910 County Advisory Committee suggested that the line was the answer, local conditions in club cricket witnessed some use of the ground perimeter for that purpose, certainly until after World War II.

After all that advance and decisiveness, the four and six boundary was solidified in cricket thinking and practice and has rarely been challenged. Indeed, one suspects that many players and watchers in the present age probably believe that there was never a time when this did not apply. As we passive cricket-lovers are part of the cult it is difficult to guess what the restless Victorian mind might have done further about boundaries or any other aspects of the game. What Australians call the 'pickets' continued to determine the boundary line, sometimes unfairly, as when crowds were allowed to encroach on the turf, say, for two busy days and then were restricted from so doing on a listless third day. There have been attempts to insist on minimum boundaries, the latter to the despair of spin bowlers looking for outfield catches and of fielders keen to demonstrate their mighty arms. On the whole, alteration has been basically negligible.

One might also cite the 1900 decision to have six balls an over in all games, the 1907 resolution over the taking of a new ball after 200 runs, or the acceptance, more or less, of declarations by 1914. Declarations, unknown in earlier years, were first mentioned in the laws of 1889, whereby a captain was permitted to declare at any time on the third and last day of a match, the first step, via declarations on the second day, towards the eventual license to curtail or even forfeit an innings that came as late as 1957. It was in 1890 that a first innings – that of Nottinghamshire against Sussex – was thus halted. Following on had been around since 1787. In 1835 the deficit was fixed at 100 runs, from 1854 to 1894, it was a mere 80 runs, and then it settled at 150 runs in 1900, and pretty much – 200 for Test matches, of course – stayed at that point thereafter. With minor adjustments only, these and other decisions were rarely altered over the next generation. Such changelessness for a hundred years is innately conservative.

Second, the major incidence of cricket was confined to the Empire. In the post-1918 period, most effort was concentrated on improving the game in the colonies and dominions. There is little need to rehearse the factors involved in this credo. Cricket was an English sport for English-speaking people resident in the British Empire. It would be 1965 before the Imperial became the International Cricket Conference. By that time FIFA had well over a hundred members. At the Imperial Cricket Conference of 1926, now a sextet of members, the autocratic Lord Harris, who had been responsible for the inclusion of the second threesome into the ICC, endorsed the decree that a Test match was a game 'between sides duly selected by recognised governing bodies of cricket representing countries within the Empire.' That was exact and pre-emptory. And the Empire was very much a going concern; migration to the Empire was sustained, peaking in 1923 when 250,000 people left British shores for the dominions and colonies. Nevertheless, had that ruling been applied retrospectively, as the 1947 regulation about first-class eligibility was to be, then the majority of the 162 'Test matches' played to that point would have been expunged from the roster.

It was amusing over the intervening period, to observe the embarrassed riposte of the advocates of 'Englishry' to the rising swell of cricket skills among the indigenous ranks of, in particular, India and the West Indies. Physiological gyrations of a mental kind were undertaken to imply there were racial traits among the Indians or West Indians that they had turned to good value. It began perhaps, with the magical properties of the enchanting Prince Ranji, incidentally, like W.G.Grace, a man who practised assiduously to perfect his technique. There was to be then, press talk of the magicianship of Indian spin bowlers and the spellbinding dexterity of Indian batsmen, similarly of the potency of West Indian quick bowlers and the exuberance of West Indian batsmen.

It was, needless to say, poppycock. There is no more a specific West Indian character than there is a South African or an Australian one. Of course people are conditioned by their habitat and they may also play out the accepted 'persona' attached to their culture. These changes, as was previously argued, are scarcely ethnic in causation. The Irish politician, Daniel O'Connell, who died in 1847, said, 'the Englishman has all the qualities of a poker, apart from its occasional warmth'. A century or so on, and that image was disintegrating, as new cultural values and social mores were imprinted by novel economic and political conditions. By gender, race, creed, region and age, there are a thousand examples of people adopting what anthropologists call 'appropriate behaviours', but that is a far cry from differences of genetic bequest. Slowly over time, the players and administrators of India and the West Indies attuned themselves to the rhythms and regimen of first-class and Test cricket. There was a professionalisation of concentration, of confidence, of careful preparation. This became evermore evident as it was harnessed to the flair that touches great cricketers in all climes and of all epochs.

Some West Indian cricketers did proceed to bat with the handsome radiance of Wally Hammond or bowl with the fiery speed of Harold Larwood, but others batted with the resolute caution of Herbert Sutcliffe or bowled with the patient doggedness of Wilfred Rhodes. Looking ahead, the splendid opening West Indian partnership of Gordon Greenidge and Desmond Haynes rather puts the 'temperament' argument in its place. Their widely varying personalities – they might, by some accounts, be mobilised to personify Carl Jung's poles of introversion and extroversion – conjoined to form the most lengthy such alliance in cricketing history, with 148 partnerships in 90 Tests.

In the last analysis, those who allowed Indians or West Indians within the sacred grove of cricket on the grounds of their ethnic adaptability to the properly English game must be asked, if Pakistanis, why not Egyptians, and if Barbadians, why not Cubans? Nurture, not, nature, is the answer. As the cane-wielding Wackford Squeers of Dotheboys Hall, in Charles Dickens' *Nicholas Nickleby*, remarked 'She's a rum 'un, is Natur.'

Third, and from the ICC downwards, the constitutional elements of cricket remained securely in place. Nothing more clearly illustrates this aspect of atrophy than the English County system. This rested on a reliance on a limited number of subscriber clubs, associated with what, in Victorian times, had been the formidable concept of the old-time shire. The change in the urban economy and in social life notwithstanding, this tight and enduring oligarchy of county clubs formed an extraordinary piece of petrifaction.

The county memberships stood jointly at about 50,000 in these years, while, to take 1935 as an example, roughly 1.3m watched the county championship programme. This was only a slight drop from the gates of Edwardian days, but the Football League had expanded attractively and from something closer to parity, football now possibly outnumbered cricket attendances by five to one. Some counties suffered financially. These included Sussex, Derbyshire, and also Leicestershire, which, in a panic-stricken moment, toyed with the idea of amalgamation with Lincolnshire.

The dysfunctional nature of the county club in regard of the needs of the game, the changing patterns of local government reorganisation, the rise of the conurbation and the gross commercialisation of top-class cricket will be discussed in a later chapter. For now a simple overall description must suffice. The Victorians, bold and assured, had experimented with the county structure as ebulliently as they had switched from round arm to over arm bowling. They had approved of eligibility and qualifications rulings and created a championship regulo. By the death of Edward VII in 1910, there were sixteen first-class counties. In the immediate post-war phase, Glamorgan became, in 1921, a first-class county. In 1992, a biblical lifetime later, Durham was admitted to the Championship Pantheon. Post-WWII flirtations with Buckinghamshire and Devon came to nothing. More significantly, no county has left or been dismissed. The 1937 MCC Findlay Commission, designed to find answers to the economic problems facing cricket, opted for reducing the first-class county list from seventeen to fifteen and playing more representative matches. That went down like a lead balloon.

Alongside the introversion of the age, there was a corresponding nerviness, perhaps most evident in the sometimes frenetic and dizzy fashions in music, dress and dance of the 1920s. Although the cricket authorities never faced up to the fundamental question of the county championship, they did contrive to fidget restively no less than eight times with the points system used in that competition in the inter-wars seasons. Altogether it is a monumental study in frozen institutionalism.

ENGLISH CRICKET BETWEEN THE WARS

Club cricket batted on. Building development and the need for allotments to provide wartime food supplies had not helped and in 1915 E.A.C.Thomson, a journalist, set in train the beginnings of the Club Cricket Conference, designed to protect the interests of non-competitive club cricket. Jack Williams, whose authorship of *Cricket and England; a Cultural and Social History of the Inter-war Years* (1999) and other studies deserves special commendation, recounts how church teams were still numerous. In Lancashire more than half the clubs in the 1920s were church clubs, with Sunday School cricket leagues common, although this dropped to something over a third in the 1930s. No other region enjoyed such clerical dominance, although, for example, a quarter of Halifax teams were church based in the opening decades of the 20th century. By 1939, the numbers of clubs with a church orientation were in general falling.

There is also evidence of plenty of clubs with an industrial origin. The Mining Industry Act of 1920 established the Miners' Welfare Fund, a levy of a penny on every ton of coal hewn for sale, with the purpose of encouraging social activities of all kinds, including cricket. By 1930 for instance, the number of works teams in the colliery town of Barnsley had risen to 18 out of the 101 recognised clubs in that district. Jack Williams also points elsewhere to the sponsorship of works teams at companies such as the Pilkington Glassworks at St Helens or the Rowntree firm in York, where there was a tradition of beneficent paternalism. As with football teams of clerical and vocational origins, it is not always easy to determine how involved were the relevant authorities, as opposed to the members of the flock or the employees using the church or the work-place as a focus for their more independent efforts. Nonetheless, church and work played their part in the formation and sustenance of English club cricket.

Jack Williams, given the fragmentary evidence, is reluctant to go beyond the cautious estimate that a minimum of 100,000 and a maximum of 400,000 adult males played weekly cricket regularly in these times, not quite as many as one would have expected, and rather less than the 600,000 young men playing soccer under the jurisdiction of the Football Association. Over against the cricket in the public and, increasingly, the grammar schools, probably no more than 10% of elementary schools were in a position to include cricket on the curriculum. Works and church teams may have tendered opportunities to the less well off and even the unemployed, but club cricket, especially in the more thriving and suburban southeast, could prove expensive. An annual subscription could be £1.50 or more, apart from the expenses of kit, equipment, travel and probably match fees, at a time when an engineer's weekly wage was often less than £3.00.

League cricket had its willing adherents. The fourteen clubs of the Blackburn-centred Lancashire League had a combined membership of 10,000 in 1933 and attracted 297,000 paying customers that summer. Between the wars and despite the economic slump, it was never lower than 200,000. In 1934 14,000 watched the Worsley Cup tie between Nelson and nearby Colne. This was when the West Indian star and Nelson professional, Learie Constantine, was biffing sixes, bowling at a blistering velocity and fielding like a galvanised panther for £25 a match and collections. Some southern clubs attracted good crowds as well. London's Mitcham Green occasionally played before attendances of 5000 or so, while 10,000 turned up to watch the Southampton Parks Final in 1933.

The desire to play – and maybe watch – cricket as a bucolic and countrified pastime was uppermost. There seems now to have been less direct reference to Christianity and more mention of the rustic idyll. Jack Williams quotes the publisher and writer, J.C.Squire, who in 1920 founded and captained the itinerant Invalids team and is the Mr Hodge of A.G.Macdonell's famous cricket sketch in *England, Their England* (1933). J.C.Squire wrote in 1930, of cricket's 'rural root', claiming that 'few men . . . would not rather play on a field surrounded by ancient elms and rabbit-haunted bracken than on a better field with flat black lands or gasworks around.' The pastoral tradition was being renewed and sustained.

Most other games continued to progress and adapt during the 20th century. To take one tiny instance, association football's strategies altered irrevocably. Jonathan Wilson's book, *The Inverted Pyramid*, analyses how soccer has travelled from having nine forwards, to eight, seven, five, two and finally the solitary striker of one of today's formations. The club structure has also been developed in another kind of inverted pyramid, with clubs enabled to rise – or fall– through the ranks of the leagues. Such is the turnover that only four of the original twelve of the Football League remain among the twenty of the English Premiership. In almost every other mainline sport it is possible to draw progressive lines of development, technical, locational and institutional, throughout the 20th century. It was not so with cricket, even if, late on, from the 1960s, there were the signs of renewed movement.

In the armchair and saloon bar debates about present and past sporting performers, it is probably simpler to compare and contrast cricketers than it is any other cadre of players. Visualise a resurrected W.G.Grace. With his quick, boyish brain, he would note the nuances of the present LBW and no ball regulations, he would nod with appreciation at the more generally consistent ability of the (never more than) eleven fielders, he would be pleased to note that bowling was less versatile than in his day, with its emphasis on medium and quick bowling, he would enjoy adjusting to the much improved mechanics of his bat and protective gear, he would eye with relishable anticipation the relative shortness of the boundaries and the generally flat condition of the covered wickets . . . an hour or so of such induction and he would be ready to score centuries galore. More sadly, his conception of fair play would not require much tweaking to render it at one with the approaches of the current era.

Fortunately, cricket was a beautiful corpse. Revivified for the 1919 season and thereafter, it gave rise to what Gerald Howat percipiently called 'the Second Golden Age', as in the same one repeated, with heroes buoyantly replacing those of the pre-1914 era. They accepted the mantle of the past, made little or no attempt to alter it, and richly celebrated it. It was if the wraiths of pre-1914 had cried 'encore.'

Domestically, Yorkshire, sternly adherent to the blood-cult of native-born players, ruled the county roost. There were tales of pregnant women being rushed over the shire border so that their baby, were it to be a boy, might benefit from whatever miasma descended upon the geographically fortunate. The supposition that somehow such advantage accrued was the rankest of superstitions. It might perhaps be argued that, if one were bred in a set of circumstances, one might be the more likely to adopt the local characteristics and values. A counter example, and there are many, is that of the Lancashire and England wicket-keeper, Richard Pilling, who was born of Lancashire parents in 1855 in Bedford, soon after which the family returned to Church, near Accrington, so that their son subsequently became more 'Lancastrian', in so far as that has any meaning, than someone born in Accrington who was removed to Bedford as a toddler.

Apart however, from a brief spell when Lancashire, prompted by the saturnine Australian quick bowler, Ted McDonald, topped the bill, it was mainly Yorkshire who took the between-wars laurels. Led by Brian Sellars, with Herbert Sutcliffe and Maurice Leyland, joined later by the young Len Hutton, the key batsmen, and with Hedley Verity a perceptively intelligent left hand spin bowler, they were a most formidable and completely expert outfit.

The Advent of the Middle-class Professional

The two leading champions of the Arthurian legend of this second golden age were the older Launcelot of Jack Hobbs and the younger Galahad of Walter Hammond.

Jack Hobbs was indeed knighted in 1953. His contemporary, George Robey, 'the Prime Minister of Mirth', and something of a cricket fan, was similarly dubbed in 1954, both of them the first professional performer in their business of cricket and music hall so to be celebrated, marked evidence to the impact on and acceptance of their trades in national life. Strangely untouched by the swirl of events around him, Jack Hobbs, for thirty years, simply scored runs. His tally of 61,237 first-class runs, his sum of 197 first-class centuries and his total of seventeen seasons in which he scored over 2000 runs, have never been surpassed. He shared in 106 partnerships of a hundred runs or more, many of them with his trusty Surrey opening partners, Tom Hayward and Andy Sandham. He lost four summers and a couple of winter tours as a result of World War I, missing out on a conservative estimate off a further 10,000 runs and forty centuries.

Wilfred Rhodes' respected opinion is that Jack Hobbs could have scored many more but that professionally, he paced himself consistently over the summers sometimes ousting himself, when times were propitious, to give someone else a chance. He admitted to yielding up his wicket 'to one of my old bowler mates', a sentiment perhaps patronising in sound to the modern ear – and certainly to the ear of the remorseless W.G.Grace or the prolific Don Bradman – but preferable to cheating and ill-temper. It is of interest that Jack Hobbs saw the beginnings of an innings as a problem for the bowler, who had to find a length, rather than the batsman, who had to play himself in, and he usually scored off the first ball of the day, characteristically with a neat push into the covers.

His combine of technical acumen and intelligent composure means that Jack Hobbs should be more exactly described as a craftsman in the best sense rather than an artist in the worst. He eschewed the temperamental excesses, associated sometimes with artistry, in favour of the dignity of labour and the pride of craftsmanship. He was schooled in the social conformity of Cambridge, born there in

1882, the son of a college servant. Even as minor businessman, Surrey committeeman and knight, he never seemed to want to abandon his rightful place, his ordered estate. In 1910 the writer F.G.D'Aeth categorised seven classes with social labels. John Berry Hobbs was 'put on collar in evening' but never 'visiting cards, some dine late.'

Churchgoer, devoted husband, who lovingly tended his ailing wife, Ada, for years, he himself died in 1963. As Alf Gover has related, he inherited correct manners from his Surrey elders and as senior professional insisted on decorum on the field and in the dressing room. His innate fineness of character obviated any sense of priggishness. Like Giles Winterbourne, in Thomas Hardy's *The Woodlanders*, 'he was one of nature's very gentleman'. Like the proud wheelwright or the careful engineer, he prosecuted his craft with unvarying application. His flawless technique was such that Neville Cardus said Hobbs never made 'a hasty or a bad shot' and the only way to dismiss him was to persuade him to play 'a wrong good shot' to a misjudged ball. He ran astutely between the wickets and brought that same judgement of a run to bear on his clever work as a swift cover point.

'The Master' bestrode both golden ages, the first in the daring manner of Prince Hal, with much offside panache, the second in the stately fashion of Henry V, with more reliance on back-foot and onside play. Jack Hobbs bridged the divide with immaculate authority. He was, both technically and socially, the final perfection of the model cricket professional.

John Arlott celebrated this maturation of the cricketing craft in his poem, 'To John Berry Hobbs, on his Seventieth Birthday 16 December 1952':

> The game the Wealden rustics handed down
> Through growing skill became, in you, a part
> Of sense; and ripened to a style that showed
> Their country sport matured to balanced art.

The old firm of Jack Hobbs and Herbert Sutcliffe became, innings for innings, the most successful opening partnership ever. They shared 26 opening stands of a hundred, fifteen of them for England, that is, fifteen out of the 37 times they were in national coalition. In these prodigious enterprises they assembled 3204 runs, at an amazing and unchallenged average of 89. Herbert Sutcliffe's intensity of concentration and assiduous composure were riveting. It is said that he could dismiss an error or a lucky escape from his mind in an instant, so clearly intent was he on playing the next ball. Once, at Old Trafford, when he had played a ball temperately and then remained still and statuesque in position, a wag cried, 'what do you think you are? A bloody war memorial?' It was an alliance of two superb batting technicians.

Their origins were similarly unremarkable. Herbert Sutcliffe was born in 1894 in Summerbridge, near Harrogate, but was orphaned by the age of ten and reared in Pudsey by an aunt. After a sparse elementary schooling he was apprenticed as a 'clicker', a fastener of soles to uppers in the boot and shoe trade, but soon made his way into clerical work and also into club and then county cricket. Perhaps the most astonishing aspect of his early life was that, despite this ordinary upbringing, he was commissioned as a second lieutenant in the Green Howards (the Yorkshire Regiment) towards the end of the 1914/18 War. Professional cricketers were normally other rankers, like Air Mechanic Hobbs or Private Patsy Hendren, and this was before Sutcliffe had even played in a first-class cricket match.

There was a self-assurance about Herbert Sutcliffe, a personality that, for instance, the youthful Len Hutton found awesome. He was radically ambitious in terms of self-improvement. He became a major in the Second World War, he established a prosperous sports outfitters in Leeds which, with exquisite irony, employed the archetypal amateur and Sutcliffe's former England captain, Douglas Jardine, as company secretary. Crushing the broadness from his accent, striving to dress and behave like such as Jardine, and exuding some haughtiness in so doing, he sought to out-do the amateur. He once chastised his younger Yorkshire colleague and hero-worshipper, the fast bowler, Bill Bowes, for following the example of his amateur skipper and not wearing his blazer to lunch. 'We must do everything better than the amateurs', he instructed, 'Your manners must be better, and, if possible, you must speak and dress better, too.' With great dignity, and after some contemplation, he refused the Yorkshire captaincy in 1927. His chief objective was to transform the lot of the paid cricketer from that of a trade to that of a profession.

To their enormous embarrassment, Jack Hobbs would, even in his later years refer to callow student cricketers as 'sir' and 'mister'. His great friend and partner, Herbert Sutcliffe, was much more upwardly mobile. While Jack Hobbs gave a substantial sense of propriety to the job of being a cricket professional, it was Herbert Sutcliffe, imperturbable of mind and immaculate of mien, who took the suburban route to middle class uprightness. In so doing, he paralleled the stance of Henry Cotton in the field of golf at much the same time. Henry Cotton, fighting the image of the golf 'pro' as the club's lackey, was the prototype for the modern, highly paid golfer.

Herbert Sutcliffe's ally in this struggle was Walter Hammond. Despite losing six seasons to World War II, he scored over 50,000 first-class runs, at an average of 56.10, and, as testimony to his physical and mental staying power, he has more double centuries, with 36, and centuries in each innings of the same match, with seven, than any other batsman. He took 819 catches and, his reactions seemingly unerring, some regard him as the best slip fielder of his age. He also took a tidy number of wickets, 732 in all. Apart from the figures, both critics and fans raved over the radiant majesty of his style. Most commentators rate him third behind W.G.Grace and Jack Hobbs in the Valhalla of English batsmanship.

So much is non-negotiable but Wally Hammond left almost as sharp a social as a cricketing imprint on the game. He was born in 1903, the son of a regular soldier who rose through the ranks to be a major, sadly to lose his life in action in 1918. His mother ensured her son was well educated at Portsmouth Grammar School and then as a boarder at Cirencester Grammar School where his delight in sport marked him out for a cricketing destiny. He played for Gloucestershire and England as a professional but adopted, like Herbert Sutcliffe, an upmarket mode of life, with London tailored suits, golf with rich businessmen and friendships with aristocratic families. His first wife, Dorothy Lister, was the daughter of a flourishing Bradford textile merchant, and his second, Sybil Ness-Harvey, the child of a moneyed and prestigious Natal family.

But Wally Hammond took this embourgeoisement of the proletariat a step further. In 1937 he rose, like his uniformed father, from the civilian ranks and became an amateur and captained England, or rather, to deploy the correct usage, he became a 'gentleman'. In fact, he forewent his £400 a year from Gloucestershire, plus Test and tour fees and some part-time earnings, for the £2000 per annum of a directorship with the Marsham Tyres Company, together with leave to play as much cricket as he wished. Economically, it was an excellent move. In the Second World War he entered the RAF and proceeded to the rank of squadron leader, although it should be noted that several professionals, among them Hedley Verity and Leslie Ames, the Kent and England wicket-keeper, also achieved officer status.

Curiously, the story has echoes of that of his great predecessor with Gloucestershire and England, W.G.Grace. Like Grace, he hovered uneasily between the social echelons, the child of a middle class family and middle class aspirations but without the Oxbridge and/or financial clout to play initially as an amateur. The biographers infer that, as opposed to the acceptance of their stable role of the likes of Wilfred Rhodes or Jack Hobbs, Wally Hammond did appear a trifle confused, even discontented, with his lot.

Others were disconcerted, too. Neville Cardus watched with alarm the disappearance of some of his working class heroes, those old-style northern professionals with respectable artisan roots. Like Lowry's matchstick men they had given him copy and made his name, as, with polished boots and with watch-chains across their waistcoats, they strolled with quiet pride the cobbled streets of their townships, unassumingly acknowledged and unenviously admired by their neighbours with jobs in mill or mine. Neville Cardus took exception to Sutcliffe speaking 'not with the accents of Yorkshire but of Teddington'. He saw the Saville Row suits of Herbert Sutcliffe and Walter Hammond as the Russian Tsar may have reacted to the hammer and sickle; they were signs of the overthrow of the feudal order. Neville Cardus bemoaned the fact that 'the county cricketer in certain instances has become a man of bourgeois profession'.

This relatively small group of cricketers who, like Wally Hammond and Herbert Sutcliffe, aspired for suburban niceties, exemplify just about the only element in inter-wars English cricket where there was a progressive shift. This was of a piece with the only element in English life where there was movement. The suburban dream, with the linear styling of ribbon development of neat gardens, 'the religion of home improvement' and 'table ready' foodstuffs, with high streets lined with multiples and chain stores, was unfolding. Over against the Depression there was a rise in some manufactures, especially of consumer goods such as light bulbs, cosmetics and fountain pens. The sale of vacuum cleaners shot from 18,000 in 1930 to 410,000 in 1935.

What is also interesting is that this all affected cricketers more than footballers. Recalling Wally Hammond as an illustration, John Arlott said that 'the established cricket professional in the thirties could afford to run a car; the average football professional could not' – and Wally Hammond was the first cricketer to own a sponsored motor car. There was even the chance, as Wally Hammond viewed it, of owning one's own home. As John Arlott also pointed out, there was little radicalism in the professional ranks. Whether they were the quietly deferential in the Jack Hobbs mould or boldly aspirational after the Hammond model, they were politically conservative, the exceptions, such as the outspoken Sam Cook of Gloucestershire's immediate post-war days, being small in number and effectiveness.

'One of the great athletes', according to John Arlott, 'of British history', Hammond played football for Plymouth Argyle and Bristol Rovers, and some judged him a potential international, but he opted for cricket and the likelihood of overseas tours. His economic calculations were correct. When he captained England at cricket in the late 1930s, he was earning as much as eight times the income of Eddie Hapgood, the distinguished Arsenal and England captain.

However, in never, like Denis Compton and a few others, mixing the two sports over a longish period, Wally Hammond's reasoning may have also been social. We return to his falling between two sociological stools. His insightful biographer, Gerald Howat, shrewdly suggests, 'the football world was more proletarian than he cared for. He was a little different from the rest of the Bristol Rovers squad.' They were working class to a man.

Thus perhaps the most significant aspect of English domestic cricket during this time was the beginnings of the gentrification of its professionals. Where George Hirst had coached at Eton and Wilfred Rhodes at Harrow, Herbert Sutcliffe would send his son, William Herbert Hobbs Sutcliffe, to Rydal School. With his troika of initials, he would play for Yorkshire as an amateur and, doubtless to his father's delight, captained the white rose eleven in 1956 and 1957. Herbert Sutcliffe's famed successor, Len Hutton, would later have his son, Richard, schooled at Repton, prior to his career with Cambridge University, Yorkshire and England.

In the meantime, Wally Hammond had other things on his mind, to the extent that many critics believe his always ambivalent personality was quite affected by this concern. For the leading historical searchlight on cricket in those inter-wars years should really be directed more on Australia than England. The formidable figure of Don Bradman was revealing his vast potential.

Two more grounds depicting two very different genres of cricket club. Top, Pudsey St Lawrence Cricket Club, one of the many urban based league clubs that brought such excellent cricket to the northern and midland towns of England, and, bottom, Merchant Taylor's Old Boys CC, Hertfordshire; the old boys teams of famous schools made a telling contribution to recreational cricket in Britain.

CHAPTER TEN
BRADMANIA

'The Don'

When Don Bradman died in 2001, at the age of 92, a legion of obituarists analysed his impact on cricket and on the Australian nation and some of their analogues – Winston Churchill, Jack Kennedy, Diana, Princess of Wales, Shakespeare, the Pope – did not seem unduly extravagant.

THE ASCENDANCY OF THE DON

His family politely declined the honour of a state funeral. Don Bradman, ever a warily private figure, had always refused offers of diplomatic or political character but he was knighted in 1949 and appointed Companion of the Order of Australia in 1979. After his astounding cricketing ventures, he had been a prosperous businessman and cricket administrator but he shunned the limelight. Nonetheless, millions mourned his death.

He was born in 1908, with the new Australian state just seven years older and declared his intent as a cricketer from his teenage days. He made a century on first-class debut for New South Wales against South Australia in 1927 and soon began his gargantuan Test career. In 1930 he made the then highest individual score; 452, not out, for New South Wales versus Queensland, and it is still the record for an Australian and in Australia. He toured England several times with conspicuous success – his 334 at Leeds in 1930 was the then highest ever Test score – and moved, for business reasons, from the New South Wales to the South Australia state team but wherever he played, he sustained a merciless run-rate. He himself regarded the 254 he thrillingly made at Lord's against England in 1930 as his best ever technical innings: 'every ball went where it was intended, including the one that got me out', a blinding catch by Percy Chapman in the covers. Moreover, Donald Bradman contrived to be a wily and quick-witted captain into the bargain.

An unselfish player always intent on team victory, he had rapidly come to comprehend a quandary hinted at earlier in this text, namely, that the cricketer has two foes – his opponents and the old enemy of swiftly passing time. To combat both he combined two extremes of batsmanship. He embarked on a risk-free tenacity of defensive approach together with a resolve to score very quickly, that his bowling colleagues might have time to take twenty wickets. One intriguing feature of his batting is that he hit very few sixes – only six in Test matches – for he was determined not to hit the ball in the air, and yet the velocity of his batting was tremendous. Like the American Civil War general, he believed that the spoils went to those 'who got thur fustest with the mostest.'

Wiry and tireless, he moved into position quickly and late from a stance of serene stillness to play the full range of shots. His concentration and composure became legendary. The sagacious West Indian critic, C.L.R. James, said other cricketers had 'inhibitions Bradman never knew', as he indomitably undertook – Neville Cardus's phrase – 'the cool deliberate murder or spifflication of the bowling.' The statistics are most persuasive. In the broadest of brush-strokes, he totalled 28,067 first-class runs in 338 innings at an average of 95.14, including 117 centuries, 37 of them double centuries. The statistician may weave all fashion of mathematical spells from such numbers. The fundamental fact is that Donald Bradman scored a century every 2.88 innings and a double century every 6.13 innings – and that descries a sportsman who has touched perfection.

Among his contemporaries were Joe Davis, who held the world snooker championship title from 1927 to 1946 and only lost four games on even terms, Gordon Richards, who rode 4,870 winners out of 21,843 mounts, with 26 championships and a record 269 winners in a season, and Joe Louis, who held the world heavyweight boxing championship from 1937 until his retirement, undefeated, in 1949, having defended it 25 times, more, in aggregate, than his eight predecessors. Not even these three geniuses could outdo him.

The Australian analyst, Charles Davis, in his study *The Best of the Best*, claimed that 'the Don' was the best sportsman of all time. With elaborate arithmetic, he calibrates Bradman's ratio as 4.4, well in front of the second-placed Pele with 3.3. Jack Nicklaus would have had to have won 25 rather than 18 major golf championships and Michael Jordan would have had to have increased his basketball points per game from 32 to 43 for either to have emulated Bradman. One might cavil. Donald Bradman was, of course, a great batsman rather than a great cricketer; he never sought to be an all-round cricketer in the style of W.G.Grace or Gary Sobers. Again, the excellent sports analyst, Peter Hartland, has shown that W.G.Grace, when 25 and having scored over 10,000 runs at an average of 61, was at that moment twice has good as the next best contemporary player, a dominance not even Bradman could match. All in all, however, few would deny that Don Bradman was clearly the most efficacious batsman there has been.

He also held a significant cultural position. The young Australian nation was struck three quick body blows in its first fifty years of existence. These were the First World War, in which 14.5% of its mobilised troops were slain; the Depression, when 29% of the labour-force were unemployed and the national income dropped by 30% in three years; and the Second World War, inclusive of the threat of Japanese invasion. Australian historians seem agreed that, from the late 1920s to the post-war years, Don Bradman acted as a unifying focus for a battered social fabric and a damaged self-belief. Yet he had secular sainthood thrust upon him, for he was no seeker after power or celebrity as such.

It might also be countered that, as Charles Williams argued in his fine biography, *Bradman* (1996), there was a severe national rift that exhibited itself in cricket. In a crudely oversimplified equation, it was Protestant, Masonic, lower middle class, English, royalist and subdued versus Roman Catholic, working class, Irish, republican and noisy. Bradman was the unwitting standard bearer of the former grouping, although one imagines some envy was also involved. E.W.Swanton, as a graphic instance, recollected how, in the press box, Jack Fingleton and Bill O'Reilly, colleagues of Bradman from across that socio-political divide, choked with mirth as their old adversary failed in his final Test match at the Oval in 1948, when Eric Hollies bowled him out for 'the most famous duck in history'. Four runs, and Bradman would have had a Test average of 100.

There have really only been two genuine icons in cricket; Grace the founder and Bradman the consolidator. Sir Donald Bradman is definitely of that tiny ilk, to the point where obituaries that compared him aesthetically with Shakespeare, Michelangelo and Keats slightly missed the point. He cannot be exclusively corralled within a classical, elitist culture, for his fame was much, much more popular than that. At the risk of offending those who regard Bradman in such high artistic, even in quasi-religious tones, it has to be urged that the logical comparisons are with the other more populist global art-forms such as cinema or pop music, coupling Bradman with Charlie Chaplin, Walt Disney and Elvis Presley. Above all, Sir Donald Bradman, most functional of batsmen and the idol of millions, is simply the most famous Australian there has been.

Rightly, he stands at the centre of a process by which the chief focus of cricket emigrated from England to Australia. It began with that expatriate nostalgia that makes, for instance, the Caledonian and Hibernian traditions of the USA more colourful than those of their respective homelands. As previously observed, cricket was the way in which the Australians venerated and emulated 'Englishry', before moving on to see it as a chief medium for rivalship with the old country. It quickly became the cultural flagship of a country just a few years old. Nations and regions sometimes have mono-economies, like Bolivia and tin. Similarly, they often have social or artistic equivalents, like Wales and choral singing. Plainly, the Welsh do not boast an extra tonsil or some form of St Cecilia's gene. A mix of economic practices and religious habits produced and bequeathed that famous tuneful flair; very soon it became the cement for communities and the route to social respect and to self-esteem, just as the 19th century township of Sutton-in-Ashfield, Nottinghamshire, it may be remembered, had produced scores of talented cricketers. New Zealand, a later developer towards nationhood than Australia, adopted the newer sport of rugby union in similar manner.

In a sense, it was slightly old-fashioned, in so far as the domination of Victorian cricket was being challenged by other sports such as the football codes, even before World War I. Even so, Don Bradman was never challenged as Australia's leading idol, such was the adoration of cricket and of its chief protagonist. Indeed, it is difficult to judge quite where the balance of cause and effect lay in the interaction of the game and its mighty performer. An infant nation, the Australians had no legendary heroes apart from Don Bradman. The British had a lengthy register, stretching back to Alfred the Great and Hereward the Wake. Even W.G.Grace, in the bustling and hyperactive Victorian epoch, did not have it all his own way in the celebrity stakes. Gladstone and Disraeli in politics, Marie Lloyd in the music hall, Gilbert and Sullivan in the musical theatre, Charles Dickens in literature, to say nothing of Queen Victoria herself may be numbered among others feted by the Victorian populace. It is this contrast – the dense tapestry of English history against the thin skein of Australian beginnings – that helps makes Grace a Mosaic and Bradman a Messianic figure. [1]

AUSTRALIAN DOMINANCE

Whatever the explanations, one can but marvel at the way in which a new nation of a just a few million souls, the huge majority locked into the seaboard areas of a massive island, with all kinds of transportation and allied problems, sought to strive, with vivacious success, against the motherland at cricket. By a systematic concentration on

1 This appreciation of Don Bradman draws heavily on the author's obituary of the great Australian in the *Wisden* of 2002.

and a social encouragement of competitive sport, especially through its intense 'grade' or league cricket, Australia laid out its cultural stall with some defiance and authority. Some critics pointed to the Australian delight in indulging youthful talents, compared with the rectitude of the more staid English system, where club cricket obligingly catered for all ages and talents.

The Australian authorities opted for an eight ball over in 1919, but otherwise adopted an orthodox approach, even to the point of trying to evade the draw. It was the Australian custom to play out matches to the full, with Tests sometimes lasting seven or even, in one instance, eight days. The Third Test of the 1946/47 English tour, which lasted six days, was the first drawn such game in Australia since the rain-affected First Test in 1881/82. Sheffield Shield matches were timeless until 1926/27, then were five days until 1930/31 and four days thereafter. Support was hearteningly high. During the five inter-wars Ashes series crowds gradually increased from some 401,000 in 1920/21, average over 20,000 a day, to 944,000, average over 36,000, in 1936/37.

Such teeming hordes were well rewarded for their passion. Having shown their mettle in the days of Fred Spofforth and Warren Armstrong, the Australians proceeded to dominate in the post-war years. E.W.Swanton, without resource to the theatrical, simply called the English tourists' visit to Australia in 1920/21 a 'slaughter', with all five Tests lost. The Australians accompanied their opponents back home on the same ship and more or less repeated the performance, with the first three matches of the rubber in England won by comprehensive margins. Results were not much better when England toured in 1924/25. The batting of G.C.Macartney and Warren Bardesley, the fierce pace of Ted McDonald and Jack Gregory and the guile of Arthur Mailey were in the van of this onslaught. With Hobbs and Sutcliffe in dominant form, and Maurice Tate showing the craft that led him to be respected as one of the best three or four fast-medium bowlers ever, England clawed back the Ashes with a single win in 1926. They also enjoyed a sumptuously successful tour of Australia over the winter of 1928/29, with Wally Hammond in rich form. That, and the controversial 'Bodyline' series of 1932/33, apart, Australia remained in the ascendant until the 1950s and for all the challenges from both England and the developing powers elsewhere, they remained cock of the Test-playing midden into the 21st century. Even when England scored 903 for 7 at the Oval, the highest ever Test innings total, with Len Hutton's then record 364 a major contribution, they clung tight to the Ashes.

'Bodyline', or, to use the less colourful epithet, 'leg theory' bowling was principally devised by the patrician Douglas Jardine, England's captain and a man who held bitter views about Australians. With as many as seven fielders on the on side, he directed the English fast bowlers, notably the speedy Harold Larwood and his Nottinghamshire colleague, Bill Voce, to bowl sustained short pitched deliveries aimed down the leg side. As is well known, this victorious assault led to diplomatic tumult and political tension at a high level, such was the potency of modern sport in the public sphere. Australia, at that moment, lacked the means to retaliate in kind, although they were well served otherwise in attack by the skilful resource of Bill O'Reilly and Clarrie Grimmett. Many regarded the 'Bodyline' approach as both dangerous and unsporting and, after some face-saving altercation, rule changes followed, mainly in the curtailment of fielders on the leg side. The occasional short-pitched ball or 'bumper' was by no means unknown but the intensity, from either end, of leg theory, was unprecedented.

It was a souring episode. Douglas Jardine seemed to vanish from the scene while his two professional charges, Harold Larwood and Bill Voce, were left unfairly to face the flak of now unfriendly authority. What should be emphasised is that Don Bradman was its unwitting cause. Had he not proved to be so awesome an opponent it is inconceivable that 'Bodyline' would have been designed. As it was, Don Bradman took on Larwood and company by retreating towards square leg and carving the ball away into the empty offside, rather as J.T.Tyldesley had played the more leisurely pace of leg spinners. The badge of failure was pinned on Bradman by English fans and he did score only one century in eight innings. It is a mark of the fear he induced that his average touched 50 in the series and it was adjudged some sort of an English triumph. All, relatively speaking, was sweetness and light again ere the Australians visited England in the summer of 1934.

A hallmark of the prestige of Australian cricket was the accumulation of large scores on sun-baked hard wickets in yawningly large stadia before massive crowds. Don Bradman was not the only accumulator. Dour Bill Ponsford was the first Australian and the second cricketer to score 400, to be exact, 429, against Tasmania for Victoria in 1922/23 and he followed this feat with 437 at the expense of Queensland in 1928/29. His opening partner for Victoria and Australia was the humane schoolmaster, Bill Woodfull, variously nicknamed 'the Wormkiller', 'the Rock' and 'the Unbowlable'. His batting was a devout application of his nonconformist beliefs. When out in the final Test at Melbourne in 1929, it was the first time he had been actually bowled for a year. Their very similar career averages – Ponsford on 65.19 and Woodfull 64.99 – locate them second and third in the all-Australian Test averages behind Bradman and leave them in the top handful of all batsmen.

It is no coincidence that it was Victoria who scored 1,059 against Tasmania in the 1922/23 season, before creating another first-class innings record at the Christmas of 1926 with 1107 against New South Wales, the only two examples of a thousand runs being accrued in a single innings.

From another angle, the advance of Australia might be assessed against the perspective not of a declining but of a stationary England. It fitted the rather static nature of England between the two wars. There was budding promise, too, in other parts of the British Empire, as first one and then another region achieved Test status. The West Indies gave some auguries of future glories, especially in the twinned pace assault of Learie Constantine and E.A.Martindale and in the luxuriant batting of George Challenor and George Headley. 'The Black Bradman', as the latter was nicknamed, and Constantine both had finely tuned tactical and leadership qualities, as Michael Manley, in his standard and detailed story of West Indian cricket published in 1998, makes clear. But they were black and at best lower middle class. As with the English amateur, in Michael Manley's words, 'it was the families that were accustomed to ruling who were assumed to produce the sons who were capable of leading;' Nonetheless, West Indian cricket was on the march. In 1934/35 they won a Test rubber against a strongish English eleven.

Global travel was still a strenuous exercise and thus cricket tours were time-consuming ventures. W.G.Grace rode his luck on board the steamship and benefited from the larger circulation of newspapers, many of them keen to report sporting matters, and from the existence of the telegraph. By 1900 the London evening papers sold 25,000 copies of their late editions, solely on the strength of cricket scores and several main cricket grounds had telegraph equipment installed. Don Bradman made do with much the same set of technical boosters; he had ended his career before the common usage of aircraft and television was to revolutionise the incidence and coverage of the game. The only shift in this respect in the inter-wars decades was the introduction of the radio and its deployment for cricketing commentary.

Freed from its initial deployment for military and naval intelligence, the wireless became available to private citizens after the Great War, with the *Daily Mail's* sponsorship of a broadcast of songs by Dame Nellie Melba, herself of Australian stock, personifying that change. In 1927 the British Broadcasting Company, primarily funded from 1922 by a group of wireless manufacturers under exclusive post office licence, became the more famous Corporation, as a model of public service broadcasting, under the direction of the Calvinistically austere John Reith. By 1939 there were 10m wireless licences held in the United Kingdom, so that much of the nation was at the behest of what John Reith approvingly termed 'the brute force of monopoly.'

It was, however, and deservedly so given their commitment and prowess, the Australians who led the broadcasting way. The first Test match ball-by-ball commentaries were aired during the 1923/34 Test series in Australia. The first English cricket broadcasts followed in 1927 and after shaky beginnings, listeners soon became accustomed to the composed utterances of Howard Marshall. The gentler pace of cricket appeared from the onset to lend itself to the new medium, possibly more so than the quicker dynamics of football or rugby, where the staccato cry of a secondary broadcaster referred the hearer to a *Radio Times* grid – 'square one' – to locate the point of action.

Its tones were at one with the concept of the 'integrated culture', for surely the majority of British families bought into the Reithian values, widely acknowledging their middlebrow intent. The quiet composure of the highly successful *Children's Hour* programme, itself named after the earnest poem by Henry Wadsworth Longfellow, is an example.

Such well-mannered cricket coverage was a complement to the more literary press accounts of cricket replacing the somewhat dull descriptions of the pre-1914 years. Neville Cardus, writing his lyrical profiles in the *Manchester Guardian*, was the doyen of a corps of correspondents who chose gloss, not matt, to paint their cricketing pictures. The affection for annuals and magazines continued. Pelham Warner was the founder-editor in 1921 of *The Cricketer*, originally a weekly journal, and destined, later as a monthly, to enjoy considerable longevity. Radio, newspapers and magazines all contributed to the new look of English cricket as a pastoral art, with, for all the ethical purity inferred, less of a religious patina.

It is then more than trite coincidence that the novel generally regarded as the best cricket-based story was published in these inter-wars years. Hugh de Selincourt (1878-1951) drew on his experience of captaining the West Sussex village side of Storrington in writing *The Cricket Match*, published in 1924. Amidst a legion of admirers, J.M.Barrie claimed it was 'the best book written about cricket, or any other sport', while John Arlott judged that 'one cricket book stands above the remainder . . . cricket at some points seems the theme, at others (it is) incidental, which means that it is the convincing background of the fully realised novel.'

A little like the *Mrs Galloway* of Virginia Woolf or the *Ulysses* of James Joyce, the time-frame is intensified to a day, to, that is, the daylight hours of 24 August 1921 when the home team of Tillingfold have a fixture with their old rivals, Raveley. The cricket provides both the framework and the kernel of the novel. The cricket does for the novel what the Church of England does for Anthony Trollope's *Barchester Towers*; it is at once of importance itself and the stage for the interplay of character. This microcosmic study of English society reveals differences of temperament and age in persuasive and never wooden style. For the purposes of this text, where there is some emphasis on the interplay of class in cricket as in everyday British life, the social cameos are distinctively telling. Thus there is the privileged Edgar Trine, scion of the squirearchy, son of the big house, mixing for sporting, but hardly for social, reasons with Sid Smith, the impoverished bricklayer and quick bowler. They come together for the pleasure of playing cricket for their local village team.

WARTIME AND POST-WAR PLEASURE

World War II broke out all too quickly after World War I. It was met in Britain with resignation rather than frenzy. The attitude to cricket, indeed, to entertainment at large, had altered. This was total war, with their families occasionally in more peril than the combatants, and there were also longuers, making for a wholly different tempo and response. In addition, the psychological understanding of morale was more sophisticated than in the previous conflict. Although a few Colonel Blimps in the War Office objected to Vera Lynn, believing her emphasis on sentimental songs to be debilitating of the martial sinews, they were out-voted. It was accepted that longing and nostalgia had its place as part of the relaxation and recuperation of a weary population, both military and civil.

The BBC livened up in answer to the martial call. Most notably, Tommy Handley's *ITMA* ran for an amazing 312 editions in twelve series from 1939, leaving a linguistic imprint – 'Mrs Mopp'; 'I don't mind if I do'; 'TTFN: ta ta for now' on the English language and cocking a genial snook at the heavy bureaucracy of a planned wartime economy. It had upwards of 30m domestic and worldwide weekly listeners, and, along with some other radio shows, its content was analysed and discussed in schoolyard, barrack room, munitions factory and shopping queue the morning after. *ITMA* was the iconic morale-booster.

Moreover, there was the also question of war charities. The Red Cross and other such bodies gained considerably from the funds raised by cricket matches. Lady Kemsley's *Daily Dispatch* War Fund XI, with a full programme of Sunday matches around the northwest of England, chiefly organised by the administratively able Lancashire and England wicketkeeper, George Duckworth, is one such example of activities that combined relaxation and fund-raising.

Thus, and although first-class cricket closed down, there was plenty of watchable cricket of a good standard, played under 'club' conditions, chiefly over a day with sporting declarations prominent. Cricket fans responded in profusion. Probably the most intriguing aspect about wartime cricket was its popularity. A surprising fact is that, over the war period, expenditure on leisure increased by 120%, inclusive of entertainments tax. With food both rationed and heavily subsidised, with clothing and petrol similarly curtailed, with holidays difficult to organise for all kinds of reasons – hence the 'Holidays at Home' initiative, which rather suited local cricket offerings – there was, with full employment and, against some increase in the cost of living, a 90% rise in incomes. So there was more money for the cinema, the theatre, the pub and the sports arenas, activities that might be enjoyed for a few hours' release from the rigours of the war effort.

In peaceful 1939 Lord's had attracted 330,000 customers over some 60 days cricket, an average of 5500 a day. In war-torn 1945 414,000 poured through the turnstiles on each of 30 days, at an average of 13,500 a day – and the gates had to be locked four times. In 1944 and 1945 Nottinghamshire averaged 2,300 takers for each of the ten or eleven weekend matches arranged by H.A.Brown, the diligent county secretary. In 1939 Nottinghamshire attracted only two paying daily attendances of more than 2000; there were four gates over 4000 in 1945. Similar evidence may be adduced from other parts of the nation.

By 1945 there was some resumption of first-class cricket, with five closely fought 'Victory' Tests against the Australian services team and a thrilling England and Dominions clash that the latter won by 45 runs. In a paradoxical twist, the Australians were captained by the non-commissioned soldier, Lindsay Hassett, who steadfastly refused that honour, whilst the other ten were often Royal Australian Air Force officers. Keith Miller took the first of many bows in these last years of the war and it is a mark of the strength of Australian cricket that, apart from Hassett and Miller and the wicketkeeper, Stan Sismey, scarcely any of the others were prominent in first-class cricket thereafter, although they had so closely matched strong English sides.

If one were looking for other portents, there was news from the West Indies, where Trinidad and Barbados, but not, because of travel difficulties, Jamaica, had retained first-class habits. In February 1946 Clyde Walcott and Frank Worrell added a premonitory 574 for the Barbados fourth wicket against Trinidad. There was some good cricket in South Africa, with the motoring magnate, Lord Nuffield, funding extensive schoolboy coaching during these years, and from India, where Denis Compton and the handsome Nottinghamshire bat, Reg Simpson, starred. In Egypt Jim Laker was making an early name for himself in forces' cricket, alongside South Africans like Dudley Nourse and New Zealanders like Martin Donnelly.

The boom continued after the war. The public were anxious, or so it appeared, to take a last fond look at the cigarette card stars of yesteryear. The counties were obliged, under laws that promised serving men a return to their peacetime employment, to provide work for the pre-1939 professionals, many of whom had managed to play some cricket during the wartime seasons. Furthermore, there were few youthful challengers. Although approaching a hundred young men were given first-class debuts in 1946, few made the grade. Statisticians rightly point to the records that would have tumbled had the likes of Bradman, Hammond, Hutton and Compton enjoyed those six lost seasons, but another form of loss were of those who never were. If one scrutinises the births of English first-class cricketers, there is something close to a black hole in the years 1921-25. Would-be cricketers born in and around that phase lost the nursery period, during which the tender roots of their talents might have been cultivated. Tom Graveney, born in 1927, is almost the only toweringly gifted English player born in the mid 1920s.

The county scene thus resembled the matching of several Dad's Armies. Had a cricket buff Rip Van Winkle slumbered on a county ground from 1939 to 1946, he may, on awakening, not have noticed much difference. It would be the mid 1950s before a rich harvest of cricketers came to England's aid. These included the lethal fast bowlers, Fred Trueman, Brian Statham and Frank Tyson and the last bloom of the amateur batting convention, Colin Cowdrey, Peter May and David Sheppard. Their birthdays were around the early 1930s.The English batting, with Len Hutton and Lancashire's Cyril

Washbrook a doughty opening pair, and Denis Compton and Bill Edrich, plus Joe Hardstaff, the attractive Nottinghamshire star, to follow, was sound enough, but the deaths on military service of Hedley Verity and Ken Farnes, the Essex quick bowler, left the attack over reliant on the diligently willing arm of the stalwart Alec Bedser, with Godfrey Evans ebullience personified behind the stumps.

The 'Vintage Summer' – John Arlott's title – of 1947 formed the pinnacle of English domestic cricket. The county championship has usually been a competition in which one or two bowlers have been prominent in the winning of the crown. In the sunshine of 1947, Middlesex, with adequate journeyman bowlers, soared away with prodigious batting feats. Both Denis Compton, that mudlark of a genius, and pugnacious Bill Edrich scored over 3000 runs each this season, as records tumbled. Denis Compton, entertaining, mercurial, boyishly smiling, certainly lightened the mood of the post-war years. He was, after Charles Dickens; 'the Sparkler of Albion' – and, with his well-remembered advertising for Brylcreem, he pointed to a later scene of team and personal sponsorship.

There were record attendances, too. Close on three millions watched first-class cricket in this Indian Summer. That approximates closely to 10,000 for every day's cricket, an unheard of series of gates. Yorkshire had total attendances, excepting members, of almost 300,000, while Kent drew 200,000 through the turnstiles, twice as many as in 1939. Even in the moister 1946 there had been sufficient customers for all counties to break even on gate receipts, without any of them having to turn, cap in hand, to a generous patron. Not since the spacious days of the Octarchy, back in mid-Victorian times, had this been achieved.

A slightly disorientated All-India courteously braved the dampness and rationing of 1946 to play the first post-war tests in England, with the elegant and prolific opener, V.M.Merchant, in stylish form. The South Africans, solid in batting, fragile in bowling, enjoyed the brighter climes of 1947, while, in 1949, the New Zealanders steadily played three-day draws to demonstrate they were ready for five day Test cricket. The realities of world cricket were however, revealed over the winter of 1946/47 and the summer of 1948, when the Australian Juggernaut crushed England twice.

Apart from a sorrowful absence of quick bowlers, the English line-up was by no means impoverished, but the Australian 'Invincibles' are regarded by many commentators as the best international team there has been. Their names are worthy of rapt inscription. Arthur Morris and Sid Barnes obdurately built the necessary plinth for the exposition of some fluid stroke play from Linday Hassett, the now veteran Bradman and Neil Harvey, bursting with youthful flair. Relaxed and carefree in his princely skills came Keith Miller, coupling his eye-catching batting with his hostile bowling. With Ray Lindwall, no slouch himself with the bat, they formed the first of the post-war rapid fire twin attacks, with Bill Johnston an excellent deputy. Don Tallon, neatest of wicket keeper and a useful bat, completed the regular stem of the team. The other places went to the all-rounder Sam Loxton or the batsman, Bill Brown, with Ernie Toshack or Ian Johnson the spin bowler. The fielding was uniformly of high class, with some brilliant standout performances, such as Neil Harvey at cover point. If one were picky, one might have hoped for a spinner in the Clarrie Grimmett/Arthur Mailey category, but, that wee hint of a blemish apart, they were magnificent and they were winners.

Then the decade ended with 'cricket's Hungary', its equivalent of the Hungarian mauling of English football hopes at Wembley in 1953. In 1950 England lost for the first time on home territory to the West Indies and Lord's rang with joyous Calypso rhythms. They included two superb units; in brilliant batting the Three 'Ws', Everton Weekes, Clyde Walcott and Frank Worrell; in bewildering bowling, the twin spin combine of the tyros, Sonny Ramadhin and Alf Valentine.

This tale of Australian authority and West Indian promise was the more authentic reality than the Brylcreem sheen of 1947. The buccaneering exploits of Denis Compton and the great hosts that foregathered to admire his audacious talents were, in essence, the last 'hurrah' of traditional county cricket. As John Arlott was wisely to conclude, we were living in 'a kind of cloud cuckoo land.' It was never really to be the same again.

THE PIVOTAL 1940S

The 1940s was the pivotal decade of the century. The United Kingdom, for all the horrors of the blitz, did not suffer the same dislocation during World War II as most of Europe and huge tracts of the Far East. Nevertheless, wartime conditions were largely sustained in the post-war years. Full employment and improved wages were retained but there was continued rationing, national service, the presence of American troops and the alarums of the Korean War and other emergencies. They were tough times. David Kynaston, in his magisterial *Age of Austerity; 1945-51* (2007), concludes that these 'extraordinarily hard' years were 'in some ways even harder than the years of the war itself.'

The domestic life of the nation certainly saw something of a continuum from war to peace. On the platform of so-called 'War Socialism', with its bureaucratic controls and extensive planning, the 1945/51 Labour government led by the laconic Clement Attlee, negotiated a vast legislative programme of collectivism. The Welfare State, its centrepiece the National Health Service, the spread of New Towns, together with a major council house building schedule, and the taking into public ownership of a raft of utilities, constituted 'the silent revolution'.

There was a pragmatic, if rather grey, air about these years. Unlike the aftermath of the First World War, when the mood, after the vain promises of 'homes fit for heroes to live in', soon turned largely to a yearning for past splendours, the practical question asked of every post-1945 activity and institution was a forward-looking 'quo vadis' . . . whither goeth thou? The public looked not for miracles but for realistic responses to tough questions. In the main, and despite the severe difficulties, they were reasonably well served. The keyword was Reconstruction, with a defiant capital 'R'. Apart from the sweeping political and organisational changes, there were economic advances in fields such as the aircraft, chemical and electrical industries and, culturally, in music, ballet, broadcasting and several sports, including street-wise football.

The Age of Austerity was, socially speaking, still a middlebrow epoch. There were censored films, respectable and respectful newspapers, carefully chosen public library books and a still rather unrelaxed BBC nurturing upright opinions. In the post-war years, Wilfred Pickles *Have A Go* programme, drawing a listenership of over 20m a week, and broadcast from different vicinities each time, sustained the overall sense of shared communal values. It led some commentators to muse whether, had he espoused such ambition, Wilfred Pickles with his comprehensive appeal to 'lords and labourers, knights and knocker-uppers', might have sought political power.

Although divorce and illegitimacy numbers tripled, the serious crime rate, already low, actually dipped slightly after the war, as community disciplines held firm. In the first two post-war general elections there were highly responsible voting turnouts in excess of 80%, figures astounding by today's lazier standards. A.J.P.Taylor said that in the war, 'the British people came of age . . . tolerant, patient and generous'. It is a kindly but well-considered verdict, and one that was largely vindicated during the immediate post-war years.

The tempo of life was not so much, as is sometimes claimed, slow, but deliberate and regimented. It was measured by the school bell, the factory hooter, the BBC's six pips, the army bugler and the holiday camp *reveille*. The human emblem of the 1940s was, uncomplaining and orderly, the queue. One queued for everything, from the bus, the train, the cinema, the football or the cricket match, to the boat to take soldiers of the Dunkirk beaches. Amid the anxieties, there was a certain seriousness in the social climate. *The Brains Trust* was, for all its cerebral character, one of radio's most popular series, with 12m devoted listeners each week and, just as one tiny instance, the army's Southern Command had thirty chamber groups and a full-scale symphony orchestra in rehearsal in the months preceding D-Day.

It was not surprising that cricket did so well during and just after the war. The cricket was often joyfully entertaining but never superficial. Its regulated patterns of play clearly suited the attitudes of the decade. The working-class/middleclass split remained at about 75% to 25%, only marginally different than in high Victorian times. As that strong internal combine of hopeful workers and confident suburbanites was still sustained, the relationship between cricket and its context, always a significant connection, was probably closer than at any time since the 1890s. Thus it is understandable that the cricket authorities were complacent and backward-looking. They did little or nothing by way of Reconstruction. They did not observe that, unlike in 1919, the tones of the mood music were, while sober, also implicitly forward-looking.

It also should be recalled there was no lack of discussion at the highest level as the dangers of war receded. There were voices arguing that these relatively good times were, as others were discovering, the opportunity to look ahead and plan carefully and wisely. All fashions of reforms were debated, including, again, the possibility of a knock-out tournament, plus the 'most mischievous proposition' of shortened boundaries and despite its rather unhappy consequences when tried in 1919, a two-day county programme. As for one-day cricket, the 1941 *Wisden* had spoken of the 'showmanship' and 'flamboyant manner' of league cricket, suggesting that it was 'foreign to the temperament and to the habit of the average county cricketer'. The powers-that-were remained short-sightedly wedded to the lofty and abiding nature of first-class cricket. 'First-class cricket', sternly intoned *the Times,* 'not first-class fun.'

In chief, they misunderstood what had enthused those wartime crowds and even what had warmed the cockles of the hearts of the 1947 gatherings. Sir Pelham Warner said of the England and Dominions contest in 1945 that 'it was one of the finest games played at Lord's . . . a feast of brilliant stroke play, it was cricket *in excelcis. A joie de vie* in the batting sparkled throughout the game which fulfilled any known axiom as to how cricket should be played.' Unluckily, Pelham Warner, the man who trustily defended the gates when cricket was under siege and organised its wartime defences, was not the man to lead it forth and claim the victory. As early as 1942 he had declared his hand; 'I can see nothing wrong with modern cricket'. The *Wisden* of 1944 confirmed his view. While appreciating the efforts to keep cricket alive during the war, it dismissed such endeavours as 'impromptu cricket.'

R.C.Robertson-Glasgow, second only to Neville Cardus in his fluency as a cricketing journalist, was even more scathing. He attacked wartime one-day cricket, and there would have been many in authority in agreement, as 'the new clockwork monkey in the nursery (that) delights for a few hours.' It was he who, in 1942, recollected how the longer day, with a 7.30 pm finish, of the 1919 two day fixtures, had meant spectators had left early so that 'their wives, cooks and servants' be not kept waiting. To be fair, he was also sagacious enough to argue that 'tradition so easily degenerates into inertia and habit into self-satisfaction.' He was not entirely against two-day cricket, mainly on the grounds that it was not one-day cricket, which he abhorred. He stated categorically that first-class cricket was 'a three act play, not a slapstick turn', and, as for those who thought otherwise, 'such spectators are, frankly, not wanted at county cricket.'

They took him at his word.

Warnford, home of the Hampshire Hogs CC, with Malcolm Marshall bowling for his Hampshire XI in aid of his benefit against the Hogs in their centenary year of 1987.

English cricket teams have sometimes been formed around occupational groups, exemplified here by, top, the Metropolitan Police cricket ground, at Imber Court, Greater London; and the Watney's Brewery cricket ground at Mortlake, Surrey.

CHAPTER ELEVEN
LOST INNOCENCE

Past serenity: Sussex v Surrey,
Horsham Cricket Week, 1931

For all its sombre ceremonial, the critical aspect of the Coronation of Elizabeth II on a damp Wednesday in the June of 1953 was domestic. Over 20.5m people, approaching half the nation, clustered about 5m television sets, peering through curtained rooms at the fuzzy images of regal pageantry. By 1970 90% of households had a television set, watched on average, twenty hours a week. In that same summer of 1953 approaching 3m British people took charter flights for holidays in sunnier climes. In 1970 there would be 7m flying abroad, chiefly to Spain, for holidays.

The television and the aeroplane respectively replaced the newspaper plus the radio and the steamship as the major providers of cricketing communication. The one brought pictures of cricket into the sitting room; the other brought players quickly from all parts of the globe. At the same time, television and civil flight revolutionised the pursuit of leisure in all its forms, rather to the detriment of cricket spectatorship.

CRICKET'S PROBLEMS

Cricket, which had catered for an attendant host of polite and generally well-behaved spectators, was assailed on all sides from the 1950s onwards. The Golden Age of Collective Leisure was drawing to a close. From about 1870 the music hall, later the variety theatre, plus football and other spectator sports, had provided a weekly focus for collegiate jollity. In the first half of the 20th century, the cinema had vied for the collective custom of the millions. There were 5000 cinemas in the United Kingdom. In the heavily industrialised areas there was one cinema seat to every nine people. In its peak years of the 1940s the cinema sold 30m tickets a week, that is 1.5bn a year. The great middle-of-the-road movies, like *Brief Encounter* or *Casablanca*, were enjoyed almost as a national experience. For those outside the reach of major cricket arenas, the newsreels of Gaumont British News or Pathe Gazette had provided the first moving images of famous cricketers they had ever seen.

Then, from a point where most people had gone to the 'pictures' once or twice a week, there was an abandonment of the movies, so that by the late 1960s only 11% of the population were visiting the cinema once a month. Two-thirds of cinemas had closed, while variety theatres also shut down in dozens. In 1980 only 101m cinema tickets were sold. By the end of the 20th century there were only 500 theatres of all kinds, left in Britain, much the same number that had been packing them in just in the London area at the end of the 19th century.

The motor car made a definitive contribution to this social disruption. Henry Ford's vision of the car for everyone came ever more true. At first it was a suburban dream. With full employment and decent wages in the aftermath of the Second World War, access to cars extended again. There were 2m cars in 1945, then 6m cars in 1960 and that doubled to 12m in 1970. In 1950 annual car mileage was 30bn miles; in 2000 it was a staggering 300bn miles. In 1959 the first stretch of the M1 motorway was opened. Soon the motorway network would form a vast web across the country.

The mesh of rail and tram lines, chiefly based on urban centres, were rigidified. The bus, which enjoyed its heyday between the wars when bus passenger numbers overtook those of rail passengers, had demonstrated the advantages of elasticity and opened up much of the country to day-by-day travel. Such flexibility was the leading characteristic of the car. Certainly one could drive the car to the county cricket ground, and some did, but increasingly, one could drive it to a thousand other destinations. The car was the emblem of a more privatised culture. Twos and threes in cars could go practically anywhere, where hundreds on buses had gone where the bus had been scheduled to go.

It was a sample of what has been called 'the miniaturisation of society'. First the radio and then, incontestably, the television had supplied theatre and cinema in the sitting room, while, in the wake of the gramophone, the record, cassette and CD players and the complete music centre constructed a concert hall in every lounge. In the kitchen the washing machine and the fridge-freezer stood proxy for the public washhouse or laundry and the ice store. For those with very aged memories, the domestic oven had replaced the use of the local bake-house. Especially as owner occupation and council house tenancy continued to grow at the expense of commercial letting, residents painted, decorated and cultivated neat gardens. The cosy home became more of a focus for leisure. The razor-sharp front-cloth comic of the variety age, Max Miller, told of the bandy-legged dairymaid, who 'couldn't keep her calves together' She was, he claimed, 'out on pleasure bent'. In post-war Britain it became the practice to ignore her venturesome example. Many people would either remain in the privacy of the home or, if sallying forth, enjoy the privacy of the car.

During the 1950s the number of households with telephones tripled and the number with refrigerators quadrupled. It was said that the modern kitchen by 1960 utilised as much power as the average mill in 1860. Surrounded with automation and electronics, people lived more privily and in so doing, the pace of existence quickened. Sophisticated machinery and gadgets enabled everyone to accomplish tasks more rapidly, to reach destinations more expediently and to switch interests more frequently.

This liberation made for a more restless tempo, one a little out of tune with the more deliberate motion of cricket. The American influence was strong. In 1956 Bill Haley and the Comets unleashed *Rock Around the Clock*, Britain's vivid introduction to the rock'n'roll era and a whole new dimension of exciting popular music. About the same time the Teddy-boy phenomenon, the first of a series of deracinated youth movements, was observed about the urban streets. Family life and street life altered irrevocably as, for example, adolescence became more segmented and socially distinct from the commonalty. The unspoken alliance of a substantial working class and a worthy middle class collapsed. That middling acceptance and encouragement of fairly narrow norms in leisure, as in other aspects of society, disintegrated. The rock upon which support for first-class cricket had been built began to break asunder.

There was a further problem for cricket. There was economic as well as social acceleration, to wit, rapid inflation. The naiveté of the cricket writer, Sir Home Gordon, to the effect that, in the 1940s, a county cricket club could manage on an annual income of £10,000, began to look plain silly. By the end of the 1950s, the counties were gazing horrified at bills of £60,000 and more and, unlike the 1930s, it was not, in new fiscal circumstances, easy to find the obliging magnate to balance the accounts with a ready cheque. Test revenues were already being deployed to help the counties; by the mid-50s they contributed about 15% of the county exchequers.

Over the 1940s, average earnings doubled from £4 to £8 a week or from about £200 to £400 per annum. During this phase the well-established cricketer was earning roughly £600 a year. It was still twice as much as the average industrial wage, although in 1900, the disparity had been three times as much. It was still marginally preferable to the professional footballer's lot but the gap had narrowed. In 1900 the first-class cricketer had, on average, made £275 to the league footballer's £208; by 1950 the latter was taking home over £500, a quarter rather than a third behind. Soon the soccer stars would fly ahead.

Meanwhile, the cricketing counties were finding particular difficulty keeping pace with inflation, as their attendances fell. From the high point of 1947 the attendances at first-class cricket matches collapsed. By 1960 roughly 500,000 paid to watch the normal programme of Test and county games. There was little solace to be found in the fact that other sports witnessed a similar collapse in support. Total Football League gates tumbled from the 40m of the 1949/50 season to 28m in 1964/65 and down further to 18m in 1984/85, although the attendances for leading First Division clubs held up better than those of lower division teams.

English cricket itself was quite perky in the 1950s. As the great Bradman ensemble began to disintegrate in 1953, England won the Ashes amid scenes at the Oval of delirious relief. With Frank Tyson and Brian Statham rampant, the Ashes were retained on the 1954/55 tour of Australia, and then, in 1956, in a series made memorable by the nineteen wickets garnered by the nonpareil off spinner, Jim Laker, at Old Trafford, the Ashes remained in English hands. Thereafter the Australians recovered strongly, winning the rubbers of 1958/59 and 1961 with some resolution. During the subsequent 1960s the Australians tended just to have the edge over England.

On the county circuit, Surrey were outstanding. They won seven titles in sequence from 1952 to 1958, proving to be one of the most competent county teams ever. Captained by Stuart Surridge and then Peter May, Surrey had the services of four bowlers – Alec Bedser, Peter Loader, Tony Lock and Jim Laker – who would have graced a flourishing international side. Surrey also had accomplished batting and scintillating fielding, especially close to the wicket. Then Yorkshire picked up the pace again, looking to remind older watchers of their inter-wars dominance. With Fred Trueman in late confident bloom, with the single-minded Geoffrey Boycott in uncompromising mood and the skipper, Brian Close, in gritty and combative mode, Yorkshire won six championships in the decade. Worcestershire too, after many attempts, won their first three pennants in 1964, 1965 and 1974. Tom Graveney in his mature prime, and Basil D'Oliveira, a good-looking and dashing talent, shone in a side of workmanlike solidity.

For all these delights there were some marked defects in the cricket itself. There appeared to be a safety-first mind-set among first-class cricketers. Approximately half the county games played in the 1950s were drawn, compared with a quarter in the 1930s and 1940s. In the 1960s the number of batsmen scoring 2000 runs in a season fell to an average of three in these years, the lowest since 1897, while by 1969, the highest aggregate of wickets taken by the leading bowler was 109, the smallest number for a hundred years.

There were also abrasive complaints about the drop in run rates and later, over rates. Varied elements were held culpable. Coaching had become stultified; the amateur ethic had all but vanished in post-war conditions; likely professionals now had the education to be tempted by other careers; and indifferent pitches, coupled with artificially fertilised outfields that kept the shine on the ball longer and forced batsmen on to the cramped defensive, while accurate military medium bowlers and an array of spinners thrived.

Probably there was truth in all those reasons. At least they made more sense than the opinion that batsmen had been rendered spiritless by the evils of the Welfare State, which led the arch conservative Neville Cardus gloomily to aver that 'life in this country is rationed.' Nonetheless, cricket in England seemed faced with every possible barrier. At its most pessimistic, the viewpoint was that more expensive cricket was being played less effectively in front of declining crowds.

CRICKET'S ANSWERS

Changes were enforced by circumstances. In 1966 a bid was made by MCC, under the banner of MCC National Cricket Association, set up in 1964 for just this purpose. It was an appeal for Sports Council funding and it was refused on the grounds that the body was not nationally representative. So MCC torturously established the bipartite MCC Cricket Council in 1968. It had a first-class wing, the Test and County Cricket Board, which replaced the Advisory County Cricket Committee and the Test Match Board of Control, both of them MCC subsidiaries. It had a non-first-class wing, the

National Cricket Association, which was eligible for Sports Council funding for the recreational game.

An even more dramatic example of English cricket coming to terms with modernity was the rather sudden decision to obliterate the amateur/professional distinction. With it went the vestiges that remained of separate travel, accommodation, dressing rooms and scorecard nomenclature. This came into force in 1963, with the last Gentlemen and Players annual fixture played in 1962. As late as 1959 there had been vehement refusals of such a reform. The tale is told of the attractive professional batsman, Tom Graveney, being rebuked by his aghast county captain for familiarly calling his England colleague, the Sussex amateur, David Sheppard, by his forename. In a less snobbish age, Tom Graveney would rise to the eminence of becoming President of MCC.

Henceforward, all first-class players would be called 'Cricketers'. The terms and conditions of cricketers improved over time. In 1968 the recently formed and still fragile Cricketers' Association negotiated a minimum salary of £485 and by 1970, most established cricketers had tipped the £1000 mark. For example, capped players might have received something like £850, plus appearance money and maybe bonuses based on results, while one or two counties made a comprehensive payment of say, £1600 and no match fees. By the later 1970s, according to Ric Sassoon, in his *The Players; A Social History of the Professional Cricketer*, a capped player might have been in receipt of up to £3500 and an uncapped cricketer £1500. Obviously, there were differences not only between young and experienced players but also between richer and poorer counties. In summary it might be estimated that that the average salary for a county cricketer at the end of the 1970s would have been £2200. By this time travel, accommodation and equipment was paid for by the county authorities, a substantial addition, while the provision of a sponsored car was also a more general possibility.

While this is to run, chronologically, a little ahead of the game, it enables one to emphasise the point that the ghosts of Herbert Sutcliffe and Wally Hammond must have smiled upon these changes. They had, it will be recalled, led the way in the embourgoisement of the cricketing proletariat and now their descendants reaped the reward of equality. Moreover, and as the cricketer's salary – no longer 'wages', incidentally – improved, the established cricketer was able to afford the trappings of a suburban existence that had largely been denied his predecessors. Returning to the earlier issue strongly pressed that the Gentleman/Player dichotomy was a social as much, if not more so, than an economic one, it is possible to state with some certainty that when all the English county staffs became 'Cricketers', they were soon to be all, at least sociologically speaking, 'Gentlemen' rather than 'Players'. Put another way, apropos income, accommodation and other such indices, the 'Cricketers' were indubitably middle class.

As a prelude to this, Len Hutton, that superb opening bat of moderate temper and rational shrewdness, had become England's first-ever 'professional' captain in 1953, not without a chorus of disapproval from the traditionalists. An outstanding cricketer, like Jack Hobbs before him, he was knighted for his services to cricket. One or two professionals had begun to lead county sides, notably Tom Dollery, who captained Warwickshire during their championship season of 1951, but the appointment of Leonard Hutton as the national skipper was a major breakthrough and an entirely successful innovation. It was also rightful acknowledgement of a fine cricketer of undoubted class.

It is of incidental interest that the sweeping statement of his being the first professional captain was qualified, at least in the broadsheet newspapers, by a dismissive reference to the antediluvian age when all-professional sides had toured Australia. The inference was that these primitive encounters did not and should not count and that Len Hutton had thus made history. However, there was no suggestion that this logic should be accepted – and that those early games should not be included in Test match records. Cricket history does throw up occasional examples of this seeming desire to want both the bun of antiquity and the halfpenny of modernity.

English cricket certainly found itself in the process of shifting from ancient to modern. The surgery was, at least on the face of it, heroic. Three operations were conducted in order to stem the flow of customers from cricket grounds.

Firstly, limited overs cricket was introduced in 1963 courtesy of the Gillette Cup, initially a 65 overs competition, soon reduced to 60 overs. Mike Turner, the Leicestershire secretary, had organised a trial run in the Midlands in 1962 but the official launch came in the May of the following year, when Lancashire played Leicestershire. They had been the bottom two in the preceding summer's county table and played a bye round to reduce the contestants to the convenient sixteen teams for knock out purposes. Given that the novel approach was often branded 'one day cricket', it was ironical that dismal weather ensured this game occupied parts of two days. Lancashire won, with the adjudicator, Frank Woolley, choosing their burly all-rounder, Peter Marner, as the first-ever 'man of the match', with a gold medal and £50 as the prize. Sussex, who had never won the County Championship, won the first Gillette Cup final in front of a packed house at Lord's.

After a season or two during which the Rothmans-sponsored International Cavaliers and also the counties, braving the wrath of the Sabbatarian defenders, played on a Sunday, the next move was to a full-blooded Sunday league in 1969 of just 40 overs a side, with Lancashire, who developed something of a taste and a technique for the shorter version of the game, taking the first honours. With a compound of grouped leagues and a knock out stage for group leaders, the Benson and Hedges competition was initiated in 1972. The first winners were Leicestershire. The first international limited overs match was at Melbourne between Australia and the 1970/71 England tourists. It was the first of a remorseless list of such contests.

Suddenly, after a century of solely first-class county cricket, there was an abundance of limited overs cricket, with three competitions ongoing in England. The emphasis was on batting. In terms of time allocation these games were not unlike the ordinary fixtures of league and recreational clubs but it was felt necessary to moderate the conditions. By insisting on an equal ration of overs there was no room for the declaration while bowlers were limited to a given numbers of overs. Fielding restrictions were gradually introduced to avoid, as one or twice happened, a boundary patrol of ten fielders, while umpires were later instructed to treat the wide more narrowly than in the first-class game.

There was no limit on batting. A logical provision might have been that if a bowler could only bowl eight or twelve overs, then the batsman must retire on completing, say, his 50. It was argued that it was quick scoring and big hitting that attracted the crowds and were, for example, the bowling to be shared by two very accurate medium-fast merchants of the persistent likes of Derek Shackleton and Tom Cartwright, who had the stamina to bowl long spells, then the public would be aggrieved. The condition did mean that teams had to include a clutch of bowlers rather than rely on a couple of experts and pack the eleven with batsmen. Others hinted that the administrators were largely ex-batsmen out to thwart the would-be attackers. There were worries that spin bowling, already bedevilled by foreshortened boundaries, would suffer and that seemed to be the case but eventually, spin, suitably modified, played a more important part. It was also said that one day games made for slovenly batting techniques, as batsmen strived to score quickly against artificially set fields. On one issue there were no arguments; limited overs cricket did tend to smarten up running between the wickets and fielding and no team could afford the passengers in the field that had once been usual.

People certainly found one day cricket attractive. In 1969, with the inclusion of the Sunday league alongside the Gillette Cup, county attendances grew to 600,000 but the number watching the first-class fixtures remained a minority of this overall total. The common complaint about three or five day cricket was that few could manage to watch the complete game and that it was like watching scenes from a play rather than the finished drama. However, limited overs cricket was a spectacular failure in the very area for which it had been promulgated. The notion was that the shorter version would act as a gateway to the longer version of cricket. Although Test match attendances held up fairly well, the overall attendances at first-class county matches continued to drop. In the early 1960s, when half a million attended first-class games, it was regarded with such anxiety that the new order of limited overs was imposed. The county committees would be hysterical with delight were half a million watching first-class cricket in England today. In 1947 15,000, 11,748 paying at the turnstiles, watched the Saturday of the Varsity fixture at Lord's, and a further 6993 paid for entry on the Monday.

Many counties nowadays do not have as many as 11,748 paying at the gate for their eight or nine home games, that is, 32 or 36 days, in the County Championship.

The one day tail soon began to wag the three day dog. In the football codes the shorter games of five a-side soccer or seven-a-side rugby has always been viewed as a bright and breezy addition and has never threatened the vitality of the genuine article nor for that matter, subverted the original character and laws of the game. And for all this busy activity, there was no underlying and fundamental reform. For instance, there was no pneumatic drill taken to the cementation of the county system itself. Where the audacious Victorian had experimented with differing designs, the New Elizabethans were wedded to their forebears' heritage and could only tinker.

Secondly, and as the mention of Gillette and Benson and Hedges exemplifies, sponsorship was sought. From Prudential in the international arena, via, from 1977, Schweppes for the county championship, to Haig for the 1971 Village Cup tournament, cricket became plastered with company logos. It was a question more of a switch from sporadic private to regularised corporate donations. Where once the well-stuffed wallets of the Duke of Devonshire, for Derbyshire, or Sir Julien Cahn, for Nottinghamshire and Leicestershire, had kept counties in the black, now it was a changing range of tobacco, drinks, insurance and banking concerns that helped keep English cricket on an even financial keel. Gillette donated £6500 for that very first limited overs competition, a mere bagatelle by today's standards. After several years of being a cricket benefactor, Gillette backed off, the reason being that they found the advertising boost sought by such corporate interest was dwindling. Their analysts found that many people had come to believe that the cup was named after a veteran cricketer, some kind of W.G.Gillette, presumably. It is a reminder that corporate aid is rarely altruistic but driven by sound business principles. Perhaps some of the earlier 'angels' also had axes to grind; Sir Julien Cahn, the furniture magnate, assuredly hoped to gain prestige and social acceptance through his beneficence.

Thirdly, in 1968, the counties were permitted the instant registration of an overseas player every three years, although, in 1982, this was limited to one per county, for, over time – Warwickshire's four West Indian stars is an illustration – one or two counties came to depend heavily on non-English signings. The brilliant Gary Sobers led the charge of often very gifted players into the county ranks. Arguments abounded, as still they do, about the pros of such players influencing mundane county cricketers for the better against the cons of them denying English players the chance to play first-class cricket. There was further anxiety about whether the rise in interest was sufficient to compensate for the higher salaries

These elements – limited overs cricket; corporate funding; overseas signings – obviously interacted. Indeed, a little treadmill was built of three trundling steps. Sponsorship required attractive tournaments for the best commercial investment; attractive tournaments needed glittering performers, like the West Indian Clive Lloyd at Lancashire or the South African Barry Richards at Hampshire; glamorous performers depended on corporate sponsorship for their high – £1500 to £2500 was the introductory norm – salaries, and so the wheel turned. But for many commentators it was too little too late. One necessary reform was probably some revision of the county system and that should have been accomplished in 1945/46 or thereabouts.

Nevertheless, the changes made constituted a switch from the purity of hitherto. Traditionalists certainly saw this phase as one of a lost innocence. The hearty Victorian male, perhaps consciously, used the word 'cherry' for both the cricket ball and for virginity. The cricketing cherry had certainly been ravished. Occasionally the nostalgia was awry. Reference was made in chapter seven to the cricketing conservatives bemoaning the wearing, from about the late 1970s, of coloured clothing as part of the razzamatazz of limited overs games. The cricketing fogeys were unimpressed by the argument that donning what they scornfully referred to as 'pyjamas' was a return to the good old days.

These somewhat shiny but superficial alterations to English cricket were perhaps at one with the possibly over lauded 'swinging' sixties. Here were other attempts to break colourfully with the past and reject other types of traditional innocence. Gambling, with the arrival of the premium bonds, as a mild curtain-raiser for the later lottery, and the removal of shackles from betting; the sudden advent of drugs and a sharp uprise in violent crime, with its noisome tokens of the Great Train Robbery of 1963 and the Moors Murders trial of 1966; even the welcome libertarian reforms concerned with divorce, abortion and homosexuality – these were all part of the same cultural shift. From the 'Lady Chatterley' case of 1960 and the Profumo Affair of 1963, to the abolition of theatre censorship in 1968, there were Beatlemania, flower power, hot pants and a score of other elements of the Permissive Society.

In retrospect, some of these changes have been judged as gaudy rather than fundamental, characterised by what cricket groundsmen, on the subject of insubstantial pitches, disdainfully term 'top-show'. Possibly the Open University remains the enduring agency of 'sixties socialism', whereas some other cultural ventures have proved ephemeral. The satire of the breakthrough television programme, *That Was the Week That Was*, seen as shocking and hard-hitting at the time, now looks a little self-indulgent and soft-centred.

Cricket once more had fallen into its social place. What appeared to be a Titanic revolution in the early 1960s was perhaps a brash extravaganza, maybe now looking a trifle seedy. It actually made only a few tiny dents in the massive if by now creaking cricketing fortress built by the Victorians and maintained, in awe and veneration, by its defendants at Lord's and elsewhere.

CRICKET'S COLONIES

While the aftermath of the Second World War witnessed a fairly limited effect on the basic organisation of English domestic cricket, its ramifications elsewhere were much more profound. The war acted as something of a catalyst for the disintegration of colonialism, as, in the post-war decades, subjugated peoples struck out for freedom from imperial yokes. For example, although the British, understandably, were preoccupied during the World War II with the reality of German bombing and the possibility of German invasion, much of the global conflict, of course, affected Asia Fighting there began in 1931, and, between 1941 and 1945 alone, 32m lives were lost to war or war-related action in and around Japanese occupied Asia. As Japanese pan-Asianism faltered under allied pressure, not least from the 2m Indians mobilised as the essential part of the British Army in India, it provided, in the words of the expert on Asian history Tim Harper, 'the platform for Asian politicians . . . to realise their own national visions, and to raise their own armies...It was at this point that Asia's people's began to grasp a future beyond empire. Young fighters prepared to strike out in the name of the nation. One of the abiding legacies of the war was the political legitimacy it gave to men in uniform and to violent, revolutionary change.'

Quite quickly, the British Empire transformed into the British Commonwealth of independent states. Indeed, the British Empire, for all its size, lasted for a much, much shorter time than the ancient empires of Egypt, Rome, China and South America. Reaching its peak in the 1890s, the British Empire was largely dissolved in the late 1940s and 1950s, a matter of some sixty years duration. Fortunately, it was during that relatively brief span of time that cricket was also at its silvery acme and was able to make a lasting impression on many of the British colonies.

In comparative terms, the dissolution of the British Empire, already committed in part to the pragmatic Victorian confederation of loosely autonomous territories, was managed with less upheaval than, say, the French and Dutch experience of de-colonisation. Nonetheless, there were disastrous episodes, whilst, in the words of the American diplomat and statesman, Dean Acheson, at West Point in 1962, 'Great Britain has lost an Empire and has not yet found a role.' The realistic diagnosis was that Britain had exhausted itself in World War II, principally during the months when the nation stood more or less alone against the German Fascist menace. It has been said that, for future reference, the critical points of the war were in 1941 when the Japanese action at Pearl Harbour and the Nazi invasion of Russia happened. By pitchforking the USA and the USSR into the general hostilities, it justified the label 'world' as a descriptor for the war and prefaced the forthcoming 'cold war' duel of those two great super-powers.

The fiasco of Suez in 1956 illustrated the bewilderment and ambivalence of a nation that had not come to terms with its more secondary role in global politics. In the 1950s the false bravado of the gifted comedian, Tony Hancock, cocksure on the outside, craven on the inside, admirably personified the national mood. Whether or not that more downbeat mood somehow conveyed itself to the country's sportsmen and women is a moot point. What one may more confidently assert is that, on the subcontinent and in the Caribbean, the seismic changes in political and cultural existence brought a new confidence and uplift to the peoples and to the cricketers of those regions. One of the lessons the cricket players and authorities of England were forced to learn was that, at best, they were *primus inter pares*.

The Indian continent and the West Indies were, in cricketing terms, the first areas to experience the joys of independence. The subsequent excitement over cricket in those regions has since been such that a key question is often forgotten. The normal reaction of a freed race is to turn its back on the culture of the perceived oppressor and develop an indigenous ethos. Chapter six described something of this in the United States during the post-colonial stage of its history. Cricket was such a symbol of imperialism.

There were moves to oust cricket from India after independence had been granted in 1947. In his wondrously brilliant exposition of Indian cricket, *A Corner of a Foreign Field; the Indian History of a British Sport* (2002), Ramachandra Guha identifies high ranking Indians, like B.V.Keskar, General Secretary of the All India Congress and later Minister of Information and Broadcasting, or Janaki Dass, Secretary of the Indian Cycling Federation, who popped the question of cricket's appositeness for a free India. 'It will never be able to survive the shock of the disappearance of British rule from our country' claimed the former, while the latter asserted that cricket as 'a black spot stamped by British imperialism on the face of India may be wiped off.'

However, Indian nationalism and cricket were quite intimately allied. Perhaps Prince Ranjitsinhji's refusal to encourage Indian cricket as part of his zeal for sustaining the Raj was now, for those seeing life through his lenses, vindicated. Ram Guha demonstrates how cricket was already too well incorporated into Indian life to be so readily abandoned. As was earlier observed, the American colonists had rid themselves of the British before cricket had become commonly entrenched, in fact, before it had become properly recognised as a national sport in Britain. America then both encouraged the incursion of a polyglot immigrant population and embarked on its own epic colonisation of the vast terrain beyond the original Eastern seaboard. In brief, an almost entirely novel state was created, whereas India was an ancient country with a mixed and lengthy saga of cultural experience.

What Ram Guha makes perfectly clear is that cricket had been assimilated into the thought and practice, not just of the high and mighty Maharajah, but also of the Untouchable. A particular hero of the author's is Palwankar Baloo, first of India's long line of slow bowlers, whose caste meant that the discrimination practised by the English amateurs apropos their professional colleagues was tame compared with his treatment. For all Mahatma Gandhi's preciously profound influence on Indian political thought, cricket had thus become an inviolate aspect of Indian life, with, for example, many of the early Indian Test cricketers coming from the urban middle classes of the nation. Their majestically high-scoring opener, V.M.Merchant, is an example.

India had played ten Tests against England, prior to independence. Thereafter there was a regular flow of top-class cricket following the war years. In the first ten years of freedom, there were three 'Commonwealth' tours, including fifteen unofficial Test matches, organised by the enthusiastic and well-organised England cricketer, George Duckworth, as well as 42 genuine Tests involving five countries. A system of five zones, with leagues of five or six teams in each zones, was established and many of these fixtures proved very attractive to the local patriotism of the Indian supporters. Ram Guha writes of 'all that went to make cricket in free India: the energy, the excitement, the noise and the nationalism.' This gusto was happily expressed in the tremendous welcome offered the first visitors to independent India, the West Indies, in 1948/49, and they also toured the nascent Pakistan.

The British government showed some tenacity in naming a day in July 1947 by which Indian independence had to be completed. Clement Attlee, thought by many commentators to be Britain's most effective peacetime premier of the 20th century, had acted decisively. It is true that there were chaotic and fatal scenes on Partition, as

Muslims and Hindus, isolated by the new frontiers, attempted to journey to their new homelands. There was a high death toll, but some historians argue that an open-ended commitment might have led to prolonged lethal internecine warring and slaughter.

Effectively, the granting of freedom to India set the benchmark for the whole decolonisation process. A.S.de Mello, the Indian cricket administrator who was so active in restoring cricketing standards to India in the post-war years, organised the last ever 'All India' tour, which was to Australia, where a weakened team was heavily defeated by the pomp of Bradman's mighty team. Thereafter, the new Pakistan had to create its own cricketing structure, whereas India enjoyed much more continuity in that respect. Pakistan was itself divided, of course, into two sectors, with East Pakistan having little experience of cricket. West Pakistan, however, had been the home for three former Ranji Trophy teams in the old united India, while, as with Pandit Nehru's new Indian government, the initial Pakistani administration was quick to encourage the game, seeing it as a focus for national consolidation. A leading legal figure, A.R.Cornelius, ensured that a Board of Cricket Control was established in 1948.

Cricketing roots prospered. Pakistan were successful in their application for membership of the ICC in 1952; they played a peaceful series in India in 1952/53, where Pakistan were captained by A.H.Kardar, aka Abdul Hafeez in his former days as an All India player. They enjoyed their first tour of England in 1954; and, again with A.R.Cornelius a key agent, they carved out that essential foundation for the Test-playing nation, an internal first-class tournament of reasonable character. In 1953/54 the Qaid-I-Azam Trophy, a competition of shifting rules, teams and fortunes, got underway. Now there were seven Test-playing countries, a situation that was to remain like that for many years.

The other main cricketing region subject to imperial control was the West Indies. Perhaps more so than in India, there was a wide-ranging sense of cricket having been adopted by the indigenous populations of most of the islands and areas. As independence beckoned, there was no hint of throwing out the baby of cricket with the bathwater of English domination. Wryly, one may observe that, throughout the receding Empire, when the heirs of all the soldiers and traders and missionaries had gone, cricket was just about the only vestige left of the old imperial order.

Politically, it was felt both locally and in London that the administrative logic pointed to a federated system. The post-war experiment with a West Indian Federation, however, was short-lived. Michael Manley, himself a prime minister of Jamaica from 1972 to 1980 and a leading expert on West Indian cricket history, has explained how Caribbean economics, as well as localised political sensibilities, told against that centralised concept. An imperial economy dictates that produce will flow to and from the metropolitan centre rather than in and around the immediate region. Such a one-way trading street offered no firm route to an integrated commercial construct. 'Logic is less than persuasive', wrote Michael Manley, 'in the face of insular preoccupations'. A combine of economic imbalance and political insularity put paid to the federal concept and to the idea that the West Indies might be a 'nation', licitly competent to play international sport. The West Indian cricket authorities, which needed no tuition in the debilitating effects of inter-island squabbling, were among those who mourned the passing of the unitary scheme.

Gradually, over the years that followed, the Caribbean territories controlled by Britain achieved singular independence. It was as if the original thirteen colonies of the eastern American seaboard or the handful of Australian colonies had each become separate nations. The process began with Jamaica and Trinidad and Tobago in 1962, followed by Barbados and Guyana in 1966, St Lucia in 1967, the Bahamas in 1973, Grenada in 1974, Dominica in 1978, St Vincent and the Grenadines in 1979, Antigua and Barbuda in 1981 and St Kitts/Nevis in 1983. A desk at the United Nations and a possible number in the draw for the football world cup was part of the prize. More importantly, certainly for the future of the region's cricket, was the fact that the USA replaced the UK as the major investor of capital in the West Indies.

The liberation of these colonies from imperial thrall contributed hugely to the already rising confidence of the peoples of the West Indies, none more so than among their cricketers, buoyed by the feats of the great side of the early 1950s. As if to personify these substantive changes, there was a significant struggle to wrest the captaincy from Anglo-Saxon hands, a battle akin to the shift in modern England from amateur to professional captains. In 1959 Frank Worrell became the first black man and the first professional to captain the West Indies for a complete series or on tour. Courteous and relaxed, yet steely of resolve and, in the past, a stern fighter for improved conditions for the basically underpaid West Indian players, he responded valiantly to the challenge. The tone was set against Ritchie Benaud's commanding Australians over the winter of 1960/61, beginning with the famous tie at Brisbane in the first Test, the first such result in the epic tale of international cricket.

These were the shoots that would blossom into the burgeoning flower of West Indian cricket in the last third of the 20th century. This phase was marked by the debonair figure of Gary Sobers, like Frank Worrell later to be meritoriously knighted. Akin to a Renaissance prince, Gary Sobers was multifaceted in his rare gifts. A buccaneering batsman, a quick bowler of deadly liveliness, a left hand spinner of mature control and, to boot, a graceful and agile fielder, he was, beyond mortal measure, the most comprehensively talented all-rounder ever, one to whom Izaak Walton's piscatorial adjective for his finished angler might be applied; Gary Sobers was the 'compleat' cricketer. Among many achievements, he broke Len Hutton's Test innings record, with 365, not out, in 1957/58 against Pakistan at Kingston, Jamaica. He scored 8032 runs, took 235 wickets and scooped 109 catches for the West Indies.

The West Indies, especially in regard to the political difficulties of incorporating players from the extensive spread of so many islands and areas, were fortunate in that Frank Worrell was followed as captain, first, by Gary Sobers from the mid 1960s, and, next, by Clive Lloyd, for another ten years from the mid-1970s. Tall and mild, Clive Lloyd was a gentle assassin among batsmen and also a fielder of tigerish speed, but, perhaps more importantly, he had enormous tact and acumen as a leader of cricketers. The open secret to the rich success of the West Indies, however, was their enviable procession of climically fast bowlers, often with four of them in tandem, bowling with such venom that older buffs whispered of the bodyline days of yore. Beginning with Wes Hall and Charlie Griffiths, the parade of high pace was sustained by several others, notable among them Andy

Roberts, Michael Holding, Joel Garner and Michael Marshall. Not that the batsmen were slouches, as the imperious assurance of Viv Richards amply demonstrated during the 1980s all over the globe and in all brands of competition. A brave and vigorous attacker, he deservedly stands high in the West Indian battling list, with 8540 runs and an average of 50.23 in Test matches. In Gary Sobers and Viv Richards the West Indies had heroes to personify their dominance of global cricket, just as W.G.Grace or Don Bradman had epitomised the supremacy of Victorian English and Australian inter-wars cricket respectively.

CRICKET'S RACIST STRUGGLE

South Africa was a very different kettle of political fish. The post-war problem was an internal hardening rather than softening of the discrimination of the European minority against the African major-ity. Australia and New Zealand did not have this same quandary in quantitative terms, although it should be remembered that, as with the American settlers and the Amerindian races, those two countries did not have proud records in regard of their treatment of these relevant native populations. The accession to power of the extrem-ist right-wing Nationalist Party in 1948 led the way to the excessive harshness of Apartheid, of absolute white racial superiority.

In 1960 the South Africans opted to leave the Commonwealth and become a republic. The rules of the ICC, for whose birth, it will be recalled, South Africa had acted as willing midwife, insisted that only members of the Commonwealth could enjoy membership. South Africa lost its membership, but the 'white' member nations of England, Australia and New Zealand turned a Nelson's eye to the clause that maintained that that only ICC members could contest Test matches. Lamely, the ICC permitted such fixtures to be called Tests, whilst mildly suggesting they were not 'official'. Anyone searching the records will find they have equal status with all other Tests, another sample of the dodgy variability of the data in respect of Test matches. The 'non-white' members – the Indians, the Paki-stanis and the West Indians – had never played Tests against the South Africans and, of course, there was no chance of them starting now.

As Joseph Conrad's narrator, the sagacious Marlow, says in the seafaring novel, *Lord Jim*, 'what a chance missed!' The ICC could have asserted both the letter of their own law and also the spirit of moral virtue in a straightforward denial of South Africa's position as a Test-playing nation. A clear-cut decision in 1960 might have saved years of prevarication during which the South African government, no less its all-white cricket board, had solid reason to believe that political and sporting life would become easier. Rather feebly, those who sustained sporting links with South Africa argued that it was wiser to keep open the channels of sunny friendship. One suspects that some of them probably agreed that Apartheid had its good points.

It seemed that, for a generation, the South African question darkened the countenance of world cricket. It was never out of the news. It served as an abrasive response to those who naively urged that sport should be kept out of politics. It can only be repeated that, as long as sport is organised competitively on national or even regional lines, a political dimension is a constant. The so-called 'Basil D'Oliveira Affair' perfectly exemplifies that political weighting. A Cape Coloured all rounder of outstanding skill, Basil D'Oliveira had, beginning in 1960, forged a professional career for himself with Middleton, in the Central Lancashire League, and with Worcestershire. He was to play 44 Tests for England.

First controversially left out of the 1968/69 party touring his home land, he was included when Tom Cartwright withdrew. The South African government refused to accept any visiting group including such a selection, arguing that it was a deliberately political move. The Nationalist administration conveniently forgot that their tacit discrimination against non-white cricketers was a somewhat larger political statement.

The devious shenanigans surrounding this event have been mulled over by several analysts, with the political journalist Peter Oborne's *Basil D'Oliveira; Cricket and Conspiracy: the Untold Story* (2004) the latest and possibly the fullest account. In the wake of Pelham Warner, G.O.Allen, the former Middlesex and England quick bowler, had, as long term treasurer of MCC, ruled as the key influence in cricketing administration, at a time when MCC still provided the secretariat for the ICC. It becomes obvious, from any reading of the situation, that MCC were keen to maintain stable relations with South African cricket and that this led the English authorities down dubious avenues of negotiation. At best, they were floundering in a political swamp too deep and too nasty for them to survive.

As for South Africa, in Peter Oborne's words, Prime Minister Vorster had foolishly 'taken the view from the start that the MCC was a subversive leftist group taking its orders from Harold Wilson, just as SACA (the South African Cricket Association) took its orders from him.' Basil D'Oliveira, whose preserved dignity was the most illuminating aspect of a sordid business, was, among other moves, tempted with a bribe to take a coaching job in South Africa, so long as he accepted it before the English touring team had been announced, while that matter was being debated with some fierceness. As a tiny cameo of the row, David Sheppard, perhaps the last of the great clerical cricketers, had just been appointed Bishop of Woolwich, and was the leading protagonist for the anti-Apartheid school of thought. His friend and colleague since students days, Peter May, was of the establishment view, and, when David Sheppard afterwards tried to restore their friendship, he was rebutted with what the famed *Guardian* sports writer, Frank Keating, called 'the rancorously hostile one-liner', the twelve word note, 'I don't think we have anything remotely to talk about ever again.'

Cricket and rugby union were the only sports now with which the South Africans had any main external contacts, but the mood against the ugliness of their regime was mounting, so much so that, with Peter Hain, later to be a Labour cabinet minister, giving an assured lead, the anti-Apartheid campaign attained the singular victory of the abandonment of the South African tour of England in 1970. Thus for many years South Africa cricket enjoyed no official status. Sod's law applied, in that it was exactly at this juncture that South Africa – with stars like Graeme Pollock, Barry Richards and Mike Procter – were entering a glittering era. Hitherto South African cricket had suffered from its dependence on the white amateur ethic, for there had been no attempt to develop an attendant professional cadre, least of all, of course, among the African majority. The alternative fashion, demonstrated by the West Indies, of tolerance of a mixed racial approach, tending latterly towards an emphasis on the black element, had been scuppered by the Afrikaans policy of white supremacy. Several of these South African players, their career hopes blighted at home, made their living in English county cricket.

Even then, there was no comprehensive aversion to the ugly racialism of South Africa. Although the South African regime was condemned at the ICC meeting of 1971, members were left to make up their own minds about playing contacts. A 1974 plea for membership from the association controlling non-white cricket was turned down on the specious grounds that it did not embrace the white element, whereas, patently, the reverse case of a white's only body had long been accepted. The subcontinent and, in particular, the West Indian membership of the ICC had now become more vociferous, blocking attempts to draw South Africa into the fold and pointing accusatory fingers at non-compliant players.

There was any number of these who succumbed to the tempting allure of the South African Rand. Such actions were mistakenly labelled 'rebel' tours, giving some impression that those involved had some ethical reason for taking such rebellious steps. Mercenary would have been a more accurate marker. Beginning with the English trip, led by Graham Gooch, the Essex and England opening bat, in 1981/82, these continued through the 1980s. The Krugerrands were a boon to cricketers who, to be fair, sometimes found employment in the long winters none too remunerative. The tours led to bans of varied severity, some of which interfered with, in several cases only temporarily, the careers of top-class players. David Graveney, as just one instance, recovered sufficiently from his management of Mike Gatting's team to become England's chairman of selectors. The ramifications were many and mixed as the decade wore on. Most understandable from an economic stance was the Sri Lankan trip of 1982/83, during which the cricketers grabbed more money in a few weeks than, in the then under-funded cricket of Sri Lanka, they might have dreamed of over many years of endeavour. The welcome tendered by the South Africans to the non-white cricket-ers of the West Indies and Sri Lanka was imbued with the rank stench of hypocrisy. The application to them of 'honorary white' status recalled MCC's bestowal of 'honorary amateur' status on the

1878 Australians. Viv Richards dramatic statement at the time – 'I would rather die than lay down my dignity' – made the point with theatrical emphasis.

It was only in 1990, with the release from his lengthy jail sentence of Nelson Mandela, that the whole wretched scaffolding of segregation in general and discriminatory cricket in particular collapsed. Under the guidance of the energetic Ali Bacher, the combined United Cricket Board of South Africa was formed in 1991, as the entire Apartheid construct fell, and South Africa was re-admitted to international councils, including the ICC.

Arguments may persist over the part, little or large, a sports boycott played in the demolition of the supremacist structure. Certainly Nelson Mandela had no doubts; 'you've done your bit', he told Basil D'Oliveira, having invited him to lunch while the cricketer was coaching in South Africa. In so far as cricket did contribute to the erasure of an uncivilised blot on the historical landscape, it makes it by far the most generally significant event in the sport's long story.

Elsewhere, in what many felt to be the saner arenas of ordinary cricket, the Australians, with Dennis Lillee and Jeff Thomson replacing Ray Lindwall and Keith Miller as the paired hunters of the pace attack, and the New Zealanders, with ex-skipper Walter Hadlee the competent administrator and his son, Richard, a splendid fast medium operator in the lineage of Maurice Tate and Alec Bedser, enjoyed excellent and moderate success respectively. The highly skilled Richard Hadlee became the first bowler to take 400 Test wickets.

What all of these cricketers, whether in the sunny Caribbean or the pleasant pastures of New Zealand, had next to face was the pressure on their sport and their livelihoods of a much more intense commercial outlook.

Chapter Twelve
COMMERCIALISM

The crowds turn out for 'Packer' style cricket

In 1965 cricket's rulers took an intrepid step that, in prospect if not immediately, marked a definitive change in the political route taken by the game. The Imperial Cricket Conference became the International Cricket Conference. The short-term reason was the sensible one, urged by Pakistan, that, if cricket were to survive and expand, nations with cricketing aspirations must be offered some place at their seniors' table. The concept of associate membership was agreed with the then Ceylon, Fiji, the United States, East Africa, Bermuda, Holland and Denmark the first beneficiaries of this scheme. One or two of these were distinctly non-imperial.

The longer-term reason was more political. The decolonisation programme was fast advancing; what Harold Macmillan, when Prime
Minister, had called 'the winds of change' had reached gale force.
The term 'imperial' was outdated, even offensive. At the same time,
and although Lord's and MCC provisionally remained the command
post for cricket, there was no strict reason for London to remain
the global focus of cricket. It had been logical for London to be the
centre for an activity limited to the Empire. Without the 'imperial'
justification, not least as the United States, European countries and
other non-Commonwealth nations sought membership, there was
no reason for England necessarily to be accepted as the focal point.
In the event, the re-constitution of the ICC was the first slight swing
in the pendulum that would, forty years on, see the Indian subcontinent become the political and economic hub of cricket.

By the mid 1960s the cricketing world was already awash with limited overs cricket. It appeared to answer the question, discussed
earlier, of how cricket had managed, unlike almost every other game,
to be open-ended as to both time and target. The brave move of
curtailing the number of permitted overs produced a positive result
over a relatively short time. It was, of course, the solution that had
occurred to lots of recreational cricketers faced, on a spring evening,
with only two or three undarkened hours. In one sense, the top tier of
the game approached more nearly to the realities of Saturday afternoon club and league cricket. Most club matches were one innings
affairs that encompassed some eighty or so overs. The limitation on
overs, and the other restrictions imposed by officialdom, was soon
incorporated more generally into league and other forms of cricket
to the detriment, for instance, of the interesting declaration strategy.
However, the insistence on excluding the draw became paramount
at almost all levels outside the first-class game.

The wildfire spread of the limited overs brand was observed by the
ICC and the brainwave of a World Cup was canvassed. It naturally
took some years to plan, both in terms of the logistics and the format
but compared with cricket's dilatory record in most aspects over the
years, the ICC reacted with commendable speed. England hosted the
first World Cup in 1975. Good luck attended the weather, the spon-

sors – the Prudential Insurance Company, who laid out £100,000 for the privilege – and the cricket. The fifteen matches attracted decent average crowds of 10,000, with a full house at Lord's to witness a superlative Clive Lloyd century and a victory for the then all-powerful West Indies over Australia.

It was decided to arrange the World Cup on a four-yearly basis with the West Indies retaining the trophy in 1979 and soon the World Cup tournament began to process around the world, a further token of the end of the London monopoly. The expansion of the ICC, with affiliated as well as associate members, was another example of a refreshing rapidity shown by cricket's bureaucracy. The ICC's exclusively proud sextet of Test playing countries of 1975 became a host of around fifty by the end of the century. From Argentina to Zimbabwe, there were representatives from all corners of the world. In 1979 fifteen associate members fought out a parallel cup contest in England alongside the major World Cup tournament. Ceylon, renamed Sri Lanka in 1972 on its becoming a republic, won this competition beating Canada in the final. After having being refused top-class status in 1975, Sri Lanka finally became a Test-playing nation. The Democratic Socialist Republic of Sri Lanka, to cite its Sunday-go-to-meeting title, played its initial Test match, drawing with England at Colombo in February 1982.

It was the first nation, not counting the division of Indian cricket, to join the Test-playing elite since 1930, a matter of 52 years, evidence of how slowly international cricket travels or is allowed to travel. The success of the Sri Lankans – they won the World Cup final in Lahore in the 1995/96 season, outstripping the favoured Australians – demonstrated the truth that, as in most fields of human endeavour, one must have opportunities in order to develop. Rather as with all the original Test-playing teams, participating, and perhaps succumbing to some early heavy defeats, it was the sole way of making progress. It had been a long while since anyone had been offered the chance so to do.

In 1992 Zimbabwe, the former Southern Rhodesia, which was declared an independent republic within the British Commonwealth in 1980, became a full Test-playing member of the ICC. Zimbabwe played its first Test matches in 1992 against New Zealand and India.

Bangladesh, formerly East Pakistan, achieved independence in 1971, prior to Pakistan and Bangladesh according one another recognition in 1974. In 2000 Bangladesh became the tenth of the senior ICC members, playing its first Test match against India in that year. Although Zimbabwe made some early impression, its cricket was later to suffer, like much of the rest of the country's infrastructure, from the abject deterioration of its political economy under the dictatorial rule of Robert Mugabe. Bangladeshi cricket struggled a little to make the top grade and its post-independence background of fierce political in-fighting and economic problems may not have been conducive to smooth improvement on the sporting front. Nonetheless, there were now ten Test-playing nations where, at the end of World War II, there had been but six.

In 2001 the ICC agreed that all ten countries should play each other home and away over each of the next two five year phases. This decision, while justly safeguarding the fixture lists of the less powerful nations, led to a huge expansion of Test matches and international one day games. Although two matches comprised a minimum series, it still meant that the majority of Test teams played up to 90 days a year, so that, in the last decade of the 20th century, the amount of international cricket doubled. This degree of extension certainly helped to generate television income. For example, when the 1999 World Cup was played in England, with Australia beating Pakistan rather convincingly in the final, countless millions of people watched the competition in over a hundred countries and the ICC made a handsome profit of £30m, much of it available to be ploughed back into the game.

Encouraging as the spread of cricket of a higher standard undoubtedly was, where cricket was being played on the North American and European continents, the participants tended often to be expatriate Englishmen or migrant subjects from former British dependencies. In 1989 a European Federation was formed and in 1992 a European Cup was played for in England. The winning German team was comprised mostly of Asian stock, captained by an Australian. However, especially with MCC valiantly prepared to dispatch missionary tours to all corners of the globe, there was a definite extension of the incidence of cricketing activity, with, naturally, some recruitment from local populations.

Over the years the ICC had to deal with a bagatelle of other issues, like the dangers of fast bowling, with changes made to the laws in 1969 accordingly and the introduction of the third umpire and referee, in part a sad and reluctant reaction to on-field discourtesies. Generally speaking, the laws of cricket include negligible sanctions. The wide and no ball are chiefly penalties for inefficiency, not impolite behaviour. As with all Victorian sports, there was a tacit assumption that the Corinthian spirit would prevail in cricket. The football codes had, towards the end of the 19th century, learned the hard way, that free kicks and penalty kicks, plus name taking and dismissal, were required to control the players. It is possibly a tribute to cricket's mores that the problem only reared its head so infrequently and only in such profusion, in relation to quick bowlers intent on bodily attacking their opponents and players intent on abusing one another and the umpires, that it was the late 1960s before official action had to be taken. Some would claim that there been an occasional interment of heads in the sands hitherto, together with a hint – and here the antics of W.G.Grace were frequently quoted – of hypocrisy about the sporting condition of the old-time game.

Others would claim that, without the constant physical contact of soccer or rugger, there was less need for punishing injunctions in cricket. It was to be a problem yielding no easy solutions. It was in response to the barrage of short, pacy bowling that the helmet, along with a veritable wardrobe of protective accoutrements, was introduced. The first primitive head protection was tried in 1974. Saucy wits have pointed out that the testicular guard was first used in 1874, suggesting that it took a hundred years for cricketers to discover they had a brain as well . . .

KERRY PACKER

If the South African quandary had proved a reminder of political actuality, it was the intervention of Kerry Packer that was to provide an economic reality check. Until his acute entrepreneurship, the cricket business had largely been something of a cottage industry, trundling along, barely keeping the wolf from the pavilion door and just about making ends meet. Moves had been made to involve sponsors and television was already a useful source of revenue but the genuine industrialisation of cricket happened as a consequence of Kerry Packer's intercession. Originally loathed as the destroyer, he came to be regarded as something of the saviour of professional cricket.

The historical canvas was a broad one. The controversy carried players and watchers alike back to the master and servant relationship associated with professional cricket since the 18th century, that is, a relationship heavily weighted on the side of the master. It may be recalled that, in previous discussion in this text of the Gentlemen and Players dichotomy, parallels were suggested with the armed forces and the stately home. The analogy holds good in that, as with either military or domestic service, any form of trades unionism was much frowned upon. As well as the strong anti-'combination' sentiments of Victorian businessmen, there was ever a feudal tendency in cricket, in fact, in other sports as well. The county cricket club, with its subscriber base, scarcely saw itself as an employer in the regular sense but more as a country house sort of establishment. The telling phrase one still often hears today in respect of long-serving professionals is that they have been a good 'servant' to the county.

That connotation of service rather than employment was even more pronounced at the national level where it was considered a privilege and an honour to be selected. There was little sense of people doing their job. Something of this valuation was constant across the cricketing world and to be fair, many players bought into this tenet, for, naturally enough, they saw international representation as the highlight of their careers. It took the steely watchfulness of a Sydney Barnes to dash cold water on the face of this patriotic illusion. The expectation of loyalty at all costs, very much the dogma required of the soldier in the barrack room or the footman downstairs in the grand mansion, was uppermost.

What was fascinating about the Packer affair was that it was not a revolt or strike by the workers that led to the collapse of the cricketing citadel. It was not like those 'schisms' of the Victorian era when the Nottinghamshire professionals had sought to gain some control of events or the senior England players had argued for increased pay. It was he who was reputed to be the richest man in Australia who felled the establishment. He inserted his wealth at the weak point of the defences of the cricket authorities, that is, on the simple point of law, whereby his old-fashioned opponents were guilty of holding their 'servants' to specious contractual conditions that clearly were in unreasonable restraint of trade. It was the application of strict business principles that broke the weakening spine of a cricket system founded in outmoded beliefs. It was as if some brash, ambitious 19th century mill owner had gathered sufficient wealth to buy an ancient pile but, instead of, as most did, merging happily into aristocratic fashions, he had upended it and made it a marketplace. It amounted to the wholesale commercialisation of cricket as part of the entertainment industry.

Portentously, the key lay with television, destined to be the most influential component of the financing of modern sport. With exquisite irony, the timing of the Packer coup was during the winter of 1976/77, when Australia and England celebrated the centenary, at Melbourne, of that game in 1877 that had been dubiously dubbed the first Test match. What Kerry Packer wanted for his Channel Nine Company was the television rights to Australian cricket to the exclusion of other companies, notably the Australian Broadcasting Commission, broadly speaking the Australian equivalent of the BBC. Denied this, and despite a pre-empting bid by the Australian Cricket Board, Kerry Packer simply decided to employ the world's best cricketers and televise them in competitive performance. The tale is told that the idea arose from a suggestion of Dennis Lillee, conveyed by his agent, John Cornell, that the poorly paid Australian cricketers should boost their income through 'exhibition' or 'benefit' matches.

Within weeks he had signed some seventy players on his tempting dotted lines, the majority of them Australian and West Indian. From the English standpoint, his subversion of Tony Greig, the then England captain, not only as player but also as agent for the cause, was critical. The arguments raged and in the summer of 1977 the ICC delivered it pontifical statement that any player who made himself available for a game 'previously disapproved by the Conference' would not be eligible for Test match selection.

This was, in trading terms, a monopolistic claim. The ICC insisted it was the sole arbiter of what constituted a *bona fide* top-class match and of who was entitled to participate in it. Any sympathy for the

ICC lay in an appreciation that, from the Conference's viewpoint, if the recognised world authority lost control, the kind of anarchy that for example, has been associated with disputatious bodies vying for power in boxing or motor car racing, could certainly ensue.

Kerry Packer, officially the World Series Cricket company, plus three nominated players, one of them Tony Greig, took the ICC and the English Test and County Cricket Board to the High Court and challenged the ICC decision on eligibility. Although the case dragged on for several weeks, it was difficult to disagree with the plaintiffs' case. It was one thing for the ICC and the national cricket organisations to 'disapprove' of somebody else arranging other games. It was altogether another thing to deny players the right to play in them under the threat of future boycott. There was also the muddy area of what constituted a contract. In England for instance, the players were the employees of county clubs and they were, so to say, released on occasion to represent England. At that juncture there were no central contracts; players, legally speaking, had either a contractual agreement for an individual 'home' Test match or for an 'away' tour. The judgement concluded that the ICC action was an example of restraint of trade. Kerry Packer was shown the legal green light.

For two Australian seasons, 1977/78 and 1978/79, World Series Cricket occupied many hours and the anxious thoughts of the world's cricket administrators. While the first year's efforts drew but sparse crowds during a season when orthodox Australia played a dramatic series with India, the second year proved to be sensationally appealing for spectators and viewers alike. It might be said that Greg Chappell's pirate Australians came to be regarded as the genuine Australian team. The games principally revolved around three sides, a World eleven, led by Tony Greig, a West Indian side and an Australian team. They played so-called Super-Tests, they competed for an International Cup over a set of limited overs games and like the Exhibition elevens of yore, they conveyed cricket to places where big cricket was relatively unknown, under the guise of an additional Country Cup Championship.

The innovations were especially diverting, for, among several other novel techniques, coloured clothing and, what proved to be very popular, floodlit evening cricket were introduced. Denied the usage of conventional grounds by his irked opponents, Kerry Packer found other venues such as other sports arenas, including Perth's pony-trotting arena, and even flew in specially prepared pitches to be inserted thereon for these occasions. Kerry Packer seemed to have had the showman's flair that enabled him to surmount the stiffest obstacles. The cricket was intensely competitive, whilst Kerry Packer, very much a hands-on operator, did not hesitate, as the fine West Indian bowler, Michael Holding, has confirmed, to berate teams or players suspected of slack endeavour.

Particularly in the second year of the Packer treatment, when an England tour of Australia coincided with the alternative WSC entertainment of skilful delights, there was much confusion. There were weakened official Test teams across the world, although the English county clubs, fearful both of legal repercussions and loss of revenue at the gate and in subscriptions, continued to employ both English and overseas players with the Packer brand. In the late winter of 1978 the WSC Australians played a rubber of Super-Tests against the WSC West Indians in the West Indies, with which the impoverished authorities felt obliged to align themselves, thereby reneging on the ICC agreement to give no succour to the enemy. When one adds in the similar upheaval over the coming years in regard of the 'rebel' South African trips, any analysis of Test cricket over this era must factor in some degree of this disorder.

With the helpful benefit of the video replays of hindsight, one may observe how likely it was that the battle would be short-lived and terminate with but one victor. Money, especially money associated with television, talks with incessant loudness. Kerry Packer was not looking to destroy international cricket; his aim was to make a fortune out of it. This was a study in economic blackmail and the victims squirmed for little more than a couple of, for them, depressing years. What he wanted was total control of the television sets and with what appeared to be surprising abruptness, the Australian Board sued for peace in the spring of 1979. In exchange for a relatively small annual sum, he was granted his wish of ten years exclusive TV coverage and in a heavy hint of television influence to come, he included the condition that the forthcoming 1979/80 Indian tour of Australia be cancelled, in favour of a World Series featuring the home team, the West Indies and England over fifteen one-day games, sponsored by Benson and Hedges and complete with the dreaded coloured clothing.

Kerry Packer proved to be not so much the Count Dracula sucking the blood from the defenceless and virginal national cricket boards, as the benign medico, boosting them with blood transfusions. The pattern upon which he insisted and which gradually emerged from the debris of the Packer conflict, was a balance of Test matches with popular limited overs contests all over the Test-playing world, all of them at the behest of the relevant television companies. Loath although some of cricket's traditional administrators might have been to pursue this road and make these very real concessions, there can be little doubt that this unholy alliance of the wicket and the telly rescued international cricket from any possible fiscal collapse. Kerry Packer has some claim to stand beside the giants of the game, the Graces and the Bradmans, in respect of his massive influence upon cricket's destiny.

The Australian stage for this cricketing and financial melodrama makes for interesting speculation. Throughout the main part of the post-war era, Australia had remained very static in its political and cultural evolution. From 1949 to 1972 the Conservatives had ruled, with Robert Menzies a long-serving prime minister of conventional view and cricketing affections. The 'Bradmanesque' school of thought, Anglophile, monarchist, especially with a delight – her early 1954 tour was a spectacular hit – in a young queen, and non-progressive, was dominant. New styles then began to emerge in rebellion. There was a fresh assertiveness associated politically with the less deferential politician, Gough Whitlam. The 'larrikin' traits in Australian life came more to the fore and they made felt their presence both in the dressing rooms as well as on the terraces of Australian cricket. One must repeat the warning about the changeability of national character. This aspect had never have been wholly absent, as the rows in the Australian dressing room and among Australian crowds over time suggested but now that 'rough' rose in influence in place of the more 'respectable' element. The Chappell brothers, Jeff Thomson and Dennis Lillee personified the change of mood and attitude. Paid only A$200 a Test match and full of the testosterone of anti-authoritarianism, they could hardly have been readier for the Packer allurement. And Kerry Packer himself was an example of the new spirit of swashbuckling enterprise and no-nonsense capitalism.

THE PACKER EFFECT

The train and the press, the steamship and the radio – these agencies had been the impetus for cricket's national and then global development. Now the pairing was that of the plane and the television. The post-1945 growth of civil flights was a crucial element. For example, the number of UK charter flights rose from 2m in 1951 to 10m in 1981 and by the end of the 20th century some 150m passengers passed through British airports, with the figures steadily rising all the time. In the European Community alone in the year 2000 there were 250m domestic and 750m international air flights. During the last twenty years of the 20th century this dual tongued prong of a TV set in practically every home, bar, pub or its equivalent and an airport in practically every area of respectable population density was completed.

From the cricketing stance, it meant that teams could be ferried quickly from one end of the world to the other, as well as rapidly and conveniently within large regions such as the West Indies, Australia and India. This was matched by the increasing ability of television, through satellite technology, to transmit live pictures of cricket matches to the four corners of the planet. It was the ideal coupling. Both the players and the pictures of them performing were always readily available. The stage was set for the Packer-motivated theatre of breathlessly continuous and interminably televised international cricket. By the year 2000 there were upward of 150 such contests yearly, with television time, complete with the usual fore and aft analyses and the highlights, of as much as 2000 hours devoted to cricket. With a practically non-stop round of televised Test and one-day matches, world cricket might have adopted the wartime motto of the London Windmill revue theatre; 'We Never Closed'.

Cricket finances swelled. The commercial wheel turned boldly. Sponsors were the likelier to find funds were matches to be televised and, for example, their corporate insignia might be stencilled on to the turf, while subsidiary sponsorship, say, of umpires, became a secondary source of revenue. Clothing and equipment was liberally stamped with the makers' brands, while another source of income arose from the practise of advertising hoardings around the perimeter of the boundary, with even the ancient device of the sightscreen exploited with a reversible poster shown during alternate overs. The superiority of commercial over spectator needs was demonstrated by the termination of the longstanding practice on some grounds, Lord's included, of allowing spectators, when the seats were crowded, to lounge on the grassy margin between boundary rope and fence. It is true that, with stricter approaches to health and safety issues, that custom might have been curtailed anyway but it was the risk that television viewers would not catch that crucial occasional glimpse of the advertisements now adhering to the palings that ended that tolerant liberty.

At the same time, there was a role for the spectators. Apart from the very useful revenue accruing from what were increasingly highly priced tickets, there was something lacking, as became quite evident in countries where the hunger for Test match cricket declined, were the venues half-empty. It sent the message to the television watcher that this entertainment was not up to par. One never sees a TV show that requires a studio audience with rows of empty seating. Indeed, as in football, the accent was on boosting the crowd's appeal, with (suitably sponsored) large cards for spectators to wave, signalling the striking of a four or a six. The wearing of fancy dress, especially in unison, as in a dozen Elvis Presleys or a job lot of brown bears, became common, to the delight of the television producers. The crowd was a necessary part of the purveyed pictorial action.

Technically, and here Kerry Packer must take some credit for such initial improvements, television production was much enhanced, with the deployment of several cameras and a series of electronic and computerised aids to demonstrate every conceivable twist and turn of each delivery. Hair's breadth decisions, like run outs, LBWs or debated catches, especially behind the wicket, were analysed in ferocious detail, while a medley of statistical testimony was colourfully descried. Exotic terms – the Snickometer, Hawkeye – became common. Cricket is the complex game for the person who enjoys complexity and one could hardly deny the luxurious value of these varied scanning implements and the speed with which obscure data might be telegraphed via the television set and later the ubiquitous internet. Eventually, television would come to be deployed as a help-meet for umpires on certain decisions, and players were permitted appeals to such electronic arbitration, although there were worries that this led to needless delays and drained the essence of the cricketing spirit.

Although cricketers, many years after footballers, began to wear numbers and/or names so that they might the more easily be identified, the vastness of the cricketing arena often makes it difficult to peruse these tagged backs. The adoption of the helmet, in particular, rendered many a batsman anonymous to the uninformed members of the throng. In fact, and apart from the benefits of ambience and sociability, one may watch a cricket match on television now with a greater expectation of an accurate receptivity than if one is actually there – although, on many occasions, the replay screens made available on grounds are, ironically, a useful, sometimes indispensable, supplement for the paying customer. First-class cricket, because of the limitations of venues and the inordinate length of games, had always been followed by many from a respectable distance, their interest maintained through newspaper reports and, later, radio commentaries. Now television gave them an opportunity to watch their once invisible heroes.

Freed from the constraints of unfair contracts, cricketers across the Test-playing countries enjoyed a boost in income, an advantage that began during the 'Super-Test' era as national authorities struggled to compete with Kerry Packer for the use of star players. Everyone seemed to have gained financially from the Packer economic revolution. The complaints were more to do with the culture of the game, expressions of dismay that the traditions and rituals of cricket were being sadly disregarded.

ENGLISH CRICKET

In its recreational sphere, English cricket apparently did not suffer as much of a decline as observers in the last quarter of the 20th century were wont to suggest. This pessimism came about through the very definite lapse in the numbers watching county and also league cricket and from anxieties about the inconsistency of England's Test performances. In the latter case this reflected paranoia traceable back many years, especially in terms of results against Australia. If there were a modern element, it arose from the improvement of hitherto mediocre national teams rather than the decline of England. Several countries had caught up with the English and Australian teams since the Second World War.

In effect, as the 20th century reached its end, the official England figures recorded the existence of 14,000 clubs and the number of regular club players was a satisfying 400,000, at least as many as the most lavish estimate for the inter-wars years, when earnings had priced out more from club cricket than in the relatively prosperous post-war decades. To that should be added the usual run of informal cricket of a cheery social nature. Looking back, it is doubtful whether and for how long cricket had enjoyed anything like the upper hand. In Hugh de Selincourt's *The Cricket Match*, the village captain, Paul Gauvinier, worried about the encroachment of football on to the village green. 'You can take that blasted football off the ground now', he shouted cheerfully to the overgrown boys.' That was 1923.

Critics gloomily castigated the schools and universities for their negligence in terms of cricket provision. This was largely a plump red herring. The phase during which many schools offered obligatory cricket on the curriculum had been short-lived. There had been little or no cricket in state schools before 1939. The temporary growth of grammar schools after 1918, with their mimicry of the public schools, had necessarily introduced cricket to another minority of boys, while the general spread of secondary schooling, especially with the building of new premises, brought more cricket into schools for some years after the Second World War. This scarcely lasted a generation. A number of factors told against schools cricket. One highly coloured piece of lore was that progressive education was opposed to competitive games, but that thought had little credence outside a very few schools, mainly in the London area. A much more punishing reason was the selling off of playing fields for building purposes, a move associated with the Thatcher-style conservatism of the 1980s. Cricket, in need of a biggish area, was something of a sufferer.

Another point, little regarded, was that the modern comprehensive school ideally developed a comprehensive attitude to the recreational and health-promoting benefits of sport, offering pupils tasters of many games rather than one or two. The olden days, when youngsters were forced to play just rugby for two terms and cricket for one have, in many instances, been supplanted by a more open-ended series of opportunities. In the past, to those who did not care for compulsory cricket or found it displeasing, it had been a debilitating experience. To be frank, and at the risk of apoplexy amongst one's readership, cricket has several negative aspects as an educational device. Given, say, an hour or so for a games period, cricket, as a game as opposed to practice, is difficult to organise, while, from the viewpoint of physical exercise, it engages very few intensely at any one juncture. Nine are sitting waiting to bat, while several fielders may also be fairly unchallenged. Once one clears one's head of the outmoded hogwash about character building and concentrates on cricket as a companionable and wholesome recreation, it takes it place, an honourable place, amid a series of other possibilities.

In effect, the notion that the state education system, at a cost of many billions of pounds, should be expected, alongside its other responsibilities, to rear eleven cricketers to represent England at cricket, is a farcical one. Its task is, or should be, to turn out young citizens of a curious, lively, hard-working, kindly, tolerant and civic-minded disposition. It is intriguing that, such has been the association of cricket with public schools and Oxbridge, that this criticism continues; it is more rarely that one hears the clarion call for schools and colleges to produce tennis, golf or snooker champions.

These points are made with no sense of disrespect to the magnificent efforts of the various bodies, national and local, to sustain schools cricket – for the final comment must be that the incidence of schools cricket is not so sparse as many commentators darkly hint. Basking in the shadow of the 2005 Ashes triumph, initiatives like the Cricket Foundation's 'Chance to Shine' scheme tried to compensate for the loss of facilities and the savage cuts in games expenditure associated with the cruel decades of the 1980s and 1990s. 'Chance to Shine', engaging from 2005 especially with primary schools as well as secondary schools, hoped to invest £50m in schools cricket by 2015. In 2008 for example, there was an expenditure of £5.4m, made up of £1m from the ECB, £1.7m from private sponsors and a matching sum of £2.7m via Sport England, the government funded agency. This excellent programme had already reached 3000 schools by the summer of 2009.

It remains true, of course, that whatever the educational arguments, the upper class affection for cricket and its supposed glories is a constant, a tradition passed down from the heady days of Victorian splendour. In 2009 *the Guardian* newspaper quoted the case of Dulwich College in the borough of Southwark. With annual boarding fees of £27,330, in a society where median yearly earnings are about £23,000, its 1450 boys use eight full grass cricket fields, whereas the Southwark borough state schools exist on just six such amenities. This imbalance may show why former fee-paying pupils are still numbered highly among the English elite. It is more surprising in those circumstances that, among others, the likes of Andrew Flintoff of Ribbleton Hall High School, now the City of Preston High School, James Anderson of St Theodore's Roman Catholic High School, Burnley and Paul Collingwood of Blackfyne Comprehensive School, now Consett Commuity Sports College, stride confidently in the valorous footmarks of Jack Hobbs, Herbert Sutcliffe and many others educated in the state sector.

From top – the ECB – to bottom – the local club – English cricket appears to have received, understood and is acting on the message that it must take full responsibility for its own destiny, recreational as well as professional, rather than leave it to others.

In 1997 the England and Wales Cricket Board had been established, the result of the recommendation of the TCCB – instigated the Murray Working Party –that is, M.P.Murray, a former Middlesex amateur – which had begun its discussions in 1991. Apart from some cricketing suggestions, such as the adoption of a four day duration for county matches, it called for this reorganisation of cricket in the United Kingdom into a pyramidal shape. This included the erection of County Boards with wider responsibilities to oversee regional and local cricket, with, for instance, the creation of 'premier' leagues in each area, beneath which would lie layers of competitive leagues, with relegation and promotion involved. This was accomplished with reasonable speed. The format in almost all cases was a version of limited overs cricket, while the huge majority of clubs found themselves engaged in league cricket of some kind, with both leagues and in many instances, clubs brandishing the logo of their proud sponsor. Aside from those to whom the competitive edge appealed, such formal arrangements, with fixtures bespoke, made for an easier administrative life for club officials, whereas the number of clubs enjoying merely 'friendlies' dwindled, not without a hint of sadness for those who preferred the more amiable approach.

Two disparate documents might be cited. The last hundred pages of the *Lancashire Cricket Yearbook* for 2001 described the exploits of the comparatively new Lancashire Cricket Board. It told of six county-wide competitions, of the LCB over 50s team, of the county's women's teams at adult, under 19 and under 15 levels, all based on fifteen women's clubs, of the Lancashire Youth Federation, with its under 19, under 16, under 13 and under 11 fixtures, and of Lancashire Schools cricket, with its chief eleven playing fourteen fixtures nationally, plus under 15, under 14, under 13 and under 12 activities in all fashions of local and national tournaments. Then came the Directory of League Cricket. There were 22 leagues in operation, comprising 276 clubs, most of them running two or three regular sides and all of them industriously engaged in youth and junior cricket.

The other publication was the *Border Counties Youth Association Handbook* for the same year – and Walter Scott fans may relax, for the borders referred to are those around Lincolnshire and Rutland. This tiny 24 page booklet reported how cricket was organised among the children of twelve clubs in the district at six levels, from under 9 to under 15, with the stated ambition of adding four more layers that would provide cricket from the ages of eight to eighteen.

The massive tome of the large and bustling county and the smaller handbook of the more minute and remote vicinity both exemplify the sheer amount of effort being made by battalions of club administrators, teachers and coaches, as well as players, to guarantee that, from an early age, those who wish to may participate in cricket. The cricket clubs are now doing infinitely more for boys and girls than was usual until the last twenty or thirty years.

The testimony is strong enough to assert that more people, especially young people, are playing organised cricket than at any other time in English history. Even allowing for population increase, this is remarkable, given the Jeremiah cries about the gloomy state of English cricket. One must repeat that the cricketing Cassandras normally begin from a much exaggerated estimate of how many were actually playing in the past.

There was clearly an excitement for and around cricket in other parts of the world, with flamboyant tales of West Indian beaches awash with incipient Frank Worrells or Indian maidans packed with budding Kapil Devs. What did become apparent was the difference in approaches. In Australia there was and is a much more systemic attitude to cricket provision. Even in proportion to population, the opportunities to play formal cricket in Australia are probably fewer than in England but the chance on offer, if accepted, calls for a much stricter personal regime and a heightened dedication to the task in hand, with the route-way, through grade and state to international cricket clearly and inexorably mapped. The basis of the pyramid is narrower and its sides steeper. That is sternly in keeping with the general Australian view of the primacy of sport in national life and the results, not only in cricket, are visible at world levels.

It is a matter of philosophical debate, rather than cultural analysis, whether the country that plays relatively little cricket, almost all of it of high and serious excellence, is happier than the country that plays lots of cricket, much of it of a moderate if cheerful standard.

WOMEN'S CRICKET

Cricket was certainly played in many, many parts of the world by the late decades of the 20th Century, as cricket historians were quick to advertise, but it would be easy to over-egg its impact. Brave although it was to play cricket in, for example, Finland, there were probably more people in England who were aware of this mild eccentricity than in Finland itself. Cricket's mainstream influence remained heavily weighed towards the few Test-playing nations. Cricket chroniclers were also likely to embroider a few details of women's cricket into their sagas. The first reported instance of a ladies' match, Bramley versus Hambledon, in 1745; the legend of Christina Willes, in the Regency era, whose attempts to bowl underhand wearing a voluminous skirt, gave her brother, John, the idea of round-arm bowling; the formation of the country house style White Heather Club in 1887; the short-lived attempt to form an 'Original English Lady Cricketers' team for Exhibition purposes in 1890 – these specks of feminine hue amidst the drab uniformity of male dominion should not be given too much earnest attention.

This is written in feminist support, for it does no favours to the cause of equal gender opportunities to quote oddities and rarities. Women have had as much difficulty gaining some leverage in sport as in other arenas, except those where men were minded to locate them. Mary Queen of Scots, in the Caledonian tradition, may have been an avid golfer, while Mrs Stokes may have excited Hanoverian audiences with her lusty prize-fighting skills but on the whole the Christian epoch frowned on serous female sport. Unlike the ancient Greeks, who permitted the involvement of some upper-crust ladies in their Olympic Games, Pierre de Coubertin, promoter of their modern equivalent, declared 'women have only one task; that of the role of crowning the winner with garlands.' The pseudo-medieval chivalry of Victorian middle and upper class men meant that their womenfolk were protected from the more strenuous aspects of life. This involved a distinction between the male 'public' and the female 'private' areas, a basic reason, for instance, why the franchise was denied women. A placid engagement in croquet, battledore and shuttlecock or lawn tennis was allowed but anything beyond that was unfeminine.

Slowly the battles were won, if not the war. Hockey – East Molesley, formed in 1885, was the first women's club – athletics, gymnastics and skating, each of which demonstrated a much admired graceful-ness, swimming, archery, cycling and netball were among the first women's games to become acceptable. In 1886 young Charlotte Dod startled the tennis courts with her 'man-like' aggression and in 1909 Eleonora Sears was expelled from the polo ground for wear-ing trousers. Sportswomen were not to be what the football writer Brian Glanville was later to call 'imitation men'. There remained a grudging corollary to women's sport about the retention of the supposed femininity factor.

This rider was neatly summarised in a song in the Gilbert and Sullivan comic opera, *Utopia Limited*, which opened in 1893. Entitled 'A Bright and Beautiful English Girl', it is difficult to decide, such is the ambiguity in the Victorian mind-set, whether it is affectionately satirical or sentimentally straight: With 'her magnificent comeliness', she undertakes a series of energetic sports: 'with a ten mile spin she stretches her limbs; she golfs, she punts, she rows, she swims' Another literary example is J.C.Snaith's cricketing novel, *Willow the King*, published in 1899, wherein the heroine, Grace Trentham, plays out a tomboyish love-match of single wicket cricket with the hero, 'Dimmy' Dimsdale, star batsman of Little Hickory.

The woman's 800 metres at the Amsterdam Olympics in 1928 was a disaster. Five of the competitors dropped out and another five collapsed during the race, while the eleventh, the sole survivor, fainted after her victory. It would be 1960, at the Rome games, before the event was next included, such was the controversy. The authorities made the error of assuming that gender was the cause of the disarray and that women were not fitted to run in such a race. It was a long time before they realised that poor training and preparation was the true reason, for the women athletes had, in the long and short term, undertaken an ill-advised and inadequate build-up, totally different to the regime adopted by men for such an event.

In all walks of life, most unhelpfully in employment, this sort of wrong-headedness has ruled. Moreover, whenever there has been discrimination, there has been some likelihood of the victims becoming part of the conspiracy, that is, believing and acting upon the discriminatory propaganda. History being about winners, little is heard now of the Women's Anti-suffrage campaign in Edwardian England, whereby women fought hard to prevent the vote being granted to their sex. It is possible that brutalising experiences on the school hockey field had scarcely aided middle and upper class women to think benignly of sports, but, for whatever reasons, it was not, for years, high on the woman's agenda.

In this climate there were mixed feelings about the physicality of cricket, what might be called the 'hard ball' versus the 'clean whites' controversy. However, there was evidently some ready acceptance of the moral worth of cricket, as advocated by the boys' public schools.

Predictably the girls' boarding schools that developed towards the end of the Victorian era, in wholesome tribute to their male predecessors, began to adopt the message of Athleticism. One or two headmistresses, the remarkable Miss Beale, founder head of Cheltenham Ladies College among them, felt that the hunger for such commonplace success as winning at games was undesirable. Dean Farrar, author of the overly pious *Eric, or Little by Little,* first published in 1861, a doleful story of a gradual sinking into despair, said he had 'but one object – the vivid inculcation of inward purity and moral purpose'. Like Miss Beale, he was suspicious of the gratuitous pride found in games-playing, a spirit of anti-competitiveness that would have made that Victorian pair strange bedfellows with the few left-wing metropolitan teachers who, many decades on, would similarly excoriate the team mentality.

Miss Beale, it must be said, was thinking more of the 'private' world of the ideal young lady, her thoughts on family, household and children. Despite that, Cheltenham, under the leadership of the next incumbent, Miss Lillian Faithfull, joined other schools, such as Roedean (until 1898 known as Wimbledon House), in playing cricket, as well as the more familiar hockey and tennis. By Edwardian times, several posh girls' schools were cricketing and there developed a handful of inter-school fixtures. But, truth to tell, cricket did not figure too greatly in the girls' school firmament.

There was no answering response from girls of the lower classes. There was none of that rough and ready alliance illustrated in the top grade by the Gentleman/Player combine, which assisted cricket in the masculine world. There was no chance for them, at school or in the local park, to play cricket. Every element, be it social, cultural or economic, was against them. At the risk of being disrespectful to an enjoyable pastime, they were lucky in those days if they had a game of rounders.

It was 1926 – eight years after the 1918 Parliamentary Reform Act had tendered the franchise to a limited number of women and a couple of years before the 1928 Universal Suffrage Act finally gave the vote to all women and, indeed, all men – before the English Women's Cricket Association was formed, almost all the players involved being ex-public school girls. Similar steps had presumably been occurring in the Antipodes, where Australia and New Zealand established women's associations in 1931 and 1934 respectively. In the winter of 1934/35 the English women toured Australia and New Zealand and defeated the representative teams of both dominions, and in 1937 the Australian women came to England.

Progress was then slow. Women's cricket remained on something of a plateau, with money for what was deemed a minority sport unforthcoming. The next highlight was the first Women's Cricket Cup in 1973, when Rachel Heyhoe-Flint's England team beat three rivals in a round robin competition. After further such competitions, there was something of a step forward when, in 1993, the final was played at the male redoubt of Lord's. England beat New Zealand by 67 runs in a match of which *the Guardian* newspaper wrote 'make no mistake, these are terrific cricketers'. Another report described a day of 'high quality skills with the bat, old-fashioned virtue with the ball, superb fielding.'

It moved some to think of an unimaginable future. Cricket is a game in which specialisms are deployed within the collective. For example, in the 1993 final, Karen Smithies bowled spinners on a niggling spot, with exact line and length, causing her opponents to falter and ending with the impressive figures of 12 overs, 4 maidens, 14 runs, 1 wicket. However much is made of the power and stamina needed for quick bowling, there is plainly no reason why a woman should not bowl slowly or at medium pace with line and length adequate to men's high-class, even first-class requirements. Wicket-keeping has a similar possibility. When, with clever marketing skill, the ICC held the men's and women's World Twenty20 competitions simultaneously in England in 2009 *the Guardian's* Mike Selvey judged Sarah Taylor, 'a wonderfully gifted youngster', unrivalled in either tournament in that position.

Games of course, were shaped for masculine physicality; high-ranking women snooker players have wryly observed that their sport is really only for the flat-chested. Cricket's nomenclature – 'man of the match', third man, twelfth man – is Chauvinist, but there may be a likelier hope of mixed gender cricket than, say, in the contact sports such as rugby.

As the 21st century dawned, women's cricket, especially in England, became better funded and gained from being part of a generally improved recognition of gender equality. MCC, its pavilion doors marginally ajar to female members from 1998, organised a women's team and the sport became more widely accepted. Following a long phase in which women's cricket was miserably financed, the ECB began to take more of an interest. Eight England women players were paid by the 'Chance to Shine' initiative to coach in state schools and generally act as ambassadors, while the top twenty England players received grants of between £300 and £800 a month. With Clare Connor, a former captain, in charge as ECB head of women's cricket, there were by 2009, 450 clubs with women's and girls' sections, while, over an eighteen month period, participation had risen by almost a half.

To look forward a little to round off a pleasant story, there was much more press and media coverage when, in 2008/09 England, briskly captained by the stylish batswoman, Charlotte Edwards, won the Ashes series in Australia and handsomely won the Women's World Cup in New Zealand. Then came the historic breakthrough. Claire Taylor, the leading English player and pre-eminent bat, was named as one of the *Wisden* 'Five Cricketers of the Year', that most prestigious of sporting quintets. Charlotte Edwards was appointed MBE and then, in the summer of 2009, England won the first World Twenty20 trophy. A fiercely fought draw enabled them to hang on to the distaff Ashes in the one game played in England in 2009.

The aspirations for women's cricket were responsibly and reasonably high. In world cricket this was the one area where conservative, fuddy-duddy England was leading the egalitarian way, with only New Zealand, Australia and India providing other than lukewarm opposition. The infamous glass ceiling may not, apropos cricket, have been shattered, but a definite crack or two had appeared.

If women's cricket is a yarn of minor triumph in the face of commercial difficulties, the final tale in this chapter of major financial intervention in cricket touches on the darker facets. In 2000, the South African captain, Hansie Cronje, born-again Christian and fraudster, holder of 53 Test and 138 one-day international caps, was uncovered as a recipient of bookmakers' bribes in exchange for information and for match fixing. He had also tried to importune other members, including two rather vulnerable non-white players, of his team and admitted that he had gained $US250,000 by his crimes. Having gained immunity from prosecution, he gave what was widely regarded as partial testimony to the Commission chaired by Justice King in South Africa, putting down his weakness to an addictive love of money. Australian, Indian and Pakistani players were also caught up in a corruption scandal that involved chiefly bookmakers on the subcontinent, while perhaps not surprisingly, cricket authorities across the world showed a feeble reluctance to confront the perils head on. There was uneasy talk of icebergs and tips, but without the kind of phone tapped evidence collected by the Indian police that brought Hansie Cronje low, it was not easy to act with directness.

He was banned from involvement in cricket for life, sadly, a sentence of brief duration, for in 2002, aged only 32, the man who had done such fine things for the emerging cricket of a unified South Africa was killed in a plane crash.

Corrupt gambling was among the first of the hints that modern cricket, for all its glitzy novelty, also had a retrogressive characteristic. Hansie Cronje might have felt at home and been enthusiatically welcomed at the Green Man and Still in London's Oxford Street, where the Hanoverian professionals foregathered to negotiate their bookmakers' bribes during those previous times when cricket and gambling had been so heavily linked together.

CHAPTER THIRTEEN
POST-PACKER

The modern county scene in recent times; Worcestershire play host to Lancashire at Worcester.

Kerry Packer is a precious gift for those desirous of the contextual analogue. Insightful interpreters of cricket, sages such as John Arlott or the West Indian writer, C.L.R. James, were ever keen to stress, rightfully, the sense of cricket as an expression of its environment. The Packer revolt of the late 1970s could scarcely have been more characteristic of the mores of an epoch when capitalism ran riot and money did not so much talk as shout from the world's rooftops.

SOCIAL CANVAS

On the economic front, the oil crisis of 1973/74, during which oil prices quadrupled, threw the entire world into the turmoil and panic of a long recession. Apart from a short debt-led rally in the early 1980s, the British economy was sluggish until the late 1990s. The average of a 3% annual rate of growth, which had held good from the 1950s, slumped to 1%. There was a grim collapse of the manufacturing sector of British industry. The proportion of the workforce engaged in manufacture had been some 50% for over a hundred years; now it abruptly dwindled beneath 30%. It has been argued that, just as the 1930s depression was linked to the switch from steam to oil based technologies, the advent of electronic techniques was a secondary cause of this economic debacle. After the long phase, since 1940, of full employment, the jobless figures soon hovered at or above 3m and stayed at high levels for several years. At the mundane level of the purse or pocket, there was raging inflation. Taking the baseline of 100 as of 1962, the retail price index had passed 500 by 1981 and 1000 by 1992.

The legitimacy of the post-war consensus rested on a harmony of the Beveridge-style Welfare State and a Keynesian approach to public finance. The first, inspired by the wartime Beveridge Report, tendered a cradle to grave protection against social distress for the citizen, its motif of 'universalism' insisting that all should pay that all might benefit. The second, associated with the eminent economist, Maynard Keynes, promulgated, at its simplest, a prudent combine of saving amid plenty and spending amid dearth. It was a moderate concept uniting a public responsibility for social matters, such as unemployment or ill-health, with a public vigilance over government spending.

There had been a growing critique of this tacit concord, not least because the bureaucratic delivery of public services now seemed laboured and drab against the gaudy pigmentation of much private consumerism from the 1960s onward. A more individualist mood, begotten of and driving that materialist credo, found the rather dour rationale of wartime and post-war collectivism alien. The political response was relentlessly market-led, not only in Britain but also in North America and elsewhere in parts of Asia and Europe. The monetarist approach, with tight budgets, lowered taxation, especially for the well-to-do and uncontrolled conveyance of capital was most destabilising both of people and communities. In a shrewd descriptor of the age, it was a situation where 'the alliance of the comfortable' was the victor.

Nor were matters helped by the centralised measures adopted by the administrations of Mrs Thatcher, very much the rider rather than the creator of the tempest. In the classic style of the right-wing government, there was an abrasive centrality of control imposed to ensure that there would be no bulwarks standing against the flow of unrestricted financial enterprise. Policing, for instance, became highly centralised in scope, with the police response to the miners' strike of 1984 a particular illustration, whereas the major accretion of Whitehall power was at the expense of the harsh diminution of local authority during this period. A prime example was in the education service, where central dicta, such as the national curriculum and severe layers of narrow testing and unhelpful inspection, became the baleful norm. The wholesome checks and balances of the old duality of national and municipal government were more or less destroyed. Trades unionism, another barrier against *laissez-faire,* had grown very powerful and occasionally selfishly so, and was accordingly now enfeebled.

Within this highly centralised state, 'The Culture of Narcissism', in Christopher Lasch's mordant phrase, came to be widely worshipped. With the individual in the affirmative and the sense of society negated, the mood of liberationist self-gratification, born of the 1960s, was in the ascendant, but its association with economic distress was fatal. The crime rate soared upwards by 36% in the 1980s. There were 791 woundings reported in 1920 and there were over 100,000 in the year 2000. Poverty was high again – officially, the number of people existing in poverty grew from 5m to 14m in these times, as the inequality gap widened considerably. There were riots, civil disorder, a rash of what criminologists called 'incivilities', such as vandalism, graffiti and other forms of social misbehaviour, evident signs of xenophobia, particularly perhaps among football fans and a collapse of communal disciplines. The solid backbone of an earnest artisan and a sedate middling class for all its flaws of censoriousness and pettiness, had been finally broken. The crowd came to be feared again.

Indeed, there were gloomy thoughts abroad that the reverse was happening and that, sociologically where there had been a sturdy stomach, now there appeared to be a thin waistline. Social analysts called this the 'hourglass society', with a largish upper bulb of well-to-do people and a largish lower bulb of an impoverished sub-class. Literary imaginations recalled the Alphas and Gammas of Aldous Huxley's alarmist *Brave New World*, published in 1932. Its cultural element was referred to as dumbing-down, together with talk of eggheads at the other end of the gamut. Of course, there had been some Philistinism at the bottom and some sniffiness at the top – the term 'highbrow' had been coined in 1908 – during the long period in which the trusty old middle ground had been comfortably occupied. Now however, the chasm was wider, with, by way of illustration, the broadsheet/tabloid gulf of the press infinitely wider than a generation ago.

With an absence of censorship, social or legal, and a welter of technological invention at one's disposal, the choice is patently huge, especially compared with the pre-1960s when the middlebrow option was, frankly, Hobson's choice. Nevertheless, there is, amid the helter-skelter of pastimes, a tendency for the ordinary, run-of-the mill diversions, the equivalent of what was once everyday fodder, to be eased out of the reckoning.

It was in many ways, a return to something like the public life of the 18th century, so much so that, and in the terms of Jeffrey Richards' simple but telling theory, the 'rough', like in Hanoverian times, gained in ascendancy over the 'respectable' elements in British as in Australian society. There were yobbos as well as larrikins. National character, ever a movable cultural feast, changed again – or possibly resumed a former fashion. In its extremes, the largely obedient, good-humoured, acquiescent stiff upper lip had yielded to the more fractious, ill-tempered, anti-social stroppy lip. In picturesque cameo, one might compare queuing calmly for a bus in the 1940s with today's testy scramble for such a service. Moreover, one might equally compare the relative absence of such a useful example of public transport from British roads with the gridlock of multitudinous private vehicles.

Cricket, which had become one the games closely identified with a 'respectable' Britain, obviously found the going hard in this ambience, for its image looked old-fasioned and its ethic was regarded as sentimental. What happened was that it became a product to be bought and sold on the global market, for it had, at bottom, sufficient televisual appeal to be worthy of financial investment.

In the immediate post-Packer phase, there were increased earnings for English cricket from television, from sponsorship and even from ticket receipts for international fixtures. It has been calculated that overall income rose from £2m annually in the mid-1970s to £8m in the mid-1980s, at which point and for the first time, 'England' and 'county' income was roughly equal. Hitherto the seventeen counties had jointly made more money than an England team playing fewer fixtures, all without sponsorship and with little income from the media. Salaries improved. Capped county players enjoyed a 100% rise in the same period from £3500 to over £7000, and the counties' combined salary bill doubled to £2m. The most spectacular jump was direct from £200 to £2000 for a Test match fee, immediately consequent to the Packer revolt.

Even allowing for the effect of inflation, these were speedy and remarkable changes – and the profitability of English cricket went on rising. By the mid-1990s, the total income was some £40m but the proportions were changing rapidly. The England element was now responsible for about 70% of this as opposed to 30% coming from the counties, who required subsidies of about £1m each to keep them hovering in the black. Of this sum of £40m, almost a third came from television revenues, a very substantial increase in a very few years, and, by the end of the century, the composite television fees were no less than £26m, an amount that would have paid for a year of early 1970s' cricket thirteen times over.

Without that kind of a commercial packaging everywhere, cricket might, as a major component in world sport and culture, have lapsed into a merely recreational pastime. Gambling had rescued cricket from oblivion in the 18th century; a form of religiosity had saved it from disgrace in mid 19th century; the market secured its provisional future in the late 20th century. Cricket, as a professional spectacle continued, therefore, to serve as an emblem of its social context.

CRICKETING PORTRAIT

For all the disruptions, from rebel tours to corrupt practices against a canvas of rife commercialism, first-class cricket continued, as in every phase of its saga, to find great teams and players to grace its fields.

Were one to watch an imagined parade of the leading lights of those closing decades of the last century, a striking feature would be its comprehensive nature. There would be recognisable bands of brilliance passing the saluting base of memory from almost all of the competing Test nations.

The West Indies gradually lost much of their dominating power as the old century lingered on but still Curtly Ambrose and Courtney Walsh maintained the brisk convention of West Indian high pace, whereas the batting mantle passed to the prolific Brian Lara. Lightly built, deft and neat, he broke records galore, among them the Test record of 365, not out, held by Gary Sobers since 1957/58. He scored 375 against England in Antigua in 1993/94 – and then, in the summer of 1994, he made cricket's first first-class 500, 501, not out, to be precise, at Birmingham for Warwickshire against Durham. These were astounding feats but thereafter his career faltered a little, just as West Indian cricket and the domestic support for it, drifted somewhat. Brian Lara never quite left the sharp imprint of his distinguished antecedents.

Emerging from the purdah of Apartheid gloom, the South Africans fielded strong sides, with the fierce fast bowler, Alan Donald, Jacques Kallis and Kepler Wessels, two excellent batsmen, and Mark Boucher, a sound wicket-keeper-batsman, among the leading lights. Happily, it was pleasing to observe the coming into the team of players, such as the quick bowler, Makhaya Ntini, who previously would not have been considered on ethnic grounds. Neighbouring Zimbabwe, too, had its moments, primarily when Andy Flower and Heath Streak, respectively the mainstay batsman and bowler, were on song.

The subcontinent was awash with glistening talent during this time. Spin bowlers – like Anil Kumble for India or Saqlain Mushtaq for Pakistan – continued to weave their sorcery, while fast bowling, not hitherto strongly represented in the region, sprang boldly forth. The all-rounders, Kapil Dev in India and Imran Khan in Pakistan led the way, but the prime example was the devastating duo of Pakistan's Wasim Akram and Waqar Younis; between them they took some 800 Test wickets.

Top-class batsmen appeared in some profusion in the wake of the likes of Hanif Mohemmed, the Pakistani batsman whose 499 in 1958/59 for Karachi versus Bahawalpur was the then record first-class innings, and Sunil Gavaskar, whose 34 Test centuries for India eclipsed Don Bradman's record 29. Hanif Mohammed and Sunil Gavaskar, both very careful batsmen, rather put the lie to Lord Harris's opinion that Indians lacked the patience for cricket. Among an opulent list, Javel Miandad, Zaheer Abbas, Imzamam-al-Haq and Yousuf Youhana among the Pakistanis and Ajay Sharma, Mohammad Azharuddin, Rahul David and V.V.S.Laxman among the Indians especially caught the critical eye. The up and coming Sri Lankans also had radiant batsmen such as S.T.Jayasuriya and P.A.de Silva.

Amid this luxuriant blossom shone the glory of Sachin Tendulkar, hailed as the perfect bloom, the ideal blend of style and effectiveness, the Bradman of his generation, and destined to be the wealthiest cricketer of all time and, rarely for a cricketer, among the top handful of the world's richest sportsmen. Of immense personable charm, Sachin Tendulkar is feted in India as if he were a prince of his nation's glamorous film industry.

Even allowing for the vast amount of international cricket on offer, his figures are extraordinary. In 2009 he passed Brian Lara's record haul of Test match runs and as of mid-2010, he had scored 13,359 runs in 167 Tests with an impressive average of 55.48. He is also the top run scorer in one day internationals, with 17,598 runs, average 45.12, in 442 outings. Moreover, he is the chief centurion of international cricket, with a splendid tally of 93 international centuries, 47 in Test and 46 in limited overs matches. With effortless balance, economy of movement and precise stroke-play, there emerges a batesman who, like only two or three others, has so magnificently combined artistry and consistency.

As the cricketing spotlight turned evermore inexorably toward the subcontinent, it is fitting that an Indian cricketer should wear the laurels. Geographically, cricket has been fortunate in that W.G.Grace, Sir Donald Bradman and Sir Garfield Sobers were the kings of the world game at the moment their regions enjoyed the brightest lime-light – and Sachin Tendulkar followed that happy pattern. Some would, of course, argue that Thomas Carlyle's emphasis on 'Great Men' is the sounder explanation, and that it was these cricketers of genius that guaranteed their nations' successes.

New Zealand seldom hit the high spots in quite the same way as their all-conquering rugby union stars but, in players like John Reid and Glenn Turner, as well as the great Richard Hadlee, in the earlier and Martin Crowe and Chris Cairns in the later part of this era, they kept up a steady level of performance. It never quite emulated the exploits of their nearest Test-playing neighbours, the Australians, who regrouped and flourished profitably. Like a brightly oiled lathe, Australia produced shining products of unfailing efficiency. Among several effective bowlers, the nagging length of Glenn McGrath caused batsmen the most anxiety and excited pressmen into the con-sistent usage of the adjective 'metronomic' to describe his precision. There was a line of splendid wicket-keepers, with Rodney Marsh, Ian Healy and Adam Gilchrist acknowledged to be among the best ever. There were batsmen, such as the prolific Matthew Hayden, who captured the world record from Brian Lara with his 380 against Zimbabwe at Perth in 2003/04, and Mark Waugh, as effortless in the making of runs as in the taking of slip catches.

What was, however, most impressive was the imposing roster of disciplined captains who also won high honours as batsmen. Wed-ded to the tougher nationalism of their age and masters alike of man-management and of all types of bowling, they formed a stern and unrelenting band. The brothers, Ian and Greg Chappell, Allan Border, Mark Taylor, Steve Waugh and Ricky Ponting – with one or two tiny gaps, they steered and piloted Australia from the 1970s to the present day, normally with unconstrained triumph. All of them stand high in the ranks of Australian run-scorers; all of them brought a keen competitive edge and a thorough grasp of cricketing essentials to the task. In particular, they recalled, after Don Bradman, the need to raise the tempo of the game, especially in respect of a quickening of run rates to afford their bowlers the essential bequest of time. The

Australian ability to produce, one after another, captains capable of exceptional generalship, each possessing a world-class aptitude for batting, did much to guarantee Australian supremacy for most years of a long generation.

Cricket remained a social expression of its time and, while by no means alone, the Australians introduced into their cricket on a constant and conscious basis some of the fashions and manners that had, unluckily, become more commonplace in the devil-take-the-hindmost attitudes of modern society. There had been occasional sledging in cricket probably from time immemorial, obviating any margin for moderns to be over prissy on the subject. Nonetheless, Allan Border and Steve Waugh's adoption of what, in a clumsy euphemism, was called 'mental deterioration' rationalised sledging as an approved dimension of strategy. There were reports of team meetings, in both the men's and women's game, for the purpose of discussing which physical or other traits of one's opponents might prove most vulnerable to verbal assault.

Umpires and other authorities seemed unable to thwart such conduct, while the sentiment was encouraged that it was somehow manly to indulge in this form of behaviour and, equally, it was unmanly to protest. It did not help that, as far as one could tell from the sidelines, the choice of epithets was crudely banal in the extreme, lacking the salty wit of the more occasional thrusts of yesteryear. Wicket-keepers, by now expected to act as non-stop cheerleaders, as well as chirpy baiters of nervous batsmen, appeared to be particularly prone to the complaint of mundane inanity.

Opinions may differ as to the sporting legitimacy and ethical probity of sledging but one aspect is ordinarily forgotten. It is not in the script. Once again cricketers have neglected to consider that long-gone day in the 18th century when the public first paid to watch cricket and immediately, as now part of the entertainment business, the overall constitution of the experience changed. The paying public, including those paying to view on television, have a right to watch an exercise that is, like a theatre performance, within the prescribed limits. In so far as both the laws and conventions of cricket are concerned, sledging has no legitimacy. Crucially, the public cannot routinely hear what is going on in respect of sledging, while much of what else that happens is more or less intelligible. Verbal commentary, provided it does not imperil the enjoyment of others, should be left to the crowd which has paid for the privilege.

The theatre is a valuable parallel and yardstick. There are rarely any unscripted and unheard asides aimed at putting off other actors – it is not unknown but it is uncommon. Although not as deeply offensive as sledging, there are one or two other modern features that are distressing, such as untidy costuming, where once the well-dressed cricketer was part of the attraction, and unnecessary appealing; the appeal when the batsman is palpably not out, is a form of cheating. Some cricketers have also abandoned the pleasant custom of politely acknowledging applause, rather turning rapturously to their comrades on the pavilion balcony for plaudits. Then there is the dreadful new practice of the fielders taking to the arena and then gripping one another into a bonding circle, crouching and presumably listening to the captain's last prayers, rather than completing their preparations in the dressing room. These two acts are akin to actors, instead of taking a bow, turning to the wings to wave to their mates, or arriving on stage and, rather than launching into the play, banding together to exchange a few last minute Thespian tips.

However this may all be dismissed as old fogeyism, professional cricketers should have some responsibility for not breaking what actors call 'the fourth wall'. This is the invisible one on the other side of which is an audience awaiting what can still be a dramatic and beautiful piece of sporting theatre, with a just anticipation that it will conform to and not demolish the watchers' glorious illusion by the self-indulgence of the players.

That yearning for a decent standard of public performance logged, what of cricketing life on the English home front during the last decades of the 20th century? Faced with multifaceted strength in all parts of the world, England performed fitfully, sometimes glowingly, sometimes modestly. England was fortunate that its heritage of powerful opening batsmanship was sustained in the persons of such as Graham Gooch and Michael Atherton, figures of technical accomplishment coupled with intense mental fortitude. Occasionally, this doughtiness was relieved by the more feathery and whimsical touch of David Gower.

Alec Stewart, another dedicated opener, doubled as wicket-keeper, in an era where such a specialist was required to be an all-rounder. This device worked well in cases such as, from pre-war years, Kent's Les Ames, a classy wicket-keeper but also the only one to score a hundred centuries, or with his brilliant successors, for both Kent and England, Godfrey Evans and Alan Knott, both of them able to score runs as well keep wicket with surpassing lustre. In the modern idiom, the pugnacious Australian, Adam Gilchrist, was an outstanding illustration. However, the practice of ignoring the best stumper but relying on a lesser breed with batting form, was frowned upon by the traditionalists. John Murray, Bob Taylor and Jack Russell may be listed as excellent English wicket-keepers who lost out to what often was the false economy of this search for an all-rounder. It was suggested that football's equivalent would be playing a good right-back in goal because he could take penalty kicks.

The bowling was perhaps less consistently effective than the batting. There appeared to be a lengthening list of bowlers who only played a handful of games. In particular, spin bowling was apparently on the wane. The Kent left-hander, Derek Underwood, who actually often bowled at something like a slow-medium rate, was probably the most incisive from early in this period. He was a reminder of an age when a school or village team would have been as likely to take the field without a left hand spin bowler as without a wicket-keeper.

The yeoman champion of the era was the burly Ian Botham, hard-striking bat, flawless slip fielder and a fast-medium bowler of mature judgement. He was perhaps England's best all-rounder since the far-off days of George Hirst. Many of England's more dramatic victories in these years centred on his daring, especially, when, with the cerebral skipper, Mike Brearley, doing the thinking and Bob Willis obliging with some tempestuous bowling, the Australians were brought low in the summer of 1981

Given the prominence of batting in England and elsewhere over the last quarter of the 20th century, not least with the allotment of so much time to limited overs cricket where the bat tended to reign supreme, it is strangely satisfying to observe that two slow bowlers competed to be regarded as the true icons of the age. Granted too, the standing of fast and fast-medium bowling during this time, some of this also attributed to the influence of the one day competitions, and the pleasure of the surprise is even more enhanced.

The Australian leg-spinner, Shane Warne, believed by many serious judges to be the best of his type the world has known, was born in Victoria in 1969 and played in his first Test in 1992. For its exquisite blend of timing and dexterity, the ball with which he deceived Mike Gatting in the Old Trafford Test of 1993 was joyously hailed as 'the ball of the century'. Physically, he always looked on the plumpish side, although he was no mean close order catcher and could bat vigorously, while his moonlike countenance and sunshine smile was capped with garish yellow tresses. Socially, he had the gossips' tongues constantly a-wagging with scandalous yarns of a sexual, drug-related and dodgy bookmaker-orientated colouring. In these ways he more resembled, indeed he was, the ephemeral celebrity of current general mode. And yet, with his strong shoulder and clever hand, with a fixed determination to excel and evolve, and with a jovial temperament to boot, he learned to bowl all the range of the leg spin mystique, while he evaded the latent inaccuracy – that natural failing of his kind – of so torturous an action. In 145 Tests he mesmerised 708 victims into submission, at an average of about 25 and in 194 one day internationals, he took a further 203 wickets, at a similar average. He took 1319 first-class wickets and also contributed usefully with 3154 Test runs.

Muttiah Muralitharan, thought by many commentators to be the finest right hand spinner in cricket's history, was born in Sri Lanka in 1972. He was born a Tamil, his minority race in frequent fanatical conflict with the Sri Lankan establishment. The son of a hill country confectioner and suffering from a slightly disabled arm, he struggled to combat both ethnic and physical conditions to become cricket's leading international wicket taker in both the long and short forms of the game.

It would require a Talbot Baines Reed to do literary justice to the ripping yarn of his closing ball in Test cricket. Bowled against India in Galle in 2010, it won the match for Sri Lanka and secured him his 800th victim, creating a never to be overtaken record. His bowling average is 22.72, spread over 133 Tests, while he has also taken 515 wickets in 337 one-day internationals, at an average of 23.07.

Loose-limbed, open-chested, his twisted arm directing his infinitely flexible wrist, he bowls an off-break of colossal deviation, plus the top-spinner, the flipper and the new-fangled doostra, the off-spinner's googly, that is, the leg-break with an off-break action. A willing, unselfish and most cheerful character, the affable grin never far away from the bright-eyed face, his brushes with controversy have been purely of a sporting nature, arising from his critics' accusations about the legitimacy of his action. Three times has he been submitted to rigorous scientific scrutiny and three times he has been cleared. The chief outcome has been the rather shame-faced confession on the part of the authorities that 99% of bowlers bend their arms a little in delivery and the matter has become a matter of the degrees of the angle of deviation, not an arbitration easily made by an umpire in the heat of cricketing battle.

'Murali' is nearing the end of his astounding career and Shane Warne has departed the mainline international scene. Their bewildering exploits have been conducted in parallel. Here are two cricketers, both of who have taken over 700 international wickets, which, even allowing for the plenitude of Test matches in the current epoch, is staggering. Here are two slow bowlers who would grace the best-ever world elevens of fireside cricketing dreamers. Unlike in method, appearance and disposition, they have been alike in their capacity to baffle batsmen and enthuse spectators.

If W.G.Grace were the cricketing Titan of the latter half of the 19th century and if his fellow-batsman, Donald Bradman, were cricket's giant for the first half of the 20th century, then it is two bowlers, more amazingly, two slow bowlers, who vie for a similar title for these last fifty or sixty years. Further, it will be an exceptional cricketer who overhauls their record and import during the rest of the still young 21st century.

English Landscape

In the meanwhile, English cricket was judged by many to be lame and halting. Between 1878 and 1980, England won 38% of the Tests it played but from 1980 to 1993 that dropped to 21%, with, it was concluded, 'only Sri Lanka and Zimbabwe having poorer playing records over the same period.' Critics galore had their say. Perhaps the two most pungent and pertinent contributions to this bracing discussion were Mike Marquese's *Anyone but England; Cricket and the National Malaise* (1994) and Graeme Wright's *Betrayal; the Struggle for England's Soul* (1993) These were the dystopias of English (Cricket) Literature, being, respectively, the equivalent of Aldous Huxley's *Brave New World* and George Orwell's *1984*. Graeme Wright claimed that MCC had 'sold its birthright in order to sustain the game it had ruled for almost two centuries', leaving the sport at large devoid of protection, whilst Mike Marquese argued that 'the neurosis of English cricket . . . is rooted in the trauma of national decline', with 'the forward defensive prod' epitomising 'the shift from a nationalism based on dominance to one based on insecurity'.

Their solutions both called on an Arcadian past. Graeme Wright looked for MCC to return to Camelot and resume the probity of its wise, selfless and noble rule as 'the conscience of cricket'. Mike Marquese put his faith in the homespun commonsensicality of good folk close to their indigenous soil, what he called, to the expressed horror of E.W.Swanton, the 'autochthonous open-endedness' of cricket. One was a top-down and the other a bottom-up answer but both were expressive of a pastoral yearning. For those familiar with the Tolkien mythology, one reached for the magical sagacity of Gandulf and the other for the honest-to-goodness stout-heartedness of Bilbo Baggins the Hobbit.

For the most part, a common thread among these and other appraisals was a continuing critique of the county format, both as to its cumbersome shape and its inward-looking selfishness. It was constantly pressed that, while the other leading cricketing nations continued to benefit from a state or provincial or city or island base for their first-class cricket, one that aligned rationally with both its geographic pattern and international sporting requirements, England struggled on with its unwieldy county system.

In 1992 Durham entered the County Championship, the first movement, either in or out, since 1921. Finance told. At this point, the average annual cost of a county cricket club was £1.4m, of which not much more than an average of £70,000, about an eighth was recouped from gate money. The Durham club was able to pledge sufficient funds for a number of years and they were welcomed to the fold. Had Shropshire or Dorset or any other county been able or wished to do likewise, they too, might have been greeted with similarly open arms. In other words, there was no competitive order of merit that ruled in favour of the new county, although, in fairness, their Minor Counties record was exemplary enough. Durham soon developed the Riverside Stadium at Chester-le-Street that came to be recognised as a venue for representative cricket and after an uneasy run of several years, they gradually consolidated their position. This they did to such effect that, in 2008 and again in 2009, they meritoriously won the County Championship, a tribute to their perspicacity and a spur, one would hope, to the authorities to remain thirsty for the taste of fresh blood.

A further initiative was the introduction in 2000 of a two-tier first-class competition of two nines, on a home and away *pro forma* of sixteen four-days fixtures, still alongside, of course, three one-day tournaments. After a compromise period of both three and four-day county cricket, 1993 had marked the first summer when all county matches were of the longer duration. Critics were quick to point out that Australian states games had been played to a finish since the inauguration of the Sheffield Shield competition in 1892. This lasted until 1927/26, when four days and a pre-lunch session were allocated, which was reduced to just four days in 1930/31 The hope was that a divisional set-up would enliven a contest that had become somewhat listless, for prestige could be at stake until the last round of matches. In the past, the season had tended to tail off once an outright winner was assured.

The counties, in accepting this formula a trifle grudgingly, were anxious that it should not be too definitively challenging. Three were promoted and three relegated, a provision that made for considerable revision of the divisions, thereby enabling the relegated counties not to feel too despondent. Their fear of the formula was the same as the advocates' hope. Many protagonists of the scheme aspired to a classification where a number of powerful teams formed a strong elite. Eager to see an improved preparation for international players, some argued for a first division of six and a second division of twelve, with one up and one down, just that single flick of the whip of relegation, as with the rugby union premiership, to concentrate the mind. With a merry-go-round of a third up and a third down – it was like six or seven leaving the football Premiership every May – there was not much chance of the cream rising to the top and staying there. It was later revised to a falling and rising twosome but there has been no creation of an elite county set of a standard not far from international level.

Rainy weather continued to be a problem for cricket in spite of much improvement in the apparatus for drainage and drying. Counties feared that climate rather than skill might lead to relegation or thwart a bid for the Championship. Nor was there meteorological equity. In 2004, when Sussex won the County Championship for the second time, they lost ten hours to rain, whereas close challengers Lancashire dismally missed out on a hundred hours (not all of it, a red rose-carrying writer swiftly adds, at the proverbially moist Old Trafford – as the Bard sings in *Twelfth Night*, 'By swaggering could I never thrive/For the rain it raineth every day'). This loss of some 1500 overs could have been critical. The counties still sustained a very fussy scoring system, with first innings bowling and batting points, already something of a tedious chore for the occasional watcher. In effect, a team that gains the maximum first innings points of eight, and loses the match, earns twice as much – four points – as a team in which the match is abandoned without a ball bowled. There is a strong case for the adoption of the football method of three for a win and one for a draw or abandonment, bearing in mind that such a welcome simplification would nor drive away the rain clouds.

There was a good deal of argument about whether there was too much cricket being played. As with recovery from osteopathic damage, it was sometimes difficult to adjust with precision the regime of 'rest and exercise'. One point was quite clear. Because of the inroads of the shortened forms of the game, there was much less first-class cricket. In 1947 Richard Howorth played the most first-class innings in that glorious English summer. This was 61. In 2003 the two players who played the most first-class innings were A.J.Strauss, of Middlesex and destined successfully to captain England, and the Durham wicket-keeper, G.J.Pratt. This was 33. Old-timers might urge that, for some players, there is insufficient first-class match experience.

During the last two or three decades of the century however, the County Championship did grow more interestingly unpredictable in outcome. In 1979 Essex won the title for the first time and had other successes, whilst the title was spread around more evenly. The ancient county club of Sussex eventually won the pennant for the very first time in 2003, having been bottom of the second division in 2000.

By this date, in fact from 2000, the England and Wales Cricket Board (EWCB), through its First-class Forum, was issuing central contracts for mainstream England players, initially to twelve players, a number soon to rise. The money was paid direct to the counties to subsidise the players' salaries, in return for the England management having control over the player's activities. This meant that, with such a full programme of international matches, normally seven Tests and a clutter of one day games and with the overseas tours and half-tours cropping up constantly, plus the management's concern not to overplay the contracted men, England players scarcely ever played for their counties.

At the same time, the counties were criticised for utilising too many overseas players and cricketers without English eligibility who were employed through glosses on European citizenship legislation. There was a feeling that they should concentrate on nurturing local talent, and the 'academy' approach, whereby the counties took seriously the need to educate fledgling cricketers, did have some encouraging results. In contrary vein, there was bitterness among county subscribers that their club was discouraged both from seeking the best players, irrespective of nationality, and denied the use of their best players of English nationality. Moreover, those who follow county cricket at non-Test playing venues no longer had a chance to see the England stars on county duty as in the past. There was the cynical view expressed that what was necessary to win the County Championship was a team of very good players, for, if you developed two or three excellent ones, they would be siphoned off via the central contract method. Very rapidly it became more difficult to recall – 'Yorkshire and England' – the county provenance of England players, so remote did they become from those origins.

Institutionally, a point repeated in this text about the urban nature of 'county' cricket was reinforced by the radical local government reorganisation that came into being in 1974 and by subsequent specific alterations. The cricketing authorities stuck to the ancient regime but administratively as opposed to ceremonially speaking, only six counties now have their headquarters, their main ground and offices, in the county they purport to represent, seven, if one counts the quirky location of Trent Bridge just across the river from the city of Nottingham. Durham, Essex, Kent, Somerset, Northamptonshire, and Worcestershire form that sextet. The locations of the other 'counties', such has been their urban proliferation, are in unitary authorities of one type or another. For instance, Surrey and Middlesex play in the London Boroughs of Lambeth and Westminster respectively; Glamorgan play in Cardiff, one of Wales' 22 'local councils', and Lancashire in the unitary authority of Trafford. For administrative purposes, the counties of Sussex, Yorkshire, Glamorgan and Middlesex do not, technically, exist.

First-class cricket in England has always been reliant on heavy pockets of urbanised population, with an infrastructure of facilities, such as hotels, and transport, like railways or, more significantly nowadays, access to motorways. As was earlier remarked, the 'county' designation was something of a fictional figment in most areas since the inauguration of the County Championship proper. Today it has largely lost organisational connection with its shire roots.

That raises the question of whether this anonymously intermediate position – gaining neither from the patriotic attraction of the nation nor the loyal partisanship of the town – has a bearing on the collapse of county support, especially for the longer version of cricket. Fewer than a million customers paid to watch Championship cricket in the mid 1960s, numbers that led to the reforms such as limited overs cricket. That total is now much lower, and it shows in the revenue accounts of the counties. True enough, most counties have always trodden a narrow path between the black and red margins of those accounts but now the income from subscriptions (even though county memberships are healthy enough) and gate receipts is nugatory.

In the opening years of the 21st century, about half a million spectators, subscribing members and paying customers, attended an average season of top-class fixtures of all kinds. With members counted in, this amounted to some 850 a day for County Championship matches. Of these only about 70,000 actually paid at the turnstiles to see County Championship games, roughly 250 a day. Visit any county ground and the vision will greet you of a fairly generously packed pavilion, tolerably replete with members, surrounded by almost empty stands and terraces. It is nowhere near an economic proposition. Indeed, it would be more economic to run, say, the Oval as a stadium, available for international cricket matches and other events but without the financial onus of a resident cricket team. In consequence and accepting that there is variation county to county, a rule of thumb calculation suggests that about 80% of county income derives from television and corporate proceeds, plus some revenue from catering and other marketing ventures. Only some 20% or so emanates from a fairly equal two-way split between membership subscriptions and gate receipts.

This leaves the counties in hock to the central authority. They exist as nurseries for the international team and are paid accordingly. To weigh the profound measure of that feudal dependence, one might turn to the English football Premier League for a comparison. Visualise the Gallic and Glaswegian rage of Arsenal's Arsene Wenger and Manchester United's Alex Ferguson were their players recruited for international duty at times when their clubs had fixtures. Here the clubs more rule the sporting roost, for, although they rely on television income for their efforts, they are not reliant on handouts from their governing bodies, even if some have incurred massive debts. For instance, the mainline football clubs generate substantial income directly from their own fixtures, while county cricket makes only a negligible amount, over against the profits from England games. The consequence may be seen in the comparative standards. Most commentators would agree that the top three or four English football clubs would normally be victorious over or, at least, offer stern resistance to, the English national side. The English cricket team would, or so many would believe, ordinarily defeat any of the counties.

The systematic use of the counties as national kindergartens has some merit but it is hard on those whose first loyalty is to the county team, which they may have followed, as with a local football team, from childhood and to which, by sheer weight of interest, they feel a more enduring affection than for the more distant England set-up. It is not a crime to prefer county to Test cricket or club to national football. County cricket has ever been an affair of the heart rather than the head.

A fine romance about cricket usually begins at the bottom and looks indulgently upwards. A severely logical test of cricket normally begins at the top and glances condescendingly downwards. There is an implicit assumption that the fortunes of the England team must take absolute precedence. In most accounts that premise is taken for granted and not even justified. The former heart-warmed adherents are relaxed about the past mores of the game and enjoy its transient joys, often at a local level. The latter brain-orientated protagonists give high priority to the national team and seek, for the sake of the future, to change the structure irrevocably. They wish to know why a country, like Australia, with something like fifty full-time professionals, frequently conquers a nation, like England, which has nine times as many – and, were we successfully to revolutionise the system, it would boost the game for everybody. Their opponents claim that broader aims, such as the health and enjoyment of thousands, and the preservation of sound principles, deserve prior consideration – and that in any event, England have won the Ashes quite often, so circumstances cannot be all that desperate.

As has been observed, the remarkably static county system sits rather lumpily in the somewhat awkwardly shaped pyramid of English cricket. As the second tier of the English game, the first-class counties have two flaws. The gap in standard between the counties and the Test team is too broad and so is the disparity of standard between the counties and the third tier of Minor County and Second XIs.

At one time there were a number of representative fixtures on the calendar. There were Test trials, Gentlemen versus Players, Champion County against Rest of England, full-scale county games against the tourists and also the use of second strings, especially on tour, to play national teams that were not yet up to the scratch of Australia.

For a number of reasons this is now rarely the case, nor do young players have much chance any longer to play against top-class England players. Touring sides find themselves facing weakened county teams with bowlers particularly being given a respite. At the other end of the county scale, and although the provision of county boards, county premier leagues, county academies and so forth, have tended to smooth out the middle and lower slopes of the pyramid, there still remains the petrified sanctity of the County Championship membership itself. It is the Fort Knox of cricket when it comes to forcing an entry and the Fort Colditz of cricket when it comes to negotiating an exit.

Not only is there no relegation but, even if there were, only another county could, presumably, be considered as a replacement. A corporate body such as a bank or an insurance company; a cricketing equivalent of Roman Abramovitch the underwriter of Chelsea football club; a public agency like the armed services – what if there were other ways of developing a first-class cricket team in England? The type of membership is as stultified as the membership itself.

The conservationist nature of the county championship has been something of a running thread in the later chapters of this text. One might make a final comparison with the English Football First Division and Premiership. No less than 43 of the current Premier and Football League clubs have played in the top flight, many of them in the modern era. It is likely that this continual element of fresh recruitment has helped to make it perhaps the world's most prestigious football club competition.

Critics of the county formula are most provoked by the number of counties in the top tier, arguing that a regional construct of five or six squads comprising about a hundred professionals, and each based at a major ground, must be the way forward. Naturally, there is much difference of detail in these varied proposals, but that is the rough gist of the formula, based on the argument that this would offer the optimal preparatory feeder service for what had become to be called Team England. This would require some 30 to 40 counties, including the present Minor Counties, to play a largely amateur tournament at the next stage down, with the elite club leagues operating below them.

The current county system also gave rise to discontent on another issue. It has been suggested that, just as there were so many players needed for the county game that a debilitating condition of incompetence was the consequence, there were also too many venues. These fell, so ran the criticism, between two stools. They were too large for county cricket and too small for Test cricket. The critics railed against the decision to add Chester-le-Street, Durham (2003), the Rose Bowl, Hampshire (2007) and Sophia Gardens, Glamorgan (2009), making nine international stadiums all told, none of them able to match the capacity of the leading Australian grounds, five of which range in seating from 32,000 to over 90,000. One or two further county clubs have plans to expand their grounds, purely on the chance offering of an international fixture of whatever type once every three years or so, believing this would considerably ease their financial straits. The revolutionary view is that just two or three existing grounds should be developed for international purposes with room for about 80,000 spectators in the largest.

Finance is one motivation for wholesale change. In 2001, according to William Buckland's *Pommies* (2008), one of the most drastic critiques of the English game, the England team generated income through broadcasting rights, ticket sales, advertising and sponsorship to the tune of £48m, whilst the counties generated some £20m, together £68m of cricket's 2001 annual earnings of £71m. But the counties made a joint loss of £25m and most of this was met by a bail out from the ECB out of the England income. William Buckland calculates that a format of five regional clubs, akin to the Australian state system, would result, at 2008 prices, in a gain of £25m for grassroots and allied investment. The critics argue that the counties soak up huge quantities of money, leaving little for grassroots investment and show little in return because the wide spread of the resources over eighteen clubs results in comparative mediocrity. Moreover, should television and allied income fall nationally, several county clubs would become endangered species under threat of extinction.

There was a national outcry when the ECB sold the exclusive rights to televise English cricket to the BSkyB television company. For the 2010 to 2013 years the price was £300m. This meant that no live cricket coverage was available for ordinary broadcasting licence payers. Apart from any ethical discussion about whether Test matches, like the Cup Final, the Derby and other major sports events, should be on the broadcasters' 'free-to-air' A List – and, as the BBC pointed out when showing little interest in the transaction, the Derby lasts only a few minutes compared with an Ashes series – there was grave disquiet about the practical effects. During the 2005 Ashes rubber, 8.2m tuned in to Channel 4 during the peak moments of the enthralling Fourth Test, while in 2009, when the First Australian Test reached a melodramatic climax, only 1.47m paying customers were savouring the occasion. The ECB, naturally enough, claims that it is obliged to attract revenue wherever possible. It points out that, by 2008, with annual income now at the level of £94.5m, the board had expended almost £33m on the first-class counties, and £13m on grass-roots cricket, of which total something well over £12m is earmarked for the 39 County Cricket Boards to administer recreational cricket. A figure of close on £46m for the underpinnings of the national teams would not, it is argued, be found without recourse to the maximal collection of television fees. However, it all accentuates the reliance on television earnings, and the huge reduction in cricket television viewing must raise some anxiety about this as a longer-term strategy.

As for the country-county question, that is so fixedly caught up in the web of this debate about funding and television, a curious paradox has evolved. The top English football clubs are lambasted for being greedily avaricious businesses, compared with the purported democracy of the leading Spanish clubs, with their extensive memberships. The top English cricket clubs are attacked for being at the petty behest of small-minded memberships, who care little for England's greater cricketing glory, contrasted with the hard-nosed, business-like efficacy of the Australian system. It is certainly true that there has been, probably since soon after World War II, a tension, particularly in the major counties, between the values of a Victorian-style subscribing membership and the calls of the big business that running a Test ground had become. The county chief executive who interprets his job remit as being the managing director of a company rather than the secretary acting on behalf of a membership may soon find himself in tepid, if not hot water.

Some counties have radically changed parts of their constitutions accordingly, while both Hampshire and Durham have become limited companies, but the many basically remain private bodies, typified by MCC, with its 18,000 members, with women members only permitted to join since 1997. The 150,000 MCC and first-class county members will take a lot of persuading that, in order to fan a flame of hope that England might become as good as Australia at cricket, they should forfeit what they regard as a precious and enjoyable birthright. Frankly, the vast proportion of county members – nine to one is the estimate of one reliable source – would prefer to see, in the living flesh, their local heroes win the County Champion-ship title rather than watch England win the Ashes, provided they had a Sky dish, on the telly.

And why not? Your patriotism should not be measured by how fervent your 'last night at the Proms' style support is for national sporting teams. Away from such near xenophobia, the yardsticks of civic virtue are much more compelling arbiters of patriotism, like whether you vote consistently in all elections, pay your taxes with-out seeking dodgy escape clauses, don't attempt to evade legitimate tasks such as jury service, send your children to state schools, have your family cared for by the National Health Service and other acts of public obligation.

That pious diatribe aside, as the first-class counties and MCC wield substantive influence in the counsels of the England and Wales Cricket Board, it is hard to see how fundamental reform might be initiated. Nonetheless, to the outsider, the county scene resembles a somewhat grisly carousel of many matches played in the empty con-fines of the Much Bowling-in-the-Morgue cricket ground, designed to find eleven English players whose primary task is to make suf-ficient money to keep the roundabout turning so that eleven players might be found . . . and so on in bleak perpetuity.

One might summon up the memory of Francis Thompson's haunting and elegiac poem, *At Lord's* (1907) to seal that image:

> *For the field is full of shades as I near the shadowy coast,*
> *And a ghostly batsman plays to the bowling of a ghost,*
> *And I look through my tears on a soundless-clapping host*
> *As the run-stealers flicker to and fro . . .*

The system might simply fracture. Amid the manifold complexity of the reasons for the English Civil War, one direct politico-economic factor is sometimes pointed out. The delicate balance between the monarchy, needful of money from taxes to fund its chosen activities, and parliament, prepared only to provide the cash on receipt of 'redress of grievances', foundered. It did so because it reached the point where an extravagant king began to need parliament more than a more self-assured and proactive parliament needed the king. The harmony of Team England and the county structure might just become thus destabilised. The counties may come to need the ECB more than the ECB needs the counties. As Sir John Fortescue, a sturdy officer in the English Civil War, muttered one night, sitting on an upturned drum beside a camp fire, 'all the Scribes and Pharisees are on one side and all the Publicans and Sinners are on the other.'

As we turn our attention to the exciting events of the first decade of the new century, a neutral view might be that the same scriptural designation might be applied to the contenders for the rights to control English and possibly even world cricket.

The seaside and summer holidays have created a special cricketing cameo in England. Stanley Park, Blackpool (top) has hosted many Lancashire matches, while Scarborough was famously the venue for its end-of-season festival, as well as being a Yorkshire out-ground.

CHAPTER FOURTEEN
TWENTY20 VISION

*The modern game: Andrew Flintoff batting
in an IPL Twenty20 match*

In 2006 the International Cricket Conference moved from Lords to
Dubai. It was as if the seat of the Anglican Church had relocated from
Canterbury to Cairo. It followed on from the formal separation of

the ICC and MCC in 1993, an event personified in the former West Indian star, Clyde Walcott, becoming the first non-British chairman of the ICC. It became an incorporated body in 1997, with a president rather than a chairman at its head.

INDIAN SUMMER

The lesser membership of the Conference was, as the new century dawned, strong enough. As well as the ten 'Full members', there were 28 'Associate Members', from states where cricket was 'firmly established and organised', and 51 non-voting 'Affiliated Members' from areas where cricket was 'played in accordance with the Laws of Cricket'. Although far behind the 207 nations that enjoyed FIFA status and contested the last football World Cup in 2006, this is a long and – three-fifth of the 'Affiliates' are of 21st century election – growing register of cricketing activity, with 89 members in total.

What remains evident is the continuing interest shown by former constituents of the British Empire. In these early years of the 21st century, of the Associate Members, 19 (including, slightly mischievously, the USA) and of the Affiliate Members, 25 had been former British colonies of one type or another. All but seven of the 'Associates' had such British links, and about half of the 'Affiliates' fell into this category, making a total of 54 out of 89 of the complete membership and 29 of the much more influential 38 Full and Associate delegations. It is difficult to spot any former British possession that does not have a formal cricketing organisation. It is both a reminder of the extensive reach of the British Empire at its proudest, as well as a tribute to the enduring allure of and affection for cricket in so many of those regions.

The imbalance of global representation, especially in the upper tier of the membership, suggests that the use of the descriptor 'International' is a trifle grandiloquent. The Post-colonial Cricket Conference would be a more accurate, but scarcely marketable, title.

The constellation of cricketing planets undertook a change of orbits, or rather, as if some cricketing Galileo had lifted a questioning eye to his telescope, the query was raised as to which was circling which. For many imperial years, England had been the happy and glorious sun around which the lesser satellites deferentially moved. Now

England was just one of the orbs in the galaxy. The sun now had a blazing Indian glow.

In truth, it was not as definitive as in the colonial yesteryear, with for example, a fervent counter-plea to be entered by Australian cricketing astronomers for their mighty place in the firmament. Nevertheless, the subcontinent had become the focus and taken over much of the leadership of the cricketing world. More compelling, all the positive cricketing indicators suggested that the centrepiece of future cricket would and should be located on the subcontinent.

In hard political terms, four Full Members of the ICC, Pakistan, Sri Lanka and Bangladesh, as well as India, found common post-colonial ground with the reconstituted South Africa and Zimbabwe, with fellow-feeling usually expressed by the West Indies. In consequence, the dominantly 'white' nations of England, Australia and New Zealand lost somewhat in influence. Likewise, some fourteen of the ICC Associates had intimate connections with the African and Asian Full Members. That is not to infer that these blocs were constantly warring nor, on the contrary, that there were not sometimes hostilities – occasional troubles between India and Pakistan being a pertinent instance – among the subcontinental members. This is just a straightforward submission of a factual constitutional position.

Of equal impact must be considered the vast and abiding popularity of cricket among the Indian people of all ranks and races. The post-war rise in cricketing interest was galvanised by the beginning of broadcasting. B.V.Keskar, the Minister of Information and Broadcasting when England toured in 1951/52, was forced to alter his anti-cricket stance by the weight of public opinion and sanction commentary on All India Radio. The transistor radio became the prime means of conveying cricket news to millions. The quest for tickets for Test and Ranji Trophy games was intense and the hullabaloo surrounding the selection of Indian teams and the state of play in matches became enormous. Then came satellite television, opening up cricket to the Indian outback of villages away from the large towns and attracting the attention of, it was said, 'the housewives and the farmers', hitherto deprived of much access to the cricketing fashion.

One day cricket ratcheted up the interest. India played its first limited overs international in 1974 and then played 450 such games by the end of the 20th century, all of them beamed live to the delight of hundreds of millions of viewers of 'the longest-running uninterrupted saga'. India and Pakistan hosted the cricket World Cup in 1987. It was the fourth of these global tournaments, the third having been comfortably, if unexpectedly, won by India in 1983 at Lord's and it was the first to be based outside England.

Ramachandra Guha tells the tale of 'a triumph of anti-colonialism'. The President of the Indian Cricket Board, N.K.P.Salve, having two tickets for the 1983 final, requested two more, when India reached the final, for friends travelling from India especially for the event. MCC's refusal to oblige led him to organise an ICC revolt that resulted in the World Cup being located outside England on a turn-for-turn basis. Here was another example of the swinging pendulum, for MCC had presumably assumed that the World Cup would always be played at 'the home of cricket'. Ram Guha, pointing up the parallel of Mahatma Gandhi being pitched off a train by an Englishman in Pietermaritzburg, South Africa in 1896, tenders the sensible advice: 'never mess around with an Indian lawyer.'

Crowds packed 21 different venues for the 27 games of the 1987 contest, with the state-owned Doordarshan TV company relaying all the games. Even after the fever-pitch of a Pakistan/India semi-final, the resultant final of Australia and England, the former winning by seven runs, at Eden Gardens, Calcutta, was watched by well over 100,000 spectators, reputedly the largest crowd ever to watch a cricket match. In 1996 the World Cup competition revisited the subcontinent, when Sri Lanka beat Australia at Lahore by seven wickets. Wider television coverage served to heighten the pandemonium, as 400m people watched the screenings. As for the marketing involved, there was huge and highly publicised contest, almost as thrilling as the cricket itself, between Coca-Cola and Pepsi-Cola for the 1996 World Cup sponsoring rights. Ram Guha, writing of the 1987 tourney, argues that 'no previous event in Indian history – with the possible exception only of Independence and Partition – attracted a comparable number of column inches in the English and vernacular press' of the subcontinent.

The cricketers themselves gained enormously in earnings and celebrity status on a par with the stars of Hindi films. In 2001 it was reported that Sachin Tendulkar's income was $4.5m, aligning him with globally wealthy sportsmen like Tiger Woods and Michael Schumacher. An Indian Test cricketer might, at this juncture, have fairly hoped to earn a thousand times the wage of the average Indian. Mainly from television revenue, it was calculated that the Indian Board of Control funds jumped astonishingly from $200,000 to $65m in the last decade of the last century. Scyld Berry, writing with his customary thoughtfulness after the English tourists' visit of India in the winter of 1981/82, had prophesied that 'cricket would soon become the most popular sport in any country in the world... the game grew up thousand of miles away, (but) India is destined to become the capital of cricket.'

Ramachandra Guha has attempted the tricky task of analysing why there is this abundant affection for cricket in his native land. It must be more, he believes, than 'a relic of colonialism' for such widespread fondness to be maintained but their softer view of imperial rule may have ensured that the Indians have not cut off the nose of cricket to spite the face of colonialism. 'Indians', he claims, 'have more time; Indians like doing things together; Hindus don't really mind a 'draw'; Hindus are culturally syncretic and choose to absorb foreign imports rather than reject them . . . ' One cannot be exactly sure whether he sees this as a genetic or an environmental factor but the latter 'nurture' explanation favoured in this text does apply. In terms of the cultural upbringing of the average Indian, there seems to be a more relaxed sense of time that suits the rhythms of cricket and a collective delight in the endless 'chatter and disputation' involved with the game, while, conveniently, the Hindu religion, many of whose 'myths stress negotiation and compromise', relishes the uncertainty of the drawn game. To this Ram Guha adds the substantive sense of nationalism generated by Indian cricket and its detailed interface with Indian politics both external and internal.

As he himself recognises, the limited overs game, with its concentration of time and its deliberate search for an undisputed outcome, galvanised the Indian public considerably. This was furthered by the fulsome Indian adoption of the even briefer Twenty20 format.

By detracting a little from Ram Guha's emphasis on the Indian's tranquil observance of time and affection for the undecided game, this leaves the participatory and nationalistic aspects as strong contenders in interpreting the Indian delight in cricket. The first of those recalls the collectivist ethic of the British crowd, if in more phlegmatic and less colourful vein, at the high point of the 'integrated culture' of the late Victorian and early 20th century eras. The second approximates to the emblematic use the world over of sport as a nationalist device. It might be rugby union in New Zealand or baseball in the USA; it is cricket in India. As in other regions, the facets of religious and nationalistic persuasion have, in India, had both 'respectable' and 'rough' outputs in respect of character. The spontaneous politesse and smiling geniality of Indian players and watchers may thus be contrasted with, for example, the corrosive and divisive machinations of some India and Pakistan cricketing encounters and some violent crowd reaction to failure.

To that may be added another trait of well nigh universal incidence. Gambling, especially the variations utilised in the context of the shortened versions of the game, obviously impacts on the public attitude to cricket in India. The Cronje and allied gambling scandals often had an Indian context of substantial betting coups and exchanges. The Indian bookmaker is destined to join his predecessor, crying the odds around the Lord's pavilion in Regency times, among those who jostle amid the busy scenes of cricket's social folklore.

Ram Guha, in his mould-breaking saga, *A Corner of a Foreign Field*, concludes in forthright mood. 'Cricket has been successfully indigenised, made part of the fabric of everyday life and language. Add to this the weight of numbers, the hundreds of millions of South Asians who have come to watch and pay for the sport. In a globalized world, this game, more subtle and varied than any other, would not have survived without their support.'

That confident assertion is possibly true of the professional game. It is likely that recreational cricket would, however sparsely, have persisted in various parts of the world but it is certainly arguable that the heavy quantity and exuberant quality of support for spectator cricket on the subcontinent has made the difference between top-class cricket languishing and reviving. Economics confirm the argument. The subcontinent now generates almost three-quarters of global cricket revenue.

The 2007 World Cup, played out in the West Indies, was an indifferent affair, the logistics awkward, the tournament protracted and the cricket uninspired, apart from the Australian charge to victory. This was their third World Cup title in sequence. Worst of all, the grounds were nowhere near full, a fact attributed to the prohibitive prices charged for tickets on islands where low incomes were the norm.

It was a sign of the harsher cricketing malaise in the area. American economic and cultural influence continued to replace that of the British. As independent states, the West Indian islands and territories naturally turned more to the USA for the investment of both financial and social capital. Professional basketball and baseball were lucrative alternatives for the sportingly gifted, and there seemed to be a diminution of the old fervour for cricket.

This was also the case elsewhere. Television moguls may have looked askance at screens showing vast empty terracing on cricket grounds all over the world. In 2005/06, when England visited Pakistan, the authorities dispensed a huge number of free tickets but the average attendance for Test matches never rose above 10,000. When England visited the West Indies early in 2009, watchers might have imagined, the bright sunshine apart, that these were based in England, for the so-called 'Barmy Army' of travelling English support tended to outnumber the locals among the scattered crowds in not oversized stadiums. In 2009 the Australian and South African Test match at Johannesburg, a clash of the then current leading world teams, could barely attract sufficient customers to fill half an arena capable of holding over 30,000 people. Those making a living out of cricket, with so weighty a reliance on television revenue, must have looked with sorrow and foreboding on these vacant expanses. Even in England, where the popularity of Test cricket had held up surprisingly well, half-filled grounds for all but the top-grade visitors, such as the ever attractive Australians, became more common. Over-pricing was once again voiced as a contributory factor as it was elsewhere in the world.

The Anglo-Australians obliged with dramatic ventures in the opening decade of the century. The 2005 Ashes series in England was won two-one by England in a remarkable series of sheer cliff-hanging encounters imbued with the essence of Hollywood silent movies. Michael Vaughan, cool of mien as captain and accomplished technically as batsman, found in Andrew Flintoff a talismanic champion, a giant who smote with direct strength and bowled with piercing venom. Like H.W.Longfellow's *The Village Blacksmith*, 'the muscles of his brawny arms are strong as iron bands . . . His face is wet with honest sweat,/He earns whate'er he can.' Andrew Flintoff's career was to suffer from a shoal of injuries, but the heroic baton was seized by Kevin Pietersen, a cricketer with South African roots, who brought a glamour as well as a brusque assurance to his inventive batsmanship. He came close to becoming a celebrity in the Indian connotation. There is a risk that both Andrew Flintoff and Kevin Pietersen may go down in cricketing annals as celebrity entertainers rather than great cricketers, in what is admittedly a somewhat subjective categorisation.

There were late-night parties, a bus procession to Trafalgar Square through tumultuous throngs and a visit to 10 Downing Street. Unluckily, the English support forgot that the feverish excitement arose from the extremely slim line between success and failure in the rubber. It had been a hit here and a miss there that had made the difference. The Australians rapidly re-crossed the line during the following winter of 2006/07 and whitewashed England comprehensively, five-nil. The Australians thereby entered the century as they had departed the previous one. Between 1999 and 2007 they won 73 out of 94 Tests played, with only ten losses, involving victory in all but two of eighteen series. It was an awesome record. However, the loss of senior players led to a transitional side losing the Ashes again in England in 2009. It was another series packed with interest, with the dramatics of inexplicable collapses and other inconsistencies suggesting that by exacting standards, these were a worthy rather than a distinguished pair of opponents.

For all that, there lingered, outside India, a scarcely whispered fear. What if live spectatorship continued to dip? Might this lead to a withdrawal of advertisers and sponsors and a basic threat to television income itself? The goose might refuse to lay the golden eggs if no one were interested in watching.

GLOBAL WINTER

There were also signs that world cricket would have to face challenges of a more politically dangerous nature. Although the modern political context for cricket was largely determined, such was its concentrated ex-imperial character, by the mixed resolution of large-scale colonial independence, it could not but be affected by world events. Familiar as these immediately are, a brief summation of them may be of help in the location of world cricket in some sort of perspective.

Population must always head the current affairs agenda. World population did not pass the billion mark until some point part way through the 19th century. Now it stands at well over 6bn. It is estimated that by 2025 it will be over 8bn. Aside from environmental issues such as climate warming, the gulf between riches and poverty is a wide one. The world's three leading billionaires together hold more assets – almost 10% of the world's total wealth – than the poorest group of nation-states with a joint population of 600m. As for nation-states, they have become the norm. In 1914 there were just 59 independent states, with the rest of the territories usually controlled by various 'empires'. Now the entire world is practically divided into some 200 sovereign nations, some of them quite tiny. The notion of the civil state is strong, with, in a recent rather intricate survey, about half being judged as 'free', with firm economic and civic liberties, and about a quarter each shown to be 'partly free' or 'not free', that is, lacking basic human rights.

When in 1989, the cold war ended with a stunning defeat for the Soviet dominated regimes of Eastern Europe and the emergence of the United States as the sole super-power (albeit with China waiting a trifle restfully in the wings), it looked as if the concept of Western democracy was the last fighter left in the ring. In 1989 Francis Fukuyama published his influential *The End of History*, in which he argued that, as this construct was 'the only viable alternative for technologically advanced societies', the whole planet would and must accept this design. 'Liberal capitalist democracy', with its variable balance of the free market economically with public regulation and provision of services socially, stood alone and, he prophesied, always would do so.

Although Francis Fukuyama dismissed them as a final backlash of outdated traditionalism before the ultimate conquest of democratic liberalism, the resurgence of Islamic militancy, in particular, the terrorist attacks on symbolic American buildings in 2001, gave many commentators furiously to think about the genuine continuance of 'history'. The flashpoints of Afghanistan, Iraq, Iran and Palestine are the warring pointers of seeming contest, to caricature a little, between fundamentalist Christian American New Imperialism and fundamentalist Moslem Nationalism. Naturally enough, those other factors mentioned – increasing population, technology's current reliance on oil, grinding poverty, the intensity of nationalist fervour – collide with that flaring politico-religious divide. Some see this as a new and gruesome global conflict, hardly the pleasantest canvas for world cricket.

This terrorist hostility is the grim edge of a much greater political and social issue. There are 1.2bn people of Islamic origin in the world today; 52 states have an Islamic majority; many have a significant minority, including Britain's ordinarily valued and hard-working 2m and by 2025, one in four of the world's population will be Islamic, ethnically, if not necessarily doctrinally. For the majority of people around the world there is the straightforward matter of everybody getting on, in both senses, of getting on one with the other and getting on with some sort of a sufficient life, including for many, especially in Southeast Asian countries, a chance to play or watch cricket.

Professional cricketers have rarely been the most politicised band of brothers, but, now that for many of them their path is a planetary one, the issues raised briefly here do impinge, whatever their views. The most evident example relates to the constant anxiety about safety, a poser that – as the Zimbabwean situation illustrated – is not caused only by bin Laden inspired suicide bombers. For obvious reasons, cricket has a higher profile in some of the relevant regions than football or other sports. Here the character of world events does touch on the fall-out from Britain's colonial past. The well-publicised cricketing event and the presence of famous cricketers in such areas attract the attention of political terrorists, despite the assurance of

Imran Khan, cricketer-cum-politician, and others, that, such was the popularity of cricket, assaults would be counter-productive.

Facile optimism collapsed with the attack on the Sri Lankan squad in Lahore in the spring of 2009. A band of fourteen armed men peppered the Sri Lankan tourist convoy as it approached the Gaddafi Stadium for the second Test against Pakistan. As a rocket launcher and grenades, as well as guns, comprised the weaponry and fusillade, injuries to seven players and officials, plus, sadly, the deaths of two and injuries to several Pakistan police officers, may be reckoned as a less devastating outcome than it might have been. The series was abandoned and top-class cricket in Pakistan was put on hold. Indeed, cricket on the subcontinent, as a whole, was imperilled. Since then international cricket has been banned from Pakistani grounds. For instance, in 2010 Australia played Pakistan at Lord's, in the first 'neutral' Test match at Lord's since 1912. This came before Pakistan played England in an intriguing series complicated by yet another furore over cricket's sporadic flirtation with fraudulent gambling. The limited overs tournament due to be played in Pakistan was transferred to South Africa, while the Pakistani cricketers embarked on a peripatetic voyage, playing all their games away from their homeland. The Sri Lankan cricketers, returning to their homeland, might ruefully have recalled that their own island had been riven for a quarter of a century by their government's conflict with the Tamil Tigers dissidents, at a cost of an estimated 70,000 lives.

REFRESHING SPRING

In spite of the fear of a reduction or even discontinuance of funds from television and sponsorship, particularly as the 2009 recession drained the confidence of those who had thought Western-style capitalism was fool-proof, and in spite of the political risks of celebrity cricket, there was actually little deceleration in the amount of professional cricket being played internationally.

In 2003 yet another confection of limited overs cricket had been baked – and it proved to be a world-beater, attracting large live and television audiences, making the fortunes of some lucky cricketers and saving the financial bacon of several cricketing bodies. It made regular use of floodlights, thus attracting evening leisure-seekers, often arriving from work or school. Many grounds felt obliged and emboldened to invest in lighting. This was the Twenty20 formula.

This was, let it not be forgotten, an English invention. Some sources cite the bright mind of Mark Nicholas, the former Hampshire player, with his suggestion, among other imaginative schemes, that a 25 overs competition be introduced. This was in 1996, when he was being considered for the post of Chief Executive of the TCCB, a process from which he withdrew, feeling that basic reform was not on the agenda. One of the new ECB committees recommended such a concept in 1998, chiefly in an attempt to stave the haemorrhage of revenue from the counties and a loss of up to a fifth in county attendances in five years, but the First Class Forum was reluctant. The ECB undertook an extensive marketing research exercise – thirty focus groups and 4000 quarter-hour interviews – that indicated support for a shorter format. It appeared that the audience profile for county cricket was 'disastrous'. Young people thought it was for old people; females thought it was for males and ethnic minorities thought it was for 'whites'. The view was expressed that county grounds seemed unwelcoming and like 'private clubs', which, legally speaking, most certainly are.

Stuart Robertson, marketing manager of the ECB, developed and argued the case for a Twenty20 competition to replace the Benson and Hedges trophy that had reached its end. Some of the counties, however reluctant to accommodate to structural reform, grasped at the possibility of financial aid and decided in 2002, but only by eleven votes to seven, MCC abstaining, for a Twenty20 tournament.

The first was held in 2003, amid slick marketing, colourful ballyhoo, tolerable weather, floodlights, pop music and carnival devices. It was very successful. The 45 group matches, with three zones of six counties each, drew 240,000 fans, with fifteen sell-outs. The semi-finals and final were held at Trent Bridge, another sell-out with 15,000 present, and with Surrey the eventual winners of a £42,000 prize. The number of zonal matches was slowly increased, as the format's popularity rose, so much so that, in 2005, 545,000 attended these games, more than the total of 470,000 for the full County Championship. Attendees at Twenty20 matches outnumbered those at a day's play in the County Championship by almost eight to one. In 2004 the first ever T20 games at Lord's, between Middlesex and Surrey, was watched by 26,500 people, symbolically enough, the largest gathering at Lord's for a county match, other than a one-day final, since 1953. Furthermore, the social goals were being met. It was estimated that almost two-thirds of Twenty20 spectators were under 34 years of age and nearly a quarter were women.

As with British initiatives such as the railways and, allegedly, parliament, to say nothing of cricket, the novel toy was quickly adopted and in some cases improved by other nations. The Australian states were among the next to adopt the formula, with their inaugural fixture being between the Western (Australia) Warriors and the Victorian Bushrangers in 2005 before a capacity crowd at the WACA of over 20,000. That same year, Australia and New Zealand played the first international game using this latest format, whilst in 2008, the match between Australia and the then world champions, India, found 84,000 spectators packed into the Melbourne arena.

Meanwhile, the ICC, quick to spot the potential of the new idea, had developed a T20 World Cup contest, first played out in 2007, with South Africa, the competent agency of the 2003 World Cup, providing the venues. The final was a neighbourly encounter between Pakistan and India. The winning Indians proved to be a steely outfit under the able captaincy of Mahendra Singh Dhoni. Attendances and television audiences alike were high and well satisfied.

It was resolved to repeat the exercise with just a gap of two years, and England was the chosen site. It was a marketing triumph, with Steve Elsworthy, the onetime South African quick bowler, again the Director, as he had been in his homeland two years before. Packaged neatly into a fortnight and staged at three grounds, Trent Bridge, the Oval and Lord's, 95% of the tickets were sold, Sky attracted record cricket watching for its live coverage and even the BBC highlights at dead of night were welcomed by a million cricketing insomniacs. ESPN Sear Sports, the Asian broadcasting company, a joint venture of the American giants, Disney and News Corp, had invested much in cricketing rights and it reported a doubling of ratings on a global, if chiefly Asiatic basis, from 2007 to 2009. The performance of 'qualifiers' like Holland, who rained on England's parade on the opening day of the festival, and Ireland, who won through to the Super Eights from an original group of twelve – nine 'full' members and three 'associates' – contenders, brought a breath of unpredictability to events. At their second attempt, the Pakistanis were successful, beating Sri Lanka with some comfort.

England's geopolitical position revealed two conjoined benefits. As the only full ICC member in the northern atmosphere, the core of its domestic programme did not overlap with that of any other contestant, so that 'overseas' players were free to join county and league clubs for the English summer. Some mourned, as was previously noted, what they saw as the abuse of this system, when indigenous players seemed to be edged out, but many felt that both spectators and English-born players gained from the experience. The siting of the Twenty20 Cup in England illustrated the allied advantage. As in most other post-colonial situations there had been considerable waves of migration into what used to be called the Mother Country from former dependencies. Thus there was ample support for most participants in the 2009 T20 competition from among the resident population, with Sri Lankan and Pakistani favours in glowing evidence at the Lord's final. It all added up to an engaging and welcome exercise in multicultural activity and a strong argument for choosing England for further international cricketing contests.

By far the most exhilarating step in the brief history of Twenty20 cricket was the launch of the Indian Premier League in 2008. The Board of Control for Cricket in India took the unprecedented step of organising not an Indian competition, nor an international one, but a transnational one, that is, the teams were formed of individuals from each and every part of the cricketing world, albeit with a few caveats to avoid undue weighting. The hope was that much joy would be generated by the sight of 'Sourav Ganguly sharing the crease with Ricky Ponting.' The Board adopted the franchise mode, well-known in American sporting business. It created the sponsored DLF Indian Premier League, based on the eight leading Indian cities and sold off the eight franchises to the highest bidder. The expectation was that $400m might be raised but the auction attracted almost twice that amount, $723.59m. For example, Reliance Industries successfully bid $111.9m for a ten year stake in the Mumbai franchise. There followed an auction for players and the resultant competition saw

Rajastan Royals the first winners, picking up a prize of £3m. 3.4m people attended the matches, an average of 58,000 at each game.

The world cup win by India in 2008 and the immediate popularity of the Indian Premier League lit the blue touch paper of the Twenty20 powder keg. Unluckily, the 2009 series coincided with the Indian general election and in the aftermath of terrorist activities, culminating in the Lahore attack, the Indian government felt it could not detach sufficient police and paramilitary force to guarantee security. South Africa, building something of a reputation for arranging international sporting events, in rugby union and football as well as cricket, edged out an England tender, and the second IPL season was transferred there.

British radio comedy series have a history – *ITMA, Take It From Here* and *Hancock's Half-hour* being examples – of their opening series being a flop, prior to second-phase triumph. Perhaps there is a suspicion that one might be involved with a flash in the institutional pan, whereas two or three flourishing attempts makes for a tradition. Certainly the second, the 2009 IPL, like the 2009 ICC T20 Cup, proved even more successful than its predecessor, as everyone accepted that the new dispensation was already settled and sure of continuity.

For all that, the logistics were daunting. thousands of players and other officials and technicians had to be transported from India to South Africa, but this was organised with reasonable effectiveness, and the programme ran for the most part smoothly. The competition was prefaced by the player auction, with a $2bn cap on each team's salary bill. The auctioneer's hammer knocked down two English lots – Kevin Pietersen to Bangalore Royal Challengers and Andy Flintoff to Chennai Super Kings – at the top bids of $1.550,000. The two English stars were awarded contracts worth £450,000 for three weeks cricket, having been granted temporary release from their English contracts. It was clear that the ECB and other national cricket boards, could not risk the Packer-like ructions of hanging on grimly to legal constraints against the compelling power of finance.

After some enthralling cricket, Bangalore lost out to Deccan Chargers in the final. Multi Screen Media conveyed live broadcasts of the games around the world to as many as a hundred countries, with an average of 200m viewers in India for each match and at a cost of $1.63bn. The Indian Board of Control, already accustomed to some wealth, was, it was estimated, the recipients of $1.75bn from its ten year deal over franchises, promotions and television rights, making it, according to one report, 'one of the richest sports bodies not just in India but the entire world.'

In this fashion did India, already something of a chief focus for global cricket, add the element of the most well-endowed T20 approach to its already bulging portfolio.

By 2009 no less than thirteen countries had thriving national Twenty20 tournaments. One of these, of course, was in the West Indies. In 2006 nineteen West Indian regional squads took part in a T20 contest won, at this first outing by Guyana. $28m was invested in the event, after whom it was named, by one Sir Allen Stanford, a Texan businessman, whose name was to flutter the dovecotes of the English cricket establishment.

In 2008 the ECB concluded a five year deal with Sir Allen Stanford for two international events worth $150m, including an annual $20m winner-takes-all competition in the autumn and a four team international contest in England, both to be played according to the already ubiquitous T20 formula. The quadrangular tournament was costed at the large sum of $9.5bn over the five years, while $3.5m was made available for English domestic cricket, which appeared to be the base for the announcement by the ECB that, from 2010, England would have a Twenty20 Premier League for its eighteen first-class counties.

Joy knew no bounds. The first Super Series in Antigua took place in 2008, with England doing ominously badly and with the Stanford all-West Indian Superstars collecting the individual and sizeable money prizes. Having narrowly beaten Middlesex, the English county T20 champions, England crashed to a low of 99, all out, against the winners. Thereafter things unravelled at some pace, as questions about the staging and financing of the series were followed by the scrapping of the Stanford cricketing operations in Antigua and with his fourteen Superstars, and by the investigation of Sir Allen's investment bank by the United States regulation agency. Early in 2009 the errant banker was charged with major fraud under American federal law; the ECB halted its involvement with the financier and the bubble was burst amid probing queries about the processes that had caught up the ECB in such a sordid business. One dire aspect was the news that some of the West Indian cricketers who had won a $1m in the Super Series had been tempted to invest in the Stanford Financial group and had lost the lot.

Cricket and cricketers were not the main losers in the ensuing debacle. In the collapse of the multi-billion dollar business, throughout Antigua, where the Stanford empire held undue sway, thousands lost their savings, their jobs, or both. Nonetheless, cricket people, still clutching to an olde-worlde sentiment, especially in England, about the place of cricket in the civilised scheme of things, were aghast. The somewhat seedy high-jinks – Allen Stanford's helicopter landing at Lord's to seal the deal, like the arrival of some visiting Hollywood star; his unseemly cavorting with the English player's wives and sweethearts in Antigua – had not helped. Critics were not too abashed to voice loudly that cricket had lost its soul.

POTENTIAL FALL

Readers of Charles Dickens' *Little Dorrit* (1855/57), featuring the fraudulent financier, Mr Merdle, or of Anthony Trollope's *The Way We Live Now* (1874/75), in which Augustus Melmotte, another extensive swindler, is central, would need no persuading that one should sup with fiscal devils with a long spoon. The lesson is evidently a difficult one to learn and the Stanford scandal illustrates the heady mix of dodgy money and glitzy styling that seems to fit so readily with limited overs, in particular, the new craze of Twenty20 cricket.

For many years, cricket had rather limped along, with coinage and species regarded as a soiled necessity. In the Packer aftermath, money and the market were in the ascendant. Often there was some sensible compromise of sport and finance but the dangers were real enough. The pricking of the Stanford bubble was of a cricketing part with the global failure in 2008/09 of an overcharged and greedy banking system at large. The gap between the reality of everyday socio-economic life and the façade of risky financial speculation has probably never been wider – and the arena of professional cricket, like that of professional football, has become a tiny microcosm of that perilous dichotomy.

Writing in 2009 in the *New Stateman*, Peter Wilby, its former editor and a Socialist commentator of analytical perspicacity, drew the broader comparison of world and sporting affairs in an astute discussion of international cricket. 'Globalisation, in sport as in economics, can be cruelly destructive of tradition. It favours mass production over craft skills, and international brands over long-established local names.' Intriguingly, there emerged some sharing of sympathies, as sometimes happens, between old Tory right-wing and old Labour left-wing adherents, in the face of yet another example of seemingly unstoppable market forces demolishing the old order. It may be recalled that the pastoral idyll of Victorian times attracted critics of industrialism from both sides of the political divide.

Traditionalists were also unimpressed by the auctioning of players for the Indian Premier League, likening it to the public sale of slaves in the deep south of pre-Lincoln USA. However dehumanising it looked, the legal truth was the converse of the slave mart, for the players had rarely been such free agents as well as such big earners. It was said that some cricketers earned more in a month of IPL engagement than in a normal career of quite recent years, even if the auction system meant they could not choose which team they represented. It was the league that was the employer. It was like the days of British music hall or variety, where the comedians and singers signed a contract to the owner of a theatre chain, such as Moss Empires and then appeared, as instructed, at the appointed venues. Away from the general contractual agreements of provincial, for example, county, or national systems, the star performers enjoyed a degree of personal liberty unknown in modern times. Cricketers looked as if they might soon attain complete contractual independence, in some ways a return to the spacious days of William Clarke and the Exhibition elevens of the 19th century.

What was startling about the IPL formula was that cricketers were not bound by race or nationality to a particular team. In English county cricket, and certainly in English football, the message had been preached and practised that, much as supporters enjoyed their locally born heroes, they were attracted by the success of their team, however formulated. It has always been interesting, both in English county cricket and Premiership football, to observe how quickly fans spot and applaud the overseas incomer who takes wholeheartedly to the role, as opposed to the mercenary who has neither heart nor commitment. The IPL took the formula of a team, not of, but for, the city or area to the ultimate.

General salaries were, in any event, improving in the early years of the 21st century. The statistics published by Barclays Bank in 2006 indicated that on average, English county cricketers were annually earning £43,000, about twice the average income for the work-force as a whole. These ranged from Surrey, where the average was between £51.000 and £60,000, to Glamorgan, where it was £32,000. One or two players, like, Andrew Flintoff, with the help of personal sponsorships and allied earnings, saw their yearly income soar above the £1m mark but these were exceptional figures. It is salutary to note that the average Premiership footballer was earning £665,000, or £884,000 if sponsorships were included, and even League Two, the old Fourth Division, players averaged £49,000. Senior British rugby union players were earning an average of £60,000.

For all that improvement, there is no doubt that football had left cricket far behind in terms of salaries, and in the moderately short time of some thirty or so years, from a point of near parity. It is a far cry from the days when Wally Hammond, it may be remembered, might have selected cricket above football because of its preferable earning capacity. When all the arguments have been urged about why English cricket may have its weaknesses, and when everything and everybody, from the schools to the government, have been found guilty of dereliction of duty, it is obvious enough that income must now be the major factor when a youth severally gifted, as many sporting youngsters are, is faced with a choice of careers.

When aged fifteen years and preparing to leave school, Phil Neville, of Manchester United, Everton and England, but rated by many experts as a really exceptional schoolboy cricketer, asked Alex Ferguson whether he should play for Lancashire at much the same fee for the summer that Manchester United were offering him a week, the astounded manager thought, in his Glaswegian way, that young

Phil Neville was 'taking the piss'. Cricket fans of an older vintage may thank their lucky stars that these seismic financial movements did not effect football years earlier. It is entirely likely that Wally Hammond and Denis Compton, to name but two, would never have played cricket at all but, quite sensibly and properly, would have devoted their entire vocational attention to soccer.

However, for many cricketers it is a wholesome and for some cricketers an affluent way of life. It is also a busy life and an all the year round one for many. The travel is non-stop and lengthy. It was calculated that, between 24 October 2008, with the ill-fated Stanford series in Antigua, and 1 May 2009, when he returned from the IPL campaign in India, Kevin Pietersen clocked up no fewer than 67,301 miles (including a South African Christmas holiday) in just over six months.

Twenty20 forced cricketers to re-orchestrate their skills. The batsmen benefited from shortened boundaries and from new powerful bats with a 'rebound capacity' 20% higher than in the year 2000. Among unorthodox shots that have been utilised have been the reverse sweep, the 'ramp' over the wicket-keeper's head and the skewed high drive square of the wicket. The bowlers are discomfited by fielding restrictions, by free hits after no balls, by highly restrictive 'wides' legislation and by having only a ration of four overs. They have retaliated with resourceful guile, using change of pace, including the cleverly bowled slower bouncer, to induce deep field catching, while, happily, spinners are still mentioned in dispatches for bravery under fire. A further dimension has been added to fielding, now an impressive exercise in collective athleticism.

Traditionalists said it would be a 'slogfest' but that has not quite been the case. Rather has T20 cricket revealed a novel construct, replete with its own range of skills. Writing in the autumn of 2008, the journalist Stephen Moss amusingly compared Test cricket to Tolstoy's *War and Peace* and Twenty20 to a Jeffrey Archer short story. But that would be unfair to T20, which is exciting and skilled enough to be granted the descriptor of, say, an Anton Chekhov short story. It is, that is, different in quantity rather than quality. Stephen Moss was nearer the mark when he contrasted the many-sided spaciousness of Test cricket with the days of George Eliot and Henry James, and the brash cupidity of Twenty20 with the hours of Jonathan Ross on the television. Each is reflective of a different tempo of cultural and social life and he believes that facing both ways – 'long-form for history; short-form for hysteria' – is dangerous for cricket.

That is the gist of the debate. The pessimists regard the limited forms of the game and their attendant sideshows and razzamatazz, as 'not cricket', either sportingly or ethically speaking. The optimists contend that the glory of cricket is that it can encompass such variations and survive as a multilateral game, serving different needs and audiences. Where the reformers may have to pause and consider is over the explanation that Twenty20 is a valuable introduction to the older and more dignified procedures of cricket. This hardly stands up to analysis. When the 65 overs Gillette Cup was introduced in 1963, the same rationale was made, as it was with the later 60, 50 and 40 overs formats. As we have noted, second-tier attendances, as in county or Australian states cricket, have continued to dwindle, while Test match crowds have also shrunk overall. In the interim, each form of the restricted game seemed to enjoy something of a transitory appeal.

People, apart from cricket *aficionados*, obviously prefer limited overs cricket to first-class cricket, with the occasional exception, at least in England, of important Test matches. The hard fact is that it is tending to replace traditional cricket rather than lay a pathway to it. The limited overs tail has always tended to wag the first-class dog. Other sports do not appear to have this problem of conflicting modes. The creation of Twenty20 cricket to make money for and attract attention to the traditional longer form of the game carries with it the awful threat that the tender carer, as if in some bleak Hitchcockian film, might turn out to be the bestial assassin.

Moreover, it does look as if the shorter the game the more popular it is. There may be something of the novelty still about T20 cricket, but could its popularity, too, prove to be fleeting, a frightening thought, for what might then be seen as salvation? It has been authoritatively said that twenty overs is the shortest possible formula, but one recalls echoes of that statement when 40 overs cricket was introduced courtesy of the John Player League. In 2009 the NatWest Pro40 overs competition in England became the last stand of a form that had survived for some forty years under the sponsorship of several companies. Rather illogically, in terms of the domestic mirroring the national agenda, it was resolved to retain a 40 overs tournament in England and jettison the 50 overs format. It was also decided in England not to add a second Twenty20 competition by way of replacement, as the ECB recommended to the counties, but to soup up and enlarge the existing tournament. Nor has it assisted in the presentation of these various competitions that a kaleidoscopic pattern of fixtures has randomly emerged, a dog's breakfast of cricket with fans finding it difficult to spot any sense of rhythm in the season's action.

At the same time, it might be added in parenthesis, the counties turned down a tentative proposal to reduce their number from eighteen to twelve. Apart from the usual traditional knee-jerk reflex, it must be said that this was a rather half-baked scheme. It had no context, such as, for example, a second division, so that there might be an exhortation to seek promotion or avoid relegation. Twelve was also too much, perhaps, of a compromise, for most reformers believed that five or six premier teams was the optimal number for the tier below the national squad.

What remained curious was the survival, especially in limited overs cricket, of probably unnecessary complications, alongside the desire to shorten and simplify the game. The complexities of the LBW rule are not generally understood by spectators, nor, if their appeals are any criterion, by some of the players. One might have expected, at least in the short forms of the games, to have had a straightforward ruling that, if the body were to stop the ball and it would have hit the wickets, then the batsman is out. A similar problem may well arise from the use of the Duckworth-Lewis method for determining targets for rain-affected limited overs matches. Few comprehend its arcane mathematics and while no one would question the earnest integrity of the design, it may come to be unhelpful in a mass spectator sport to utilise a tool of such incomprehensibility.

These are minor points. The chief issue is whether or not, were the T20 method to fall away a little in popularity, the anxious authorities would embark on a ten overs game, bringing cricket well within the reach, in time terms, of the football or rugby match. The 40, 50 and

60 overs matches have always had some near parallel in recreational cricket, being close in time-scale and in overs bowled to many club fixtures and now, as was noted, the vast number of local leagues and competitions are founded in some such construction. The 20 overs game was and is something of a standard for evening cricket, especially as played by scratch club and social sides, for forty overs is about all that could be crammed into most summer evenings. Thus, psychologically, the ten over reduction may be out of the question, until that is, the financiers and marketers grow restless.

When the shorter game was introduced the ever astute John Arlott suggested it should be labelled something other than cricket. It was, in his view, too unlike the genuine tradition to be called cricket. It is an intriguing question. Are these different games or facets of the one game? Certainly it is difficult to think of another modern sport of such variety. For example, at club level, the second innings was dropped in most fixtures by the late 19th century, although teams were expected to play out time after the completion of both first innings, with games then described as being 'won on the first innings'. At county level, the second innings was dropped for some parts of the programme, namely the limited overs fixtures, in the late 20th century. In the event, the period when everyone, both at local and national level, was playing the time-honoured two innings convention, was not prolonged. There had always been other kinds of deviation, notably in the numbers participating, from single wicket to teams of twenty-two. There are many precedents. What price the possibility of a ten overs game, six a side, with mixed gender teams?

Such bewildering change and variety as now exists is, perhaps, reminiscent of the very early days of cricket, when, as was argued in the early chapters of this text, there were many games called cricket that possibly differed in tactics and methodology and possibly some games that looked suspiciously like cricket and were called something else. There was no cradle for a single birth of cricket and centuries later, there appears again to be competing types of very different games called cricket being played.

By the same token, it was earlier claimed that, in respect of national character and culture, the late 20th century and now the opening of

21st century has more in common with the 18th century and opening decades of the 19th century than with the period from about 1850 to 1950. It is interesting to detect a sporting correspondence in the welcome accorded Twenty20 cricket. Like many of the great matches of the 18th century, T20 games are negotiated in less than a day; they are played before great crowds, often rowdy and enthusiastically involved; alcohol and gambling are a part of the scene; and, in the IPL, players are more randomly recruited as individuals to constitute the teams, as was the Hanoverian fashion.

In 2009 Andrew Flintoff, trying to pursue a career with the goal of becoming 'the best limited overs and Twenty20 cricketer in the world', rejected an incremental contract with England. He had already forsaken Test match and indeed, first-class cricket at large. He thus became a freelance cricketer. It was thought his agent, Andrew Chandler, would thereby be able to commit him fully to his Indian Premier League employers, Chennai Superkings, for the small matter of £935,000 annually, and perhaps raise his annual earnings to £2m, although some thought his possible loss of international status might impact on his other lucrative sponsorship deals. In flamboyant addition, there was also the suggestion that Dubai would become his base, with a coaching stint with the United Arab Emirates team one of his sidelines. However, as of 2010 successive injuries remained a career-threatening obstacle.

It was quite a dramatic venture, again with some sense of retrospect. The prospect of entirely freelance professional cricketers conveys us back in imagination to the comings and goings at the Green Man and Still tavern in Oxford Street, where professionals sought hire in the late 18th and early 19th centuries, if not at quite the same prices. Perhaps a closer analogue would be with the entrepreneurial as well as cricketing skills of William Clarke and the Exhibition elevens of mid-19th century. That was probably the last time professional cricketers had deployed their freelance powers in as unfettered a fashion as that open to the celebrity cricketers of today.

The history of cricket once more demonstrates its multiplicity of trajectories. In some bucolic fashion, it has swung back almost to its formal origins in Hanoverian and early Victorian times.

EPILOGUE

On 14 June 1922, at Edgsbaston, which then 'still resembled a country park', Hampshire, captained by the jovial Hon. Lionel Tennyson, grandson of the poet, dismissed Warwickshire, captained by the equally well-connected Hon. Freddie Calthorpe, for a modest 223. Hampshire having won the toss and inserted their opponents, were content. They began their innings at 4.0pm. By 4.40pm they were all out for fifteen, one of the lowest first-class scores ever. At he end of the day, following on, they were 98 for 3, and Freddie Calthorpe, assuming a premature end to the contest, suggested to the amateurs that golf should be arranged. An incandescent Tennyson bridled and released an 'immediate flood of Anglo-Saxon', claiming that the match would be won. 'Substantial wagers at long odds' were laid.

Hampshire then proceeded to bat until the morning of the third day, accumulating 521. Most of the team made a contribution, with George Brown's 172 the major input, and with the number ten, Walter Livsey, who doubled as wicket-keeper and Lionel Tennyson's valet, making 110, not out. A perplexed Warwickshire eleven were ousted for 158, falling to the bowling of Jack Newman, 5 for 53, and Alec Kennedy, 4 for 47. It was not even a close contest, for Hampshire won by a comfortable 155 runs. Bets were settled and champagnes corks popped, at least in the Hampshire camp.

The tale is deliciously related in Neil Jenkinson's *Cricket's Greatest Comeback* (1998), and, in the foreword, the then *Times* cricket correspondent, John Woodcock, argues that, of the 20,000-odd County Championship games played, this is 'the most wonderful example of the glorious and everlasting uncertainty' of cricket. It serves to demonstrate a tenet of cricket present from its emergence as a formalised sport, that is, the offer of a second chance. There is considerable agreement that the game originated in pristine design as a two innings encounter, with mentions of the fact as early as 1721. Indeed, the laws took the matter for granted and it was 1835 before it was included therein. Although Freddie Calthorpe, paying out on his gamble with Lionel Tennyson, missing his golf and having his team roundly condemned by the *Birmingham Post,* may have demurred, there is much sporting appeal in the concept of the second chance. In the early days of cricket, a one innings meeting may have been too brief to be worth making the effort, while of course, the possible entanglements of two innings must have found favour with the bookmakers and their clients.

As the focus of cricket archivists and chroniclers has naturally been on the upper echelons of the game, the two innings format is the most widely recorded, whilst the gradual move to the one innings format in the recreational game is less frequently related. The reason – the growing potency of batting – is evident enough. The professional game could afford to increase the time available, whereas the wholly amateur game had to seek the radical option of, in effect, halving the game. Like Charles II, the two innings format was 'an unconscionably long time a-dying'. To take just one absolutely random instance from Arthur Haygarth's invaluable *Cricket Scores and Biographies*, there is the 'curiosity' of the two innings of a 'very inferior match' in 1879 in which Bangor beat Dolgelly by an innings and 55 runs, Dolgelly managing but one run – a single from the intrepid W.James – in their first attempt.

The allure of the second chance is now confined to Test and provincial first-class cricket, for slowly, many international and county or equivalent regional games are now not only restricted to one innings but to a limited number of overs aside, as is now the case with the great majority of league, club, school and other recreational fixtures. In quantitative terms, this is probably the principle alteration that has taken place to the actual playing of cricket in 300 years. The amputation of a half the body of a game is indeed heroic surgery.

Other structural aspects have been more settled. For example, the number of players in a team is now rarely other than eleven, and the playing of matches against odds of up to twenty-two is completely outmoded. As was hinted in the foregoing chapter, the future chances of smaller teams, or even Hanoverian-style single or double wickets champions should not be ruled out. It could be a temptation for a highly celebrity conscious society; Andrew Flintoff versus Kevin Pietersen might have the turnstiles revolving. Over arm bowling is another constant and when underarm tactics have been tried in limited overs cricket, they have been frowned upon by the authorities. There are still three stumps, a twenty-two yard – the old agricultural measure of a chain – pitch, and much the same sized ball (although of varied hues) while there is a general accommodation of the six ball over, the four and six boundary and other such quasi-legal requirements. There is then, much that has become quite consolidated. With carefully preserved effects, like the arcane patois of its terminology, cricket still has a highly conservationist character.

In part because of these efforts to circumscribe and protect the game, the Cricketer's Progress has not been straightforward. Like John Bunyan's Christian, on his Pilgrim's Progress, the journey has been littered with obstacles. Unlike that theological trek, the cricketer's excursion is ongoing, with no signs of an ultimate heavenly destination, but the hurdles have been just as several and varied. Moreover, the likes of Andrew Flintoff and others might feel that, with the fruitful bonanza of Indian Twenty20 cricket, some form of earthly paradise has, in fact, been achieved. They may feel, with P.G.Wodehouse, that it is 'like being in heaven without going to all the bother and expense of dying'.

By way of recapitulation, cricket emerged from a slough, not of despond, but of primitive 'play', and, as a recognised professional spectator entertainment, became organised on the back of the gambling spree of the 18th century. It then came close to expiry, only to be rescued for respectability by the evangelical spirit of the Victorian era, with the public schools a prime motivator, where after it blossomed into being the chief sporting craze of the British Empire and enjoyed a famed and phenomenal golden age.

The Great War of 1914-18 traumatised top-class cricket, as it did other long-standing institutions, but it maintained its imperial status and appeal until well after World War II in a meticulous reprise of that first golden age. It was during these twinned golden epochs that cricket, more so than most if not all other sports, deepened its cult close to a religious sentiment, alongside the development of its substantial artistic, archival, statistical and literary superstructure. One aspect of this sense of cult rather than sport has been occasional tension between the high status of the game and its realistic existence as a marketed entertainment for which, by ticket or telly, customers pay ready money. Some current problems arise from this clash of the high priests of cricket, anxious to preserve its sacred integrity, and the money changers entering the temple, keen to increase the popular paying support.

From the stance of historical interpretation, a telling element has been the natural eagerness of chroniclers, as with those of other religious and semi-religious vogues, to press back the dates of origins and other developments as far as was conceivable, that chronological distance might lend enchantment to the view. History is always as much about interpreters, themselves the children of their cultural environs, as about hard facts and sound data. The considered opinion, for it is, like any other belief, no more than that, offered in this text as been that, not only in respect of cricket's origins and infancy, but in other matters, such as the back-dating of county cricket and its championship, of Test cricket and of first-class matches, some preceding work and analysis has borne the stamp of this yearning for cultural longevity.

Next, in the post-colonial world of electronic wizardry and transatlantic or 'coca-colonisation' influences, top-class cricket again stared demise in the face. The pessimistic Rowland Bowen prophesied in 1970 that first-class professional cricket would be finished within a hundred years. Actually, and given that fully-fledged first-class cricket, certainly on a worldwide basis, had only been sustained for about a hundred years thus far, it was a fairly guarded prediction, and it still has sixty years to run. As Lenin, questioned about his deviation from the hallowed text, said of Karl Marx, Rowland Bowen 'could not know all'. He could not have known that razor blades, tobacco, alcohol and especially insurance companies would become involved. He could not have known that professional cricket would be re-capitalised by a combine of corporate sponsors and, importantly, television companies on a global basis, nor could he have forecast that India would, on those financial terms, have inherited the cricketing earth. Even so, his emphasis on first-class cricket may yet still make his supposition a sound one, for the mounting popularity for Twenty20 cricket and the declining appeal of the longer forms of the game, especially on its essential nursery slopes just below the high peak of Test match performance, could yet mean that professional cricket might endure solely in its limited overs formulae.

The television-led financing of cricket, with Kerry Packer somewhat incongruously joining W.G.Grace and Donald Bradman in cricket's most sacrosanct gallery of immortals, is the modern fashion, but its geographical accent is very significant. The novel overlordship of India, the swing of the power pendulum thence from England, has proved to be one the most important and surprising movements in cricket's history. It is a switch of trajectory difficult to find elsewhere in sporting history, for, otherwise in the post-colonial world, the metropolitan powers have mainly clung tight to the administrative and financial controls of professional sport. Whether, say, China, as part of its rush to super-power status will in time grab some of the command posts of international sport away from Europe and from Europeanised nations like the United States and Australia, is a matter for conjecture. However, it is salutary to recall that Lord Harris would be amazed to learn of India's powerful position in today's cricketing circles.

Cricket's history has been a torturous and uneven switchback of fits and starts, of charges forward, misleading byways and sudden arrests. Possibly for this reason has it given rise to many internal contentions. Heaven knows there are plenty enough rows in football, with, for example, complaints about the preposterous sums paid to or for often mediocre players but at least, there is little or no argument about the actual conception of the game. In England today much of the cricketing debate is of that essence. For all the dismissal of one side as dinosaurs and the other side as destroyers, it is, in fact, a fair and legitimate dispute.

On the one hand, stands the market, excusing its appetites, as markets ever will, on the grounds of what admittedly is an extremely popular but possibly shallow, demand for, in this case, limited overs, especially now, Twenty20 cricket, full of thrills and spills but for all that, replete with genuine resolve and skills. On the other hand, ranged against this argument are a minority of highly committed and involved adherents to the contemplative coils of the County Championship or its counterpart elsewhere, with maybe a modicum of Test matches, wishful of enjoying and preserving the ancient craft of traditional cricket in all its *longueur* and intricacy. It is a battle between the proper demotic if occasional needs of the many and the equally valid but intense wishes of the few. These latter are the ones that George Bernard Shaw was thinking of when he wrote, 'the English are not very spiritual people, so they invented cricket to give them some idea of eternity.'

It is a sport that also gives rise to a degree of emotional strife and a further set of opposing sentiments. The father of the satirist, Peter Cook, was a district officer in Nigeria, with an abiding love of cricket. Peter Cook said 'my father used to receive news by boat, six months after it had been published. He'd open *the Times* and say, 'Good God; Worcester are 78 for 6.'

In contrast to that mildly and charmingly eccentric devotion to cricket, there is the darker side, as revealed in its extreme in *By His Own Hand* (1990) by David Frith, one of the keenest and most thoughtful cricketing scholars of his times. In this and a subsequently updated volume, he examined the cases of the many cricketers who have committed suicide. The numbers appear to be above the norms. Although the variables knit together a complex tissue for investigation, the fact that the matter is worthy of legitimate inquiry is itself a reminder that cricket's aesthetic may either attract the vulnerable or create vulnerability. The locking of lonely phases of isolated pressure within the confines of a team game has been felt by some commentators to have this sobering effect. Evidence of family dislocation and nervous breakdown might be added to the possible list of ills. One should not over press the argument but at least, it is necessary to admit that, in professional cricket, there has always been sackcloth and ashes as well as beer and skittles.

Overall, there is a cultural, even an aesthetic, element to contemplate. One turns again to C.L.R.James, whose benign sense of the place of cricket within both its social and artistic context is an enduring influence on all who attempt to analyse the game from a broader historical perspective. Employing his favoured Greek analogue, he argues that 'it is an unspeakable impertinence to arrogate the term 'fine art' to one small section of this quest and declare it to be culture . . . The end of democracy is a more complete existence', inclusive of the expansion of an aesthetic sense – and, in the industrial era, 'the need was filled by organised games . . . the popular democracy of Greece, sitting for days in the sun watching *The Oresteia*; the popular democracy of our day, sitting similarly, watching Miller and Lindwall bowl to Hutton and Compton – each in his own way grasps at a more complete human existence. We may be able to answer some day Tolstoy's exasperated and exasperating question: What is art? – but only when we learn to integrate our vision of Walcott on the back foot through the covers with the outstretched arm of the Olympic Apollo.'

Thus there are emotional as well as structural elements to consider, as one peers dimly into the coming decades. Some optimists hope and pray that cricket, ever adaptable, will continue to stay multifaceted and contrary to axiomatic prejudice, satisfy all the people all of the time. What is difficult, given cricket's mixed and convoluted antecedents, is to look ahead and guess which of the several options, if any, will trace the future path of cricket. There is an apt Goldwynism to the effect that prediction is very difficult, 'especially about the future.' Nonetheless, as has been wisely remarked, 'it is better to light a candle than curse the darkness.'

It is perhaps not irrelevant to compare cricket, in English terms, with pantomime, another worthy institution that has been pronounced dead on several occasions, only to be miraculously resuscitated through the intervention by way of tonic of, in lengthy sequence, music hall, variety and radio, television and 'celebrity', including sports, stars. Like cricket, it has contrived, over much the same length of time that formally organised cricket has existed, to absorb the intrusion of such foreign bodies, despite the predictable anguish, at each such concurrence, that the inner being of the artistic form would be sullied, diseased and destroyed by the treatment. It is not uncommon to visit a pantomime at the present time and find, as in the regulation bridal trousseau, something old, new, borrowed and blue. The familiar dame figure, itself regarded initially as intrusive by last-ditchers, was first popularised in 1812 by Joe Grimaldi as Queen Roundabellya. The dame may now be, to the chagrin of panto die-hards, the mother of a principal boy loaned from a soap opera, but most people do not seem to mind too much. Pantomime is still going strong.

The situation, both of cricket and its formative social context, is, like that of pantomime, a human one, contestable and changeable by people. The circumstances in which we live and play or watch games such as cricket have not been abstractedly decreed by Thomas Hardy's 'President of the Immortals', having his 'sport' with the tragic figure of Tess of the D'Urbervilles. These conditions have been made by men and women and they can, by that token, be altered. As many a cricketer or cricket-lover approaches each season in an expectant mood of pleasurable anticipation, perhaps it is time to look on the bright side. We might do worse than return to the 17th century where some of the story commenced and borrow from John Milton, who wrote in *Comus*, his masque of 1634;

> *Where an equal poise of hope and fear*
> *Does arbitrate th'event, my nature is*
> *That I incline to hope rather than fear,*
> *And gladly banish squint suspicion.*

AUTHOR'S SPORTS BIBLIOGRAPHY

W.G.Grace; His Life and Times   1981

Fair Game; Myth and Reality in Modern Sport   1986

The Lost Seasons; Cricket in Wartime, 1939-45   1987

Red Roses Crest the Caps; the History of Lancashire CCC   1989

Brylcreem Summer; the 1947 Cricket Season   1991

The Illustrated History of County Cricket   1992

First Knock; Cricket's Opening Pairs   1994

Darling Old Oval; the History of Surrey CCC   1995

150 Years; a Celebration; Surrey CCC (ed) 1996

Quill on Willow; Cricket in Literature   2001

Red Shirts and Roses; the Tale of the Two Old Traffords   2005
(Winner of The Times/Cricket Society Book of the Year Award)

Parish to Planet; How Football came to rule the World   2007

George Duckworth; Warrington's Ambassador at Large   2007

Also the booklets:

God's Classroom; Four Essays in Cricket's Social History 1996

From Meadowland to Multinational; A Review of Cricket's Social History 2000

Dr Eric Midwinter OBE edited the MCC yearbook/annual 1997/2006; was President of the Association of Cricket Statisticians and Historians for seven years; was Chairman of the Cricket Society Book of the Year judging panel, 2003/2009 and has written extensively for major cricket journals, including *The Cricketer*, for which he was a 'mainline reviewer' for several years, and very regularly as a major contributor to *Cricket Lore*. A social historian and social policy analyst, he has written over fifty books on a wide range of subjects.

SOURCES AND ACKNOWLEDGEMENTS

Particular gratitude is owed to Stephen de Winton for his careful reading of the text, for his pointing out of several infelicities, and for his wise advice about the use of additional authorities. As a scholar, richly steeped in cricketing and literary culture and a former and much-esteemed colleague on the Cricket Society Book of the Year judges' panel, his help and counsel has been highly appreciated.

The running series of cricket ground images throughout the text has been generously supplied from the Morphot 'Grounds for Pleasure' series, and the author and publisher wish to acknowledge, with manifold thanks, the capable and kindly assistance of Tony Morris, the talented photographer and manager of the 'Morphot' enterprise.

Unless otherwise stated, the chapter heading illustrations are taken from the Keith Hayhurst and Richard Hill collections, for which the author and publisher wish to express their genuine gratitude to both these keen cricket-lovers. All efforts have been made to trace the copyright of the illustrations used but the author and publisher would be appreciative if anyone able to help them in this matter would contact them.

In the belief that extensive footnotes might have proved distracting to the general reader, the foregoing text has instead included where appropriate, plentiful references to authors and works. To supplement that, there follows an extensive list of the books and other materials used to support this narrative account of cricket's social and political history. Having watched cricket for over seventy years, and having read about it for almost as long, this is naturally a list restricted to books that the author has consulted for this immediate purpose, while recognising that, at the same time, a lifetime of cricket and wider reading remains the bedrock of the data and arguments to be found in this book.

Altham, H.S. *A History of Cricket; vol i from the beginnings to the First World War* (1926)

Arlott, John *Vintage Summer: 1947* (1967)

Arlott, John *Basingstoke Boy; the Autobiography* (1990)

Bailey, P, Thorn P, & Wynne-Thomas, P *Who's Who of Cricketers* (1984)

Barker, Ralph *Purple Patches* (1987)

Berry, Scyld Berry & Peploe, Rupert *Cricket's Burning Passion* (2006)

Birley, Derek *The Willow Wand; Some Cricket Myths Explored* (1989)

Birley, Derek *A Social History of English Cricket* (1999)

Blunden, Edward *Cricket Country* (1944)

Booth, Keith *The Father of Modern Sport; The Life and Times of Charles W. Alcock* (2002)

Booth, Keith *George Lohmann; Pioneer Professional* (2007)

Bowen, Rowland *Cricket; a History of its Growth & Development throughout the World* (1970)

Bose, Mihir *A History of Indian Cricket* (1990)

Bright-Holmes, John (ed) *The Joy of Cricket* (1985)

Bright-Holmes, John (ed) *Lord's and Commons; Cricket in Novels and Stories* (1988)

Brodribb, Gerald *Next Man In; a Survey of Cricket's Laws and Customs* (1995)

Brooke, Robert *A History of the County Cricket Championship* (1991)

Brookes, Christopher *English Cricket; the Game and its Players through the Ages* (1978)

Brookes, Christopher *His Own Man; the Life of Neville Cardus* (1985)

Brown, Lionel H. *Victor Trumper and the 1902 Victorians* (1981)

Buckland, William *Pommies* (2008)

Cardus, Neville *English Cricket* (1945)

Cardus, Neville *Cardus on Cricket* (1949)

Cardus, Neville *My Life* (1965)

Cashman, Richard *Sport in the National Imagination* (2002)

De Selincourt, Hugh *The Cricket Match* (1924)

Down, Michael *Archie; a Biography of A.C.MacLaren* (1981)

Eddows, John *The Language of Cricket* (1987)

Edwards, Alan *Lionel Tennyson; Regency Buck* (2001)

Epps, William *Grand Matches of Cricket 1771 to 1791* (1799)

Figueroa, John *West Indies in England; the Great Post-war Tours* (1991)

Frindall, Bill *The Wisden Book of Test Cricket, 1876/77-1977/78* (1979)

Frith, David *By His Own Hand; a Study of Cricket's Suicides* (1990)

Frith, David *Bodyline Autopsy* (2002)

Frith, David *The Ross Gregory Story* (2003)

Goulstone, John *Hambledon; the Men and the Myths* (2001)

Grace, W.G. *Cricket* (1891)

Green, Benny (ed) *The Wisden Book of Obituaries* (1986)

Green, Benny (ed) *The Concise Wisden; an Illustrated Anthology of 125 Years* (1988)

Green, Benny (ed) *The Wisden Papers; 1947-1968; Rise and Fall* (1990)

Guha, Ramchandra *A Corner of Foreign Field; the Indian History of a British Sport* (2002)

Haigh, Gideon *The Big Ship; Warwick Armstrong and the Making of Modern Cricket* (2002)

Haigh, Gideon *Ashes 2005; the Greatest Test Series* (2005)

Harte, Chris *A History of Australian Cricket* (1993)

Hartland, Peter *The Balance of Power in Test Cricket, 1877-1998* (1998)

Heald, Tim *Denis Compton; The Life of a Sporting Hero* (2006)

Hignell, Andrew *A 'Favourit' Game; Cricket in South Wales before 1914* (1992)

Hignell, Andrew *Rain Stopped Play; Cricketing Climates* (2002)

Hignell, Andrew *Cricket in Wales* (2008)

Holt, Richard *Sport and the British* (1989)

Howat Gerald Walter *Hammond* (1984)

Howat, Gerald *Len Hutton; the Biography* (1988)

Howat, Gerald *Cricket's Second Golden Age; the Hammond-Bradman Years* (1989)

Howat, Gerald *Cricket All My Life* (2006)

James, C.L R. *Beyond a Boundary* (1963)

Jenkinson, Neil *Cricket's Greatest Comeback* (1998)

Jones, Richard *Exiles and Kings; the African Imprint on English Cricket* (2008)

Kynaston, David, *W.G.'s Birthday Party* (1990)

Laughton, Tony *Captain of the Crowd; Albert Craig* (2008)

Le Quesne, Laurence *The Bodyline Controversy* (1883)

Lewis, Tony *Double Century; the Story of MCC and Cricket* (1987)

Low, Robert *W.G.; a Life of W.G.Grace* (1997)

Malies, Jeremy *Great Characters from Cricket's Golden Age* (2000)

Manley, Michael *A History of West Indies Cricket* (1988)

Marquese, Mike *Anyone but England; Cricket and the National Malaise* (1994)

Martineau, G.D. *They Made Cricket* (1956)

Martin-Jenkins, Christopher *Wisden Book of County Cricket* (1981)

Mason, Ronald *Jack Hobbs, a Biography* (1960)

Maun, Ian *From Commons to Lord's vol I 1700-1750* (2009)

Moorhouse, Geoffrey *The Best Loved Game* (1979)

Oborne, Peter *Basil D'Oliveira; Cricket and Conspiracy* (2004)

O'Neill, Joseph *Netherland* (2008)

Perry, Roland *The Don; Based on Interviews with Sir Donald Bradman* (1995)

Phelps, Gilbert *Arlott and Trueman on Cricket* (1977)

Plumptre, George *The Golden Age of Cricket* (1990)

Pollard, Jack *The Complete Illustrated History of Australian Cricket* (1992)

Rae, Simon *W.G.Grace; a Life* (1998)

Rae, Simon *It's Not Cricket* (2001)

Ranjitsinhji, Prince *The Jubilee Book of Cricket* (1897)

Rayvern Allen, David *Sir Aubrey; a Biography of C. Aubrey Smith* (1982)

Rayvern Allen, David *Cricket; an Illustrated History* (1990)

Rayvern Allen, David (ed) *'The Field' Book of Cricket from 1857* (1991)

Rayvern Allen, David *John Arlott; the Authorised Biography* (1994)

Rayvern Allen, David *Jim; the Life of E.W.Swanton* (2004)

Rijks, Miranda *The Eccentric Entrepreneur; a Biography of Sir Julien Cahn* (2008)

Rodrigues, Mario *Batting for the Empire; Ranjitsinhji* (2003)

Ross, Alan *Ranji, Prince of Cricketers* (1983)

Ross, Alan (ed) *The Kingswood Book of Cricket* (1992)

Sandiford, Keith *Cricket and the Victorians* (1994)

Stoddard, Brian & Sandiford, Keith (ed) *The Imperial Game; Cricket, Culture and Society* (1998)

Streeton, Richard *P.G.H.Fender; a Biography* (1981)

Swanton, E.W. *A History of Cricket; vol ii from the First World War to the Present Day* (1962)

Underdown, David *Start of Play; Cricket in Culture in 18th Century England* (2000)

Waghorn H.T., *The Dawn of Cricket* (1906)

Webb, Geoff *They All Played at Lord's* (1991)

Webber J.R. *The Chronicle of W.G.* (1998)

Webber, Roy *County Cricket Championship* (1957)

West, G. Derek *Six More Days of Grace* (1992)

Williams, Charles *Bradman* (1996)

Williams, Jack 'Churches, Sport and Identities' in (ed) J.Hill & J.Williams *Sport and Identity in the North of England* (1996)

Williams, Jack *Cricket and England; a Cultural and Social History of the Inter-war Years* (1999)

Williams, Jack *Cricket and Race* (2001)

Wright, Graeme *Betrayal; the Struggle for Cricket's Soul* (1993)

Wright, Graeme (ed) *Bradman in Wisden* (2008)

Wynne-Thomas, Peter *The History of Cricket; From the Weald to the World* (1997)

JOURNALS AND MAGAZINES VARIOUSLY CONSULTED
INCLUDE

The Cricketer Magazine

The Cricket Statistician (the journal of the Association of Cricket Statisticians and Historians), plus many of the informative booklets and pamphlets published by the ACS.

The Journal of the Cricket Society

Cricket Lore

Particular mention must be made of *Cricket Lore*, the labour of devotion of its owner-editor, the energetic and well-informed Richard Hill. Between 1991 and 2005, he contrived to produce, against seemingly insuperable odds, five volumes of *Cricket Lore*, 47 editions in all, each of up to 60 advertisement-less pages in length, usually averaging a matter of 40,000 words an issue. This offered me an extensive opportunity, as it did to others interested in researching and writing about cricket, to write, in my own case, 86 articles, some long, some short, for this near-equivalent of an academic journal for cricket. I have naturally gone back to this valuable source to quarry not only pieces of research that I had published, but also, naturally, the excellent articles by colleagues. These have all been used with the enthusiastic permission of Richard Hill, and I am extremely happy to have this chance of expressing the most genuine appreciation to him for all his kindnesses and encouragement over the last twenty years.

Eric Midwinter

GENERAL CRICKET INDEX

Holden, Captain 81
Holding, Michael 242,255
Hollies, Eric 206
Holt, Richard 91
Hornby, Albert Neilson 87/8,158,187
Hornchurch 45,77
Howat, Gerald 64,139,194,200,333
Howorth, Richard 286
Hughes, Thomas 61-63, 145,148
Huizinga, Johann 22
Hutton, Len 194,197,201,209,215, 230,241,327,333

Imperial Cricket Conference (later International Cricket Conference, ICC) 159,166/7,188-190,239-255,268,297-300,309-311
Iddison, Roger 106
Imzamam-al-Haq 277
India 7-9,12,89,113,121-129, 130, 136, 142/3, 161,166/7, 169/70, 180, 189/90, 204,210,215-7,234-257,264,269/70,276/7,298-304,310-316,320-325
Indian Board of Control 311
Indian Cricket Board 300
Indian Premier League (IPL) 2, 7-12,297,310-320, 188,247,248,297
Invalids, the 193
I Zingari 66,140

Jackson, John 105
Jackson, Sir Stanley 155,169,171
Jamaica 121,215,240/1
Jamaica College 121
James, C.L.R. 155,204,271,326
Jardine, Douglas 197,209
Jayasuriya, S.T. 277
Jenkinson, Neil 321

Jenner, Herbert 63
Jessop, Gilbert 143,157,169,171,180
Johannesburg 122,171
John Player League 317
Johnson, Ian 217
Johnson, Samuel 22/3,77
Johnston, Bill 217
Jones, Bulkeley Owen 62-64
Jupe, W.H. 103

Kallis, Jacques 276
Kennedy, Alec 321
Kent 15,17/8,36,40-49,74,78-81,94-99, 101,106/7,129,153,175, 178/9,199,216,281,288
Keskar, B.V. 237,299
Khan, Imran 277,307
King, J.Barton 116
Kingston College 121
Knott, Alan 281
Kumble, Anil 276

Lacey, Francis 166
Lahore 249,307,311
Laker, Jim 215,227
Lancashire 4,74,79-82, 87, 96,105,106,170,175/6,191-194,231,234,263,286,288,296,315
Lancashire County and Manchester Cricket Club 81
Lancashire Cricket Board 263
Lancashire Youth Federation 263
Lancaster 94
Lara, Brian 276,277,278
Larwood, Harold 190, 209
Laughton, Tony 175
Launceston 117
Lawrence, Charles 127
Laxman, V.V.S. 277
Leeds 57,94-97,197,204

Quidnuncs, the 66

Rae, Simon 155
Rajasthan Royals 7
Ranjitsinhji, Prince 125, 155, 166,169,171,189,237-9
Rayvern Allen, David 15,26
Read, W.W. 128,173
Reid, John 278
Rhodes, Cecil 128/9,144,149,
Rhodes, Wilfred 171-173,190,195,199,201
Richards, Barry 234/4
Richards, Frank (aka Charles Hamilton) 146
Richards, Viv 242-246
Richmond, 2nd Duke of 36-38,43
Richmond, 4th Duke of 46/7
Riverside Stadium 285
Robertson-Glasgow, R.G. 220
Robertson, Stuart 308
Roberts, Robert 146
Rodrigues, Mario 166
Roedean 267
Rose Bowl, the 292
Royle, Vernon 186
Rugby 58-62,87,121,140
Russell, Lord Charles 125,158,281
Rutland 67,263

Salisbury, Lord 60,111
Salve, N.K.P. 300
Sandham, Andy 195
Sandiford, Keith 143,144,334
Sassoon, Ric 229
Scotland 98,167
Seaman, L.C.S. 138
Selincourt, Hugh de 212
Sellars, Brian 194
Selsey 17
Selvey, Mike 168,268
Sevenoaks 9,18,43,45

Shackleton, Derek 232
Sharma, Ajay 277
Sharp, Evelyn 148
Shaw, Alfred 105,126
Shaw, George Bernard 326
Sheffield 55,81
Sheffield, Lord 176
Sheffield Shield Competition, the 118,176,208
Sheppard, David 64,215,229,244
Sheriff, Lawrence 58
Shrewsbury, Arthur 105
Silva, P.A. de 277
Simpson, Reg 146,215
Sismey, Stan 214
Skelton, John 18
Slade, Lucas, R. 128
Slindon 43/4
Smith, Sir Cecil Aubrey 117,128
Smith, George 46
Smithies, Karen 268
Snaith, J.C. 266
Snow, Eric 66
Sobers, Gary 205,234,241/2,276-278
Somerset 79,109,154,170,186,288
Southampton 94/193
South Africa 12,113,120-123,128/9,163-166,171,176,189,216,234,242-246, 251,255,269,276, 303/4,307,309,311,316
South Africa Cricket Association 163
South African College 122
South African Coloured Cricket Board 163
South African Independent Cricket Board 163
South Australia 118,164,204
South-east Lancashire League 176
Spiers, Felix 160

THIRD AGE PRESS

... an independent publishing company which recognizes that the period of life after full-time employment and family responsibility can be a time of fulfilment and continuing development ... a time of regeneration

Third Age Press books are available by direct mail order from
Third Age Press, 6 Parkside Gardens London SW19 5EY
... or online from **www.thirdagepress.co.uk**
... or on order through book shops
Please add 20% for UK postage   UK Sterling cheques payable to *Third Age Press*.

Other Third Age Press books by Eric Midwinter

.. is a series (by Eric Midwinter) that focuses on the presentation of your unique life. These booklets, seek to stimulate and guide your thoughts and words in what is acknowledged to be not only a process of value to future generations but also a personally beneficial exercise.

A Voyage of Rediscovery: a guide to writing your life story
... is a 'sea chart' to guide your reminiscence & provide practical advice about the business of writing or recording your story.
36 pages   £4.50

Encore: a guide to planning a celebration of your life
An unusual and useful booklet that encourages you to think about the ways you would like to be remembered, hopefully in the distant future.   **20 pages   £2.00**

The Rhubarb People ... Eric Midwinter's own witty and poignant story of growing up in Manchester in the 1930s. Also on tape including useful tips on writing or recording your story.
32 pages   £4.50   audio cassette   £5.00

OR all 3 booklets for only £10

THE PEOPLE'S JESTERS
Twentieth Century British Comedians
by Eric Midwinter
Illustrated with
photographs
and playbills

"Meticulously researched and vastly entertaining The People's Jesters is a major work on the British variety theatre"
(Patrick Newley,
The Stage Newspaper)

At one level, *The People's Jesters* is an absorbing exercise in nostalgia, with its perceptive and amusing profiles of scores of well-loved and well-remembered comics, from George Robey and Will Hay, via Max Miller and Tommy Handley, to Tony Hancock and Morecambe and Wise. Beyond that, it is an astute and definitive analysis of how comedians worked. With its combine of colourful content and shrewd comment, there are rich pickings here for all manner of readers.

Eric Midwinter's lifelong interest in comedians began 70 years ago when he saw Albert Modley in pantomime. He thus brings untold memories, as well as his noted skills as a well-known social historian and commentator, to the task of describing and judging the major age of the comedians.   In **The People's Jesters**, *he revisits, updates and widens his critically acclaimed 1979 study,* Make 'Em Laugh; Famous Comedians and Their Worlds.

232 pages 248mm x 178mm ISBN 1898576 25 4   £14.50

BEST REMEMBERED: A hundred stars of yesteryear
by Eric Midwinterr

... presents a galaxy of 100 stars from the days before television ruled our lives. These cultural icons achieved lasting fame through radio, cinema, stage, dance hall, theatre, variety hall and sporting fields. Most of today's 'thirdagers' were growing up between 1927 and 1953 – a quarter century rich in talent, innovation, humour and unforgettable melodies. Whether **Best Remembered** is used as a trigger for personal or group reminiscence or read as a rich but light scholarly text on our social and cultural history, its lively style and fizzing illustrations cannot fail to please.

illustrated by **Rufus Segar 168 pages 248mm x 178mm £12.50**

I SAY, I SAY, I SAY
The Double Act Story
by Eric Midwinter
illustrated with photos and play bills
£9.50 paperback   154 pages

Why were there so few double acts before the end of the First World War and why such a profusion between 1920 and the mid-1950s and why, since then, with the exception of Morecambe and Wise, have there been so few comic duos? Midwinter cheerfully answers these questions and analyses the effects of television and other social dimensions on popular entertainment by way of explanation. Knowledgeable and readable, *I Say* is an attractively presented account of a significant element of popular entertainment over the last 100 years.

NOVEL APPROACHES:

a guide to the popular classic novel

Novel Approaches

a guide to the popular classic novel

Eric Midwinter

Oh for a good read and an un-putdownable book! Despite the lurid blandishments of television, there are still many of us who turn, quietly, pensively, to the novel in leisure moments. This short text is aimed at such people whose interest has been kindled sufficiently to permit some extra contemplation and study.

Novel Approaches takes 35 novels that have stood the test of time and embeds them in historical and literary commentary – a combination of social background giving scientific objectivity, and the author's artistic subjectivity.

Third Age Press